C000183796

EGYPTIAN LOVE SPELLS AND RITUALS

EGYPTIAN LOVE SPELLS AND RITUALS

CLAUDIA R DILLAIRE

quantum

LONDON • NEW YORK • TORONTO • SYDNEY

quantum

An imprint of W. Foulsham and Co. Ltd
The Publishing House, Bennetts Close, Cippenham, Slough,
Berkshire, SL1 5AP, England

ISBN 0-572-03046-0

Copyright © 2005 W. Foulsham & Co. Ltd

Cover illustration by Jurgen Ziewe

Illustrations by Ruth Murray

A CIP record for this book is available from the British Library

All rights reserved

The Copyright Act prohibits (subject to certain very limited
exceptions) the making of copies of any copyright work or of
a substantial part of such a work, including the making of
copies by photocopying or similar process. Written
permission to make a copy or copies must therefore normally
be obtained from the publisher in advance. It is advisable also
to consult the publisher if in any doubt as to the legality of
any copying which is to be undertaken.

Neither the editors of W. Foulsham and Co. Ltd nor the
author nor the publisher take responsibility for any possible
consequences from any treatment, procedure, test, exercise,
action or application of medication or preparation by any
person reading or following the information in this book.
The publication of this book does not constitute the practice
of medicine and this book does not attempt to replace any
diet or instructions from your doctor. The author and
publisher advise the reader to check with a doctor before
administering any medication or undertaking any course of
treatment or exercise.

Printed in Great Britain by Creative Print & Design (Wales), Ebbw Vale

Contents

Dedication

This book is for the Egyptian gods and goddesses, especially Amun, Hathor, Imhotep, Isis, Nephthys, Osiris, Ra and Thoth, who govern such matters as enchantment, love, magick, spells, success and writing. I thank Them for giving me the inspiration and determination to see this project through to completion. Without Them, nothing would be possible.

Many people inspired me to write this book and deserve my thanks:

To Abigail Brewer, my best friend and college roommate. Your trials and tribulations spurred me into action to bring this book to light. You mean more to me than I can ever express in words.

To James Butland, who has been my friend in good times and bad. You have always been there for me with wit, advice and comfort. Your quiet strength and encouragement have been my salvation in many a trying time.

To Natalie Damon, my friend, confidant and 'adopted daughter'. You read and re-read and gave me moral support when I needed it most. You never let me give up and for that I am eternally grateful.

To Rita Dillaire, my late mother. You showed me and taught me what love really means. I share this with you and still miss you after all these years. I hope I have made you proud.

To Philip Dubuque, a man without equal. Thank you so much for your assistance with the image reference for this book. I couldn't have done it without you.

To William Dykens, who has been my partner in life, my heart, my soul. Without your urging and support, this book would never have been started or completed. Thank you for your understanding, tolerance and unwavering devotion.

To Wendy Hobson, Editorial Director at Foulsham. Thank you for believing in this book as much as I do. And to Amanda Howard, my editor. You are the one who has really made this book so beautiful.

To Gary McKinstry, adviser and friend. You gave me the strength to go forward and I will always cherish the time we have spent together.

You have a rare gift and I am proud to be the recipient of your wisdom and guidance. Thank you from the bottom of my heart.

To Richard McNeil, my friend and colleague. You were the male perspective on much of my poetry. Your comments and insight were invaluable and I owe you more than I can ever repay.

To Jacky Sach, my agent and friend. Thank you for helping me in so many ways through a very stressful time. You are a true treasure.

To Arnold Vosloo, whose portrayal of undying, eternal love touched my heart and soul. I can only hope my rendition of Egyptian love will move someone as much as you moved me with your performance as the High Priest Imhotep in *The Mummy* and *The Mummy Returns*.

And finally, but most importantly, to Peter Woodward, my true inspiration, without whom this work could not have been created. It is to you that I owe my sanity during the writing of this book. You opened my eyes to the beauty of Egypt and Egyptian love poetry and lyrics. Even these humble words cannot express the depth of my appreciation. Life, health and strength to you, my brother.

Hathor

Introduction

This book is for anyone interested in love and Egyptian magick. The Ancient Egyptians knew as well as we do that love is a driving force in life, and I have attempted to cover as many aspects of love and desire as possible, including the loss of a loved one. My aim has been to make the book simple and straightforward for those new to Wicca and magick, but even the experienced may find fulfilment in the poetry, spells and rituals, which are the result of research, personal beliefs and practices, as well as my passion for Ancient Egypt and its rich history.

I will share with you my knowledge of how to connect with the deities of Ancient Egypt and how to perform love spells. Although the spells are specifically designed for the solitary practitioner or for two persons, they can easily be adapted for use by covens. By the same token, most, but not all, of the poems are written from the female perspective but can be altered for male practitioners.

The concept of love for the Ancient Egyptians was eternal love, a love to span the ages, even a love to transcend time and death. In our time, love is so confused with sex that it is a wonder anyone experiences real love. You may wish to read some poetry from the New Kingdom, the period of Egyptian history prior to the take-over by the Roman Empire; it is wonderfully expressive, as well as often being highly sensual and erotic.

The myth of Osiris and Isis

The earthly king Osiris was hated by his jealous brother, Set. Set killed his brother, sealed the body in a casket and threw it into the Nile. Osiris's grieving wife Isis, Mistress of Magick, searched all Egypt and then overseas, found the casket in the roots of a massive tree and brought the body back to the Beloved Land.

The furious Set heard of this, found the body and dismembered it, scattering the pieces throughout Egypt. Isis and her sister, Nephthys, then set about to find all the body parts to restore Osiris to life in the Land of the Dead. They were able to find all the pieces but one – his phallus, which had been swallowed by a fish. Isis fashioned a new phallus out of earth, and in breathing life into her husband conceived their son, Horus.

Youthful Horus battled with his uncle Set to avenge his father's death. Ultimately, Osiris was declared King of the Underworld, Horus was appointed King of the Living, but Set became Ruler of the Deserts and god of chaos and evil.

Isis and Osiris

The story of Isis and Osiris is a perfect example of eternal love that transcends even death. It also shows how integrity overcomes evil, that what is honourable will prevail. That's what Egyptian mythology and magick can teach us. Open your heart to the deities; they will guide you and show you the way to bring eternal love into your life.

CHAPTER 1

My Background to Egyptian Magick

I was not born into the Wiccan tradition but was drawn to it. Like many Wiccans, I was raised in another religion and was expected to attend services and participate in rituals whether I felt like it or not. The end result was that I started looking elsewhere because the connection just wasn't there.

I was brought up Catholic, but found much lacking in that religion. It is certainly not my intention to belittle Catholicism (or indeed any other faith): I am simply stating the fact that, for me, it was not the right religion. It confused me and I felt confined and empty. I couldn't understand why I needed to have a priest or minister intercede on my behalf in order to speak to my god. Why couldn't I talk directly and get the same result? If I questioned, I was told it was not my place to question, that religion was a matter of faith.

So I started in magick as many of my generation did, as a teenager, toying with spells and trying to conjure up demons. But back in the mid-1970s, Wicca did not exist as a religion as it does today; it was called the Occult and the word itself was enough to cause fear and trepidation. I practised off and on in college, but fell away from most religious thought for many years.

When I approached Wicca anew, the intervening years had taught me a great deal. I was much older and more willing to open my mind and heart to the spirituality I so desperately desired. I read many books on Wicca, witchcraft and any number of other New Age pursuits but, although I dabbled with these traditions, I never really felt connected to the worship or the rituals. I had always been fascinated by Ancient Egypt but there was little to be found on the magick of those times. Eventually, though, I happened upon a book of Egyptian mythology and recognised that this was the path for me. After much reading and meditation, I knew in my heart that I was ready to devote my life to the service of the Egyptian deities, a commitment I had just not been ready for until then.

If there was so little information available, why did I choose Egyptian magick? I have asked myself that same question and can come up with only one answer: because it felt right and natural for me. All the many and varied witchcraft traditions encourage you to question – yourself, your beliefs, the boundaries of possibility – and all allow you to be the person you desire to be. But Egyptian magick is spontaneous, uplifting, vital, passionate and exciting, and less restrictive than other witchcraft traditions. It does not require special knowledge, study or progression through levels in order to become a priest or priestess, as do some traditions; it does require dedication, imagination and an open mind and heart. My beliefs make up a part of my life that sustains me; they even helped me deal with the loss of my mother more than twenty years ago.

I found the Egyptian deities easy to connect with – on my own, whenever I needed to, and in my own home, on a beach at sunset or in a driving rainstorm. I read as much as possible about each deity before I attempted to invoke one. I meditated with each of the deities on an individual basis and asked what was expected of me in my service to them. I must add that I do not hear voices, I do not channel, and I do not see visions or dead people. But the deities do 'speak' to me in a way that only they can – by bestowing feelings of peace, serenity, solace, grief, hope and love. Connecting with a deity may put me through a range of emotions, only to realise how much better I feel after the encounter. While writing this book, I have called upon Thoth more times than I can number for his guidance, inspiration and support. When I had difficult days, he was always with me, forcing me to push the limits of creativity and imagination.

Above all, the Egyptian deities touch my soul, even Amun, the Hidden One, who seems so inaccessible to many. The deities flavour every facet of my life and I have been enriched by my devotion to them.

Connection through meditation

I allow a block of time, at least an hour, and close myself off from the distractions of the outside world. I light a candle, gold for a god or silver for a goddess, as well as a white candle to represent myself (white signifies my willingness to hear whatever lesson I need to learn). I light an incense appropriate to the deity or a blend of frankincense and myrrh resins. I think of all that the particular god or goddess represents and how that deity could instruct me. I open my heart and mind to whatever comes; I let the stillness envelop me, inhale the incense deeply and let the deity enter my life.

Sometimes what I experience is very subtle and I don't realise I have connected with my deity until days later: at other times the connection has happened like a bolt of lightning and I have found myself weeping uncontrollably or overwhelmed to the point where it was difficult to catch my breath. But each encounter touches the core of my soul and gives me a better understanding of my deities and what they expect of me.

This is a meditation that you, too, could use as your very first step in Egyptian magick. I do know how hard it is to allow an uninterrupted space in a busy life, but it will be worth making the effort. Turn off the telephone, the computer and the television; the hour you spend with a deity might make a profound difference to your life. You may find the answer to a nagging problem, the reason for choosing one job over another, or what path to follow in life.

I spent many months connecting with deities, when I could set aside the time, because connecting with all the deities is not something that can be done in an evening or a weekend. It's an ongoing process. I still take time to connect on a personal level with deities I feel a special affinity with or with those who have lessons for me to learn. Now that I am familiar with my deities, they don't require so much time: I can connect with them for just a moment or for longer if necessary. It is a great comfort to have their assistance whenever I feel the need, and sometimes I just take the time to sit in quiet meditation, taking the time to thank a deity for accepting me as an Egyptian witch.

Spells and rituals

Since very little has been written for the Egyptian magick practitioner, I have created most of my own spells and rituals. This is one of the reasons why I find Egyptian magick so exciting – it is a blank canvas upon which to write one's own worship of the ancient gods. For example, I have no need to ask the god Set to destroy my enemies in battle, but I do call upon him to assist me when my life is in chaos.

I do use scholarly works and poetry from the New Kingdom to capture the feeling of the times and to explore many of the gods who were minor deities in their time. It is also possible to read some of the spells and rituals used by the Ancients as a starting point for worship today.

I am a firm believer that you should make your spells or rituals moving experiences. Who wants to be worried whether they said the right words or if they lit the candles in the wrong order? I don't memorise incantations or follow prescribed sequences: I would rather have the words that are appropriate to the moment come from my heart. I do follow certain guidelines in my spells and rituals – I use candles and incense for my deities and always thank them for their presence; I perform my most important spells in the evening, because I feel more connected to the Moon – but I also go with the flow. I may invoke a goddess first and then a god, and the next time invoke the god first. So far I haven't noticed any ill effects, and the deities still seem to be assisting me. Life is stressful enough without bringing that pressure into your magickal work. Relax, connect with your deities and enjoy the experience.

I don't speak about my spells to all and sundry because they are personal and talking about them will diminish their effectiveness. My intent in performing a spell or ritual is for my satisfaction and improvement or to thank the deities, not to impress others. I feel sorry for anyone who would choose this path in order to impress the uninformed. Wicca is a religion, not a popularity contest or to be used to shock people. It should be approached with the same reverence and respect as for any other religion.

My faith in everyday life

Egyptian magick is also a lifestyle. I have surrounded myself with Egyptian statuary and have headdresses, artefacts and reproductions of daggers to bring my worship to life. Some of the jewellery items I wear day to day are Egyptian, because I am proud to identify myself as an Egyptian witch.

These items bring me serenity and solace on a personal level but they are not really necessary to my spirituality. All that is needed is my devotion to the Egyptian deities and my knowledge that they are with me always. My belief in them allows me to connect with them any time, day or night, regardless of formal ritual or devotional act. I am able to offer them my thanks for assisting me in mundane tasks or in personal acts of kindness and pleasure. To me, each and every thing I do is in honour of my gods and I strive to do the best I can. I let my actions speak for me, for if I lead a good life then I am displaying my beliefs with each act of caring and compassion.

I do not keep my spirituality a secret, nor do I broadcast it loudly to all I meet. My beliefs are private and I share them only with people I feel can understand and accept my choice. There are those who are very close to me yet know nothing of my religion; I haven't told them out of deference to them and the knowledge that this would be detrimental to our relationship. People who have known me for some time and find out about my religion are generally surprised. My devotion to Egyptian magick makes me who I am; I refuse to apologise for my religion and will not tolerate people who belittle it or are narrow-minded about it. My beliefs are just as strong, if not stronger, and just as personal as anyone else's religious beliefs, be they Wiccan, Catholic, Protestant, Jewish, or any other faith.

Fear is another reason why Wiccans may be reticent about their practices. Even in this day and age there are still so many people who harbour strange notions about witchcraft in general. Some think that Wiccans worship the devil and perform animal sacrifice. Those concepts are absolutely appalling to me! Wiccans do not believe in the devil or pure evil; that is an entirely Christian concept. And animal sacrifice has no place in a religious belief system where all life is sacred. To the Ancient Egyptians, animals were links with the deities or were seen as aspects of the gods themselves – they certainly would not have sacrificed a god.

My personal intent

My purpose in bringing my personal beliefs to light is to instruct, to offer what I feel is an alternative in Wiccan worship, and to share what knowledge I may have acquired in my devotion to the deities.

True spirituality is a calling. I have chosen to be a witch and Egyptian magick is my choice. It is not my intention to advise you to follow any specific religious doctrine or to convert you to Wicca. The rituals I have included in this book should be approached after much study and soul searching. Dedicating yourself to witchcraft, as with any other religion, is not something to be taken lightly. I can't imagine anyone would convert to any faith on a whim, without study and instruction. But trying the spells in this, or any other book, even without dedicating yourself to Wicca, will help you to understand the time and attention it takes to fully devote to your spirituality.

CHAPTER 2

Magick in the Time of the Pharaohs

 When I first approached Egyptian magick, I was pretty much on my own. I had to read numerous general books on Ancient Egypt and other forms of Wicca just to find passing references to Egyptian deities or mythology. But the more I read, the more I was moved by the culture, the people, the deities. I wanted more than anything to connect with the spirituality of the Ancient deities. The passion and urgency of their life moved me as no other religion had.

The Ancient Egyptians were a simple people who followed the will of the pharaoh. The rituals they observed were based upon the rise and fall of the Nile, the appeasement of the gods, and fertility for themselves, their beloved land and most especially the pharaoh. The gods and goddesses provided sun, rain, fertile lands, favourable weather and, ultimately, abundant crops. To worship and offer thanks to the deities helped ensure their survival.

In our urban society, we have a rather different perception of what is important. Most of us do not raise our own crops or livestock and advances in agricultural management all but guarantee that we will be provided for. I try to adapt my rituals to give thanks to the deities for helping me to stay employed, keep my ancient car running, find the love of my life, or be creative enough to write a book. It may not correspond exactly with the needs of the Ancient Egyptians, but then my life doesn't revolve around agriculture and harvest.

The Egyptian deities

The deities of Ancient Egypt were central to life in the Beloved Land. All aspects of life, love, prosperity and death were governed by one or more deities. In battle, the god Set could be called upon to smite enemies; in love matters, Hathor, Bast or Isis could be invoked to move a loved one's heart. The deities provided their assistance on a daily basis and their worship today should be no different.

However, if religious worship does not change and evolve with the times, it will grow stagnant and cease to be. So, too, the worship of the Egyptian deities should change with the times. Even during antiquity the worship of the gods was ever changing. Some gods were discarded, others were 'absorbed' and melded with other gods, or became aspects of the same god. Some gods fell out of favour with the pharaoh; the heretic pharaoh, Akhenaten, attempted to force his people into the worship of just one god, the Aten. Other gods were held in high esteem throughout hundreds, even thousands, of years.

Life and death

The Egyptian concept of life was really a concept of death. Every day and every act performed in an Egyptian's life was in preparation for the afterlife. The average Egyptian's life was a difficult one and the promise of an afterlife that was sweet and free from toil was very appealing.

We take so many things for granted that were terrifying to the Ancients. If we fall ill, we go to the doctor and in short order are on the mend. Think of what life must have been like with little or no medication, only herbal remedies that might or might not have been effective; some could even do more harm than good. But they were all that was available from the local priest/magician/physician. Infant mortality was high; an injury could maim for life; a minor infection could kill. Evidence has been found of tooth decay, healed fractures and even brain surgery performed on the Ancients prior to their death. Just imagine how painful drilling into someone's skull must have been without the use of modern anaesthetics!

Yet the Egyptians celebrated all facets of life and death, for they knew that their deities could be called upon to help in times of distress. Death was not the end of life: it was the beginning of another form of life. The Ancients understood that, no matter what the outcome might be, the deities would assist them, protect them, cure them, nurture them and welcome them into the afterlife.

The practice of mummification was to keep the body intact so the soul would recognise its body after death. Some of the internal organs removed in the process were carefully preserved and placed in canopic jars, while others were discarded as they were not considered important or necessary for the afterlife. Even the most humble Egyptian was buried with familiar items to be used in the afterlife: the mummy was wrapped with scarabs inserted between the layers of bandaging to ensure entrance to the Underworld, food was left in the tomb to nourish the soul, and furniture and personal items were placed in the tomb for a comfortable life in Eternity.

The Cairo Calendar

Most traditional Wiccans follow the Wheel of the Year, which is based primarily on Celtic practices and revolves around the cycles of birth, fertility, planting, growth, harvest, death and rebirth. The eight festivals (Samhain, Yule, Imbolc, Ostara, Beltane, Midsummer, Lammas and Mabon) that comprise the Wheel are generally designed to honour the god and goddess aspect of religious belief. Monthly worship of the goddess aspect coincides with the Full Moons; some years there are 12 celebrations, some 13. Monthly Moon worship is an excellent time to cast spells because the Full Moon exerts a great deal of energy and adds power to any spell cast at that time.

I try to follow the festivals outlined in the Cairo Calendar, which delineates the Ancient Egyptian feasts and holidays that focus on the Annual Inundation and the Intercalary Days – the birth days of five of the major deities: Osiris, Horus the Elder, Set, Isis and Nephthys. The annual Nile inundation was the single most important event to the people of the New Kingdom, for without it crops could not flourish, famine and disease would be rampant and death would quickly follow. Beltane (May Day) and Samhain (Halloween), being Celtic in nature, were unknown to them. As I am an Egyptian witch, the Cairo Calendar is the most meaningful to me. I do celebrate Samhain though, but not as a Wiccan holiday; it happens to be my birthday, which could explain why I was drawn to witchcraft, and it gives me an opportunity to honour the deceased members of my family.

Some books have adapted Egyptian ritual to correspond with the Wheel of the Year. An excellent example is *An Egyptian Book of Shadows* by Jocelyn Almond and Keith Seddon. However, I find it difficult to celebrate in Egyptian ritual a concept that had no basis in the Egyptian form of worship. I can understand it and I have even participated in Wiccan rituals of other traditions, but it does not move me the way Egyptian ritual does.

Gods and goddesses

Mainstream religions do not celebrate the feminine aspect of divinity, only the masculine. You might see the statue of a female saint in a church, but it will not be a goddess statue. Most of the earth-based religions associate the God, or masculine energy, with the Sun, and the Goddess, or feminine energy, with the Moon. However, the Ancient Egyptians recognised that there should always be a balance of male and female energy in all aspects of life, including spirituality. Always innovative, they had both Sun and Moon gods and goddesses. Traditional Wiccans often refer to Mother Earth: to the Egyptians Earth was represented by the god Geb.

When you commit yourself to the Egyptian pantheon of deities, your perception changes. You can see masculine and feminine energy in almost anything, as the Egyptians did.

Nepthys and Set

Some useful hieroglyphs

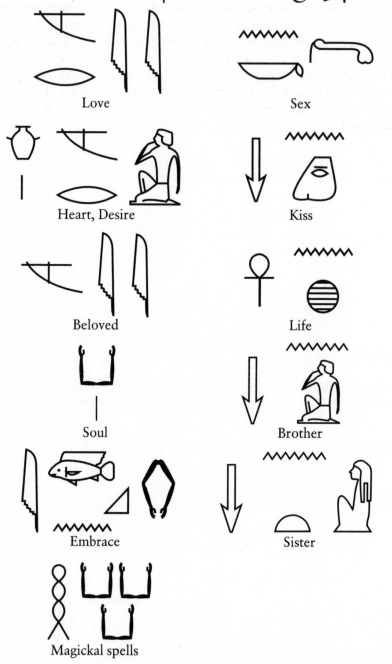

Love

Sex

Heart, Desire

Kiss

Beloved

Life

Soul

Brother

Embrace

Sister

Magickal spells

Brothers and lovers

The Ancient Egyptians used terminology that some may find distressing – a woman may call her lover her brother! This does not mean that she is in love with her brother. The pharaohs did in fact marry half-sisters and daughters, but that was, in part, to strengthen the royal lineage. The average Egyptian used 'brother' and 'sister' as terms of endearment, since they felt the closest bonds were between siblings. I have tried to be consistent with the essence of the poetry from that period and have used 'brother' and 'sister' to designate words such as 'lover' and 'beloved'.

CHAPTER 3

Egyptian Magick for Today

Contrary to how it is sometimes depicted in novels or films, witchcraft is not a parlour game to be taken lightly. Wicca is a religion, an ongoing quest for peace of mind, love, respect, and, ultimately, eternal rest in the Summerlands – or eternal life in the West, which was the land of the dead for the Ancient Egyptians. Wiccans do not fly, except in aeroplanes, nor do they cause time to stop, throw fire, turn men into toads, or any of the other nifty special effects that Hollywood dreams up. But with proper meditation, relaxation and visualisation, you can use your mind and magickal energy to bring about change.

Choosing witchcraft should be personally rewarding for you, though it may cause those closest to you to treat you differently. Your lover/spouse may understand and tolerate your new beliefs, or may not. This could change your life entirely: people you are now close to may shut you out of their lives; your parents and siblings may not be able to understand the choice you have made; your friends may not want to spend time with you. If you feel that someone close to you may not be understanding of your choice, you may prefer not to tell that person. Whom you choose to tell is your business, but choose wisely: discrimination in all forms still exists and it can be very difficult to prove that you were fired from your job because of your beliefs. Having said that, don't feel that you should not become a witch because you will inevitably be isolated and ostracised. Witchcraft is not an easy path, but for me it has been rewarding and deeply spiritual. My gods and goddesses guide my life, help me through the difficult times and rejoice with me during good fortune. They lead me down paths of knowledge that I never dreamed possible.

Wicca does not force you to celebrate at certain times of the month (Esbats) or of the year (Sabbats) (see pages 241 and 242); rituals should be your personal expression and desire to connect with the gods and goddesses. You are free to perform daily devotions to them, if you so desire and have the time. Our lives are so full that we may feel we do not have the time to speak to our deities as often as we would like. But they are always with us, always ready to hear us, whether we choose to devote an hour or a moment in thanks. Witchcraft allows you to expand your thinking, be creative and express yourself as the unique person that you are. It encourages you to look within and get in tune with your feelings, fears, hopes and desires – because you are a gift of the Gods, you are their creation. They want you to be happy and healthy, they want you to know yourself and discover how to achieve your ultimate goals. And they are always ready to lend a hand, guide you, assist you in times of need and despair and celebrate with you in times of joy. Just call out to them in perfect love and perfect trust; they will hear you and help you in any way possible.

Witchcraft is a learning process. I read more now than ever before and not just about witchcraft. I have an extensive library on aromatherapy, herbs and natural healing, Egyptian history and hieroglyphics, comparative religion, divination methods, even beadwork and sewing. One book leads you in many other directions and all add to your skill and knowledge as a witch or Egyptian practitioner. I highly recommend that you read as much as possible on the subject that most stimulates your interest. Obviously, for me that was Egyptian religion and mythology and each book I turn to adds to my knowledge, understanding and appreciation of my devotion to the Ancient Ones.

Divination

Divination is the act of predicting or foreseeing future events. It is a good idea to familiarise yourself with one or more divination methods. There are many beautiful Tarot decks on the market, as well as scrying mirrors, runes (for the Norse tradition), crystal balls and tea leaves (for the Romany tradition), the I Ching (for Asian traditions) and medicine cards (for Native American traditions).

Try more than one method until you find those that most suit your needs and particular path. I have used some of the Egyptian divination tools on the market with great success, as well as Egyptian Tarot decks, but I have also experimented with runes and crystal balls. As with any of your magickal items, they are not for other people to handle because you have infused them with your energy, specifically for divination. You may want to divine for other people and that again is your choice; my advice is to wait until you are comfortable with the divination method you choose – you would not want to give a 'bad' reading, by which I mean inept rather than distressing or dangerous. You may also want to keep one deck of Tarot cards, if that is your divination choice, just for spellwork alone and have a second deck for divining for others.

Daily devotions

Egyptian magick doesn't have to be centred on specific rituals and the performance of them to connect with spirituality. Egyptian magick is daily, it flavours all aspects of one's life and brings a sense of peace and serenity. Since it is less structured, less constricting, than other Wiccan traditions, it can be performed with just an incantation or a few moments of quiet reflection. The simple candle devotion I perform each evening really helps me to ground myself after the demands of work and family.

I light a gold candle to the gods and a silver one to the goddesses. I do not anoint these candles unless I am calling upon specific deities. I then light a coloured candle to represent my intent or need at the time, or a white candle for thanks, which I usually anoint with an appropriate essential oil or blend. I don't often burn incense because I live with someone who is sensitive to the smoke, but I can get the same ambience by using a diffuser or aromatherapy lamp.

I then speak to the gods from my heart. No special spell is needed, no special tools, no written words. I meditate for a time and leave the candles to burn for one to two hours before I speak to the gods again to thank them for hearing me. I then extinguish the candles. While the candles are burning, I think of my intention but I am also free to do the laundry, make dinner, write, read a book or watch television. I get a chance to connect with my gods, unwind from the day and let my mind and body relax, with just a few candles and a subtle fragrance. How could anything be so simple yet so rewarding?

A grateful incantation

Even the deities like to get the recognition they deserve every day. It takes so little time to thank them for all the wondrous things they do and provide for us. The following incantation can be used on its own or coupled with any spell or ritual:

> *O Great Amun*
> *Thank You for another beautiful day*
> *My Lord and My Lady*
> *Osiris and Isis*
> *Thank You for giving me life*
> *And all the gifts that I so richly enjoy*
> *And to all my other deities*
> *I say thank You*
> *Thank You for everything You have given me.*

Magickal names

Many witches choose to rename themselves specifically for magickal work, usually with a name in keeping with their tradition or a personal characteristic. For some it becomes almost akin to an alternative personality.

Only the deities know the magickal name I have chosen for myself, and that is how I feel it should be. I included 'renaming' in my Self-dedication Ritual (see page 130) when I decided to become an Egyptian witch. I rededicate myself on a regular basis; although this is not essential, I find it a deeply spiritual and moving experience. I feel connected with my deities and it gives me an opportunity just to thank them for their help and guidance.

If you are drawn to a particular deity, you may wish to incorporate the name into the magickal name you adopt. You may change this name as you change and evolve as a Wiccan: a name that suited you as a young

Wiccan may not be as appropriate in middle age so you can find another that suits you better. If you belong to a coven (I do not as I have chosen to work alone), the members may know you only by your magickal name.

I have included a list of Ancient Egyptian names for your information. Whenever possible, I have given the translation or meaning of the name to help you choose what suits you and your aspirations. Since kings were more widely known, the male names are more extensively translated.

Egyptian magickal names - female

Aahotep	*Great and pleasing*
Ahhotep	*The moon is pleased*
Ahmose	*The moon is born*
Ankhesenamun	*Her life belongs to Amun*
Ankhesenaten	*Her life belongs to the Aten*
Ankhesepaaten	
Ankhesneferibre	*Her life is the beautiful heart of Re*
Ankhmut	*Image of Mut*
Ankhmutes	*Image of her mother*
Ankhnesmerire	
Aset	*Isis*
Baktwerel	
Beket-Aten	*Maidservant of the Aten*
Berner-Ib	
Bint-Anath	*Daughter of Anath*
Bunefer	
Djedmaatesankh	
Duatnefret	*Beautiful in the Underworld*
Hatshepsut	*Foremost of noble ladies*
Hatshepsut-Meryetre	*Foremost of noble ladies, Beloved of Re*
Henhenet	
Henutmire	*Beloved mistress of Re*
Henutsen	
Henuttawy	*Mistress of the Two Lands*
Herneith	
Hetepamun	
Hetep-Heres	
Iput	
Ipwet	

Isetnefret	*Isis is beautiful*
Isetnofret	*Isis is beautiful*
Isis	
Isisnofret	
Istnofret	
Kawit	
Kemsit	
Khamaat	*Appearing like justice/truth*
Khamerenebty	
Khenemet	
Khenemetamun	
Khentkawes	
Khnumet	*Of Khnum*
Khutenptah	
Kiya	*Jovial lady*
Maatkare	*Truth is the soul of Re*
Maatneferure	
Mekytaten	
Menhet	
Menwi	
Mereret	
Meresamun	*She is beloved of Amun*
Meresankh	*She is beloved of life*
Meritates	
Merneith	*Beloved of Neith*
Merti	
Meryamun	*Beloved of Amun*
Meryetamun	*Beloved of Amun*
Mery-Sekhmet	*Beloved of Sekhmet*
Merytaten	*Beloved of the Aten*
Mutemwiya	*Mother of the sacred barque*
Mutnefert	
Mutnodjme	
Mutnodjmet	*Sweet one of Mut*
Muyet	
Nakht	
Nebettawy	*Lady of the Two Lands*
Neferhetepes	
Neferet	*Beautiful woman*
Neferhotep	*Beautiful and pleasing*

Nefertari	*The most beautiful*
Nefertiti	*Beautiful one has come*
Neferu	*Beauty*
Neferu-Ptah	*Beauty of Ptah*
Neferure	*Beauty of Re*
Nefru	
Nefru-Ptah	
Nefru-Sobek	
Neith	
Nemathap	
Nenseddjedet	
Nesitanebashru	
Netikerty	*She who is excellent*
Netjeret-Merites	*Goddess, beloved of her father*
Nithotep	
Nodjmet	
Nofret	*Beautiful*
Reweddjedet	
Sadeh	
Satire	
Satsobek	*Daughter of Sobek*
Sennuwy	
Seshseshet	
Setepenmut	*Chosen of Mut*
Sitamun	*Daughter of Amun*
Sit-Hathor	*Daughter of Hathor*
Sit-Hathor-Yunet	
Sithenen	
Sitkamose	*Daughter of Kamose*
Sitra	*Daughter of Ra*
Sitre	*Daughter of Re*
Sitre-Meryamun	*Daughter of Re, Beloved of Amun*
Sobekkare	*Sobek is the soul of Re*
Sobeknefru	*Beautiful of the god Sobek*
Taheret	
Takhat	
Tanetnephthys	
Tem	
Tenetamun	
Tia	

Tiaa
Tio
Titi
Tiy
Tuya
Twosret   *Mighty lady*
Wepwawet
Weret-Imtes

Egyptian magickal names – male

Aakheperenra	*Great is the form of Ra*
Aakheperre	*Great is the soul of Re*
Aasehre	*Great in council is Re*
Ahmose	*The moon is born*
Akhenamun	*Helpful to Amun*
Akhenaten	*Servant of the Aten*
Akhenre	*Beautiful for Re*
Akheperenre	*Great is the form of Re*
Akheperkare	*Great is the soul of Re*
Akheperure	*Great are the manifestations of Re*
Amenemhet	*Amun is at the head*
Amenemnisu	*Amun is king*
Amenemope	*Amun in the Opet Festival*
Amenhirkhopshef	*Amun is his strength*
Amenhotep	*Amun is pleased*
Amenmesses	*Fashioned by Amun*
Amenmose	*Born of Amun*
Anedjib	*Safe is his heart*
Ankhkare	*Re gives life to the soul*
Ankhkheperure	*Living are the manifestations of Re*
Ankhtify	
Aqenenre	*Spirit of Re*
Auserre	*Great and powerful like Re*
Auyibre	*Re succours the heart*
Baenre-Merynetjeru	*Soul of Re, Beloved of the Gods*
Bakare	*Glorious is the soul of Re*
Bakenkhons	*Glory of Khons*
Bakenkhonsu	*Glory of Khonsu*
Bakenmut	*Glory of Mut*

Bakenptah	*Glory of Ptah*
Banefre	*Beautiful soul*
Demedjibtawy	
Den	*Horus who strikes*
Djedefhor	*Enduring like Horus*
Djedefre	*Enduring like Re*
Djedhor	*Horus says (he will live)*
Djedi	
Djedkare	*Enduring is the soul of Re*
Djehuty	
Djer	*Horus who succours*
Djeserkare	*Holy is the soul of Re*
Djeser-Kheperu	*Holy of manifestations*
Djeserkheperure	*Holy are the manifestations of Re*
Djet	*Horus cobra*
Djoser	*Most sacred one*
Haaibre	*Jubilant is the heart of Re forever*
Harsiese	*Horus, Son of Isis*
Hedjkheperre	*Bright is the manifestation of Re*
Heka-Khaswt-Anather	*Ruler of the Desert Lands Anather*
Hekamaatre	*Ruler of justice is Re*
Hemaka	
Hemnetjertepyenamun	*First prophet of Amun*
Henenu	
Heqakheperre	*Manifestation of Re rules*
Herihor	*Horus protects me*
Hetephermaat	*Joyous is truth*
Hor	*Hawk (Horus)*
Hor-Aha	*Fighting hawk*
Horemheb	*Horus is in jubilation*
Horus	*Hawk*
Hotep-Dif	
Hotepsekhemwy	*Pleasing in powers*
Huni	*The smiter*
Imhotep	*He comes in peace*
Ineni	
Intef	
Irmaatenamunre	*Truth is the form of Amun-Re*
Irmaatenre	*Carrying out the justice of Re*
Iwaennetjerwymenkhwy	*Heir of the two benificent Gods*

Iwaennetjerwymerwyitu	*Heir of the two father-loving Gods*
Iwaennetjerwyper	*Heir of the two houses of the Gods*
Iwaennetjerwysenwy	*Heir of the twin Gods*
Iwaenpanetjernehem	*Heir of the God that saves*
Kamose	*Spirit is born*
Kaneferre	*Beautiful is the soul of Re*
Khaba	*Soul appears*
Khaemwaset	*Appearing in Thebes*
Khafre	*Appearing like Re*
Khakhaure	*Appearing like the souls of Re*
Khakheperre	*Soul of Re comes into being*
Khaneferre	*Beautiful is the soul of Re*
Khasekhemre	*Powerful is the soul of Re*
Khasekhemwy	*Two powerful ones appear*
Khendjer-Userkare	
Kheperkare	*Soul of Re comes into being*
Kheperkheperure	*Everlasting are the manifestations of Re*
Khepermaatre	*Justice of Re abides*
Khnemibre	*He who embraces the heart of Re*
Khnumhotep	*Khnum is pleased*
Khuenre	*Protected by Re*
Khufu	*Protected by Khnum*
Khufukaef	
Khutawyre	*Re protects the Two Lands*
Maakherure	*True of voice is Re*
Maatibre	*Justice is the heart of Re*
Mayebre	*Seeing is the heart of Re*
Meket-Re	
Men	*Established*
Menes	
Menkauhor	*Eternal are the souls of Re*
Menkaure	*Eternal like the souls of Re*
Menkheperre	*Lasting is the manifestation of Re*
Menkheperure	*Everlasting are the manifestations of Re*
Menmaatre	*Eternal is the justice of Re*
Menmire-Setepenre	*Eternal like Re, chosen by Re*
Menpehtyre	*Eternal is the strength of Re*
Mentuemhet	
Mentuhotep	*God Montu is content*
Merenre	*Beloved of Re*

Mereramunre	*Beloved of Amun-Re*
Mereruka	
Merneferre	*Beautiful is the desire of Re*
Merneptah	*Beloved of Ptah*
Meruserre	*Strong is the love of Re*
Meryamum	*Beloved of Amun*
Meryatum	*Beloved of Atum*
Meryenptah	*Beloved of Ptah*
Meryhathor	*Beloved of Hathor*
Meryibre-Khety	*Beloved is the heart of Re*
Merykare	*Beloved is the soul of Re*
Meryre	*Beloved of Re*
Mesehti	
Mesutire	*Offspring of Re*
Nakhthorheb	*Strong is his Lord Horus*
Nakhti	*Strong*
Nakhtmin	*Strong is Min*
Nakhtnebef	*Strong in his lord*
Nakjtnebtepnefer	*Beautiful and strong champion*
Narmer	*Angry catfish*
Nebhetepre	*Pleased is the Lord Re*
Nebka	
Nebkaure	*Golden are the souls of Re*
Nebkheperure	*Lord of manifestations is Re*
Nebmaatre	*Lord of justice is Re*
Nebpehtyre	*The Lord of strength is Re*
Nebtawyre	*Lord of the Two Lands is Re*
Nedjty-Ra	*Protector of Ra*
Nefaarud	*Great ones prosper*
Neferefre	*Beautiful is Re*
Neferhotep	*Beautiful and pleasing*
Neferibre	*Beautiful is the heart of Re*
Neferirkare	*Beautiful is the soul of Re*
Neferkare	*Beautiful is the soul of Re*
Neferkhau	*Beautiful of appearances*
Neferkheperure	*Beautiful are the manifestations of Re*
Nefertemkhure	*Nefertum is his protector*
Nekau	
Nekure	
Nemtyemsaf	*Nemty is his protection*

Nesbanebdjed	*He of the ram*
Netjerikhet	*Divine of the body*
Netjerkheperre	*Like a God is the manifestation of Re*
Niuserre	*Possessed of the power of Re*
Nubkaure	*Golden are the souls of Re*
Nubkheperre	*Golden is the manifestation of Re*
Nubmaatre	*Lord of truth is Re*
Nymaatre	*Belonging to the justice of Re*
Nynetjer	*Godlike*
Pami	*He who belongs to the cat (Bastet)*
Pasebakhaenniut	*Star that appears in the City (Thebes)*
Pedibastet	*Wise One of Bastet*
Peftjauabastet	
Piankh	*He who belongs to life*
Piankhi	*He who belongs to living beings*
Pinedjem	*He who belongs to the Pleasant One*
Ptahhotep	*Ptah is content*
Qa'a	*His arm is raised*
Qakare-Iby	*Strong is the soul of Re*
Rahotep	*Re is pleased*
Ramesses	*Re has fashioned him*
Raneb	*Re is the Lord*
Rekhmire	*Wise like Re*
Sahure	*He who is close to Re*
Sanakhte	*Strong protection*
Sanakhtenre	*Perpetuated like Re*
Sankhkare	*Giving life to the soul of Re*
Sehertawy	*Maker of peace in the Two Lands*
Sehetepibre	*Satisfied is the heart of Re*
Seheteptawy	*He who pacifies the Two Lands*
Sekhemankhamun	*Living image of Amun*
Sekhemankhre	*Living image of Re*
Sekhemkheperre	*Powerful are the manifestations of Re*
Sekhemkhet	*Powerful in body*
Sekhemre-Khutawy	*Powerful is Re, Protector of the Two Lands*
Sekhemre-Sankhtawy	*Powerful is Re, Giver of life to the Two Lands*
Sekhemre-Sewadjtawy	*Powerful is Re, He makes the Two Lands flourish*
Sekhemre-Shedtawy	*Powerful is Re, Rescuer of the Two Lands*
Semerkhet	*Thoughtful friend*

Senenmut	*Brother of Mut*
Senusret	*Man of Goddess Wosret*
Seqenenre	*Who strikes like Re*
Setepenamun	*Chosen of Amun*
Setepeninhur	*Chosen of Onuris*
Setepenptah	*Chosen of Ptah*
Setepenre	*Chosen of Re*
Setepptah	*Chosen of Ptah*
Sethirkhopshef	*Set is his strength*
Seth-Peribsen	*Hope of all hearts*
Seti	*He of the god Seth*
Setka	*Spirit of Set*
Setnakhte	*Victorious is Set*
Setutre	*Likeness of Re*
Seuserenre	*Powerful like Re*
Shabaka	
Shebitku	
Shepenwepet	
Shepseskaf	*His soul is noble*
Shepseskare	*Noble is the soul of Re*
Shepsesre	*Noble like Re*
Siamun	*Son of Amun*
Sibastet	*Son of Bastet*
Sineit	*Son of Neith*
Siptah	*Son of Ptah*
Smendes	*Lord of Mendes*
Smenkhkare	*Vigorous is the soul of Re*
Snedjemibre	*Pleasing to the heart of Re*
Snefru	*He of beauty/Bringer of beauty*
Sobekemsaf	*Sobek is his protection*
Sobekhotep	*Pleasing to the god Sobek*
Taharqa	
Tanutamun	
Tefnakht	
Tepemkau	*Best of souls*
Titkheperure	*Image of the transformations of Re*
Tutankhamun	*Living image of Amun*
Tutankhaten	*Living image of the Aten*
Tuthmosis	*Born of the god Thoth*
Unas	

Userkaenre	*Powerful is the soul of Re*
Userkaf	*His soul is powerful*
Userkare	*The soul of Re is powerful*
Userkhaure	*Powerful are the manifestations of Re*
Userkheperure	*Powerful are the manifestations of Re*
Usermaatre	*The justice of Re is powerful*
Wadjkare	*Prosperous is the soul of Re*
Wadjkheperre	*Flourishing is the manifestation of Re*
Wadjmose	*Born to flourish/prosper*
Wahankh	*Strong in life*
Wahemibre	*Carrying out the wish of Re forever*
Wahibre	*Constant is the heart of Re*
Wahkare	*Constant is the soul of Re*
Wahneferhotep	
Wosret	*Powerful one*

CHAPTER 4

The Egyptian Pantheon

In this chapter I have given information on the Egyptian deities most associated with the many aspects of love, creation, marriage, birth, death and magick. The first name that appears is the more common and, in most cases, the Greek name; if another follows in parentheses it is the Egyptian name (if there is no name in parentheses then the two are usually the same). I have added a pronunciation guide in bold for the more difficult names and included some of their more common titles, animals that were sacred to or associated with them, and any items of note that might help you to connect with them.

There are many books available that will give you a more comprehensive list of all the gods and goddesses (see Bibliography and Suggested Reading, pages 243–7), but this is a good place to start.

Geb and Nut

Ament (Amenti)
Goddess of the Underworld (Land of the West).

Titles include:	The Westerner, Hidden Goddess, Goddess with Beautiful Hair.
Relationships:	The consort of Amun. She welcomes the deceased into the Land of the Dead.
Direction:	She represents the direction West.

Amun (Amen)
Creator God, God of Fate, Fertility, Prophecy, Prosperity, Reproduction, Spells, the Sun.

Titles include:	Hidden One, King of the Gods, Lord of Time, He Who Hears All Prayers.
Relationships:	Husband of Ament.
Images:	Often depicted as a bearded man wearing a double plume headdress, holding an ankh in his right hand and a sceptre in his left.
Sacred animals:	Among others, the ram with curled horns, elephant, falcon, frog, goose, snake.
Sacred colours:	Gold, saffron yellow.
Sacred gemstones:	Amethyst, emerald, sapphire, turquoise.

Anubis (Anpu)
God of Animals, Death, Endings, Wisdom.

Titles include:	Lord of the Divine Pavilion, Guardian of the Underworld, Protector and Judge of the Dead.
Relationships:	Son of Nephthys and Osiris.
Images:	Most often depicted as a jackal-headed man or a crouching jackal.
Sacred animals:	Dog, dolphin, fish, jackal.
Sacred gemstones:	Fire opal, opal, pearl.
Direction:	He represents the direction West.

Apophis (Apep)
God of Darkness, Death, Eclipses, Night, the Underworld.

Titles include:	Great Serpent of Tuat (the Underworld).
Relationships:	The enemy of Ra.
Images:	Often depicted as a large snake.
Sacred animals:	Beetle, lobster or crayfish, scorpion, serpent, wolf.

Bast

Goddess of Animals, Childbirth, Dance, Fertility, Fire, Happiness, Intuition, Joy, Marriage, Music, Pleasure, Sex, the Sun.

Titles include:	Mistress of Pleasure, Eye of the Sun, Lady of the East.
Relationships:	Daughter of Ra; wife of Ptah.
Images:	Most often depicted as a cat-headed woman carrying a sistrum.
Sacred animals:	All lions and cats are sacred to her, but especially the black cat.
Sacred colour:	Red.
Direction:	She represents the direction East.

Bes

God of Childbirth, Cosmetics and Female Adornments, Fertility, Luck, Married Couples, Music.

Titles include:	Guardian Against All Evils, Lord of the Land of Punt.
Images:	Most often seen as a grotesque dwarf.

Geb (Seb) (geeb)
God of Creation, Crops, Earth Fertility, New Beginnings.

Titles include: Chief of the Gods, Father of the Gods.

Relationships: Nut is his consort, sister and beloved; father of Nut's children; son of Shu and Tefnut.

Images: Often depicted stretched out under Nut.

Sacred animal: Goose.

Hapi
God of Crops, Fertility, Prosperity, the River Nile.

Images: Generally depicted as a fat man with large breasts.

Sacred animals: Baboon, fish, marsh birds.

Hathor (Het Heret)

Goddess of Astrology, Beauty, Enjoyment, Flowers, Happiness, Intoxication, Joy, Love, Marriage, the Moon, Motherhood, Music, Pleasure, Prosperity, Protection, Wine, Women.

Titles include:	Queen of the West, Mistress of Heaven, Golden One, Lady of Malachite, Lady of the Sycamore, House of Horus.
Relationships:	Wife of Horus the Elder; mother of Ahy the Sistrum Player.
Images:	Often depicted as a cow-headed or cow-horned woman carrying a sistrum.
Sacred animals:	Cow, dove, hippopotamus, lion, lynx, snake, sparrow, swan, vulture.
Sacred colours:	Bronze, red.
Sacred gemstones:	Emerald, malachite, turquoise.
Direction:	She represents the direction West.

Heket, Heqet

Goddess of Childbirth, Conception, Creation, Fertility, Resurrection.

Images:	A frog-headed goddess and one of the midwives for the birth of the Sun each morning.
Sacred animal:	Frog.

Horus (Heru, Sa Aset)
God of Prophecy, Protection, Retribution, Revenge, Success, the Sun.

Titles include:
God on the Horizon,
Horus the Younger,
Protector of his Father.

Relationships:
Son of Isis and Osiris;
father of The Four Sons
of Horus, Duamutef
(dwa'mu'tef), Hapi,
Imsety and Qebhsennuf
(keb'snoof). Conceived
by magick after Osiris's
death.

Images:
Most often depicted as a
falcon or a falcon-headed
man.

Sacred animals:
Bear, bull, crocodile,
falcon, hawk, horse,
ichneumon (mongoose),
lion, shrew, sphinx, wolf.

Sacred gemstones: Ruby and other red
stones.

Sacred herb:
Horehound.

Imhotep (I-em-hetep)
God of Healing, Knowledge,
Magick, Medicine, Peace, Writing.

Titles include: He Who Comes
                       In Peace.

Relationships: Deified architect,
                       physician, scribe and
                       vizier; builder of the Step
                       Pyramid at Saqqara.

Sacred animal: Ibis.

Isis (Aset)
Earth and Creator Goddess, Goddess of Abundance, Death, Dreams,
Enchantments, Magick, Marriage, Reincarnation, Rituals, Success,
Tarot.

Titles include:	Great Mother, Giver of Life, Mistress of Magick, The Great of Magick.
Relationships:	Sister/wife of Osiris; mother of Horus.
Images:	Often depicted as a woman wearing the solar disc or as a kneeling woman with outstretched wings.
Sacred animals:	Ape, cat, cow, eagle, goose, hawk, kite, lion, owl, ram, scorpion, snake, sphinx, swallow, vulture.
Sacred colours:	Green, red, sky blue.
Sacred gemstones:	Amethyst, aquamarine, beryl, crystal, pearl, peridot, ruby, sapphire, star sapphire, turquoise.
Sacred herbs and plants:	Date palm, fig, heather, onion.
Direction:	She represents the direction North.

Khensu (Khonsu)
God of Exorcism, Healing, the Moon.

Titles include:	The Wanderer, He Who Traverses, The Navigator, God of the New Moon.
Relationships:	Adopted son of Mut and Amun-Ra.
Images:	Often seen as a man in mummy wrappings, wearing a skullcap topped with a disc in the crescent moon.
Sacred animals:	Baboon, cat, falcon.

Khepera (Khepra)
Creator God, God of Change, Compassion, Gentleness, Healing, Literary Abilities, Miracles, New Beginnings, Reincarnation, the Sun, Transformation.

Titles include:	He Who Becomes.
Sacred animals:	Crab, dolphin, fish, lobster or crayfish, scarab beetle, scorpion, sphinx, turtle, wolf.

Khnum
Creator God, God of the annual Nile floods, Arts and Crafts, Fertility and Creation, Gentleness.

Titles include:	The Potter God, The Moulder.
Relationships:	Husband of Anukis; father/husband of Satis.
Images:	Often depicted as a ram-headed man and it is said that he created men on his potter's wheel.
Sacred animal:	Ram.

Ma'at (may'at)
Goddess of Fate, Harmony, Judgement and Justice, Law, Order, Reincarnation, Truth.

Titles include:	Eye of Ra, Mistress of the Underworld, The Mother, Lady of the Judgement Hall.
Relationships:	Daughter of Ra; wife of Thoth.
Images:	Often depicted sitting on her heels wearing an ostrich feather on her head.
Sacred animals:	Elephant, ostrich, vulture.
Sacred colour:	Red.
Sacred gemstone:	Emerald.

Meshkent
Goddess of Childbirth and Delivery.

Relationships:	She brought relief to women in labour.
Images:	Often depicted as a woman wearing two long palm shoots, curved at the ends.

Min
God of Crops, Fertility, Harvests, Sexuality.

Titles include: Lord of the Foreign Lands, God of the Eastern Desert.

Images: Portrayed wearing a crown of two tall straight plumes, holding a flail in his right hand and with an erect phallus.

Sacred animal: White bull.

Direction: He represents the direction East.

Mut (moot)
Creator Goddess, Goddess of Marriage, Motherhood, the Sky.

Titles include: Lady of Thebes, The Great Sorceress, Eye of Ra.

Relationships: Wife of Amun-Ra.

Images: Most often depicted wearing a vulture headdress.

Sacred animals: Among others, the cat, eagle, lion, vulture.

Sacred gemstones: Agate, opal, pearl, star sapphire.

Neferten
God of Fragrance, Perfumes, the Sun.

Titles include: Atum the Younger.

Relationships: Son of Ptah and Sekhmet.

Images: Often depicted as a man holding a lotus sceptre.

Sacred plant: Lotus flower.

Neith
Creator Goddess, Goddess of Arts and Crafts, Healing, Herbs, Knowledge, Magick, Marriage, Meditation, Mysticism, Rituals, Women.

Titles include:	That Which Is, The Terrifying, The Huntress, Opener of the Ways, Lady of the West.
Relationships:	Virgin mother of Ra; sometimes identified as the mother of Sobek, the daughter of Ra and the wife of Khnum.
Images:	She wears the red crown of Lower Egypt and carries a bow and two arrows in her hands.
Sacred animals:	Among others, the bee, cat, perch, snake.
Direction:	She represents the direction West.

Nekhbet
Goddess of Childbirth, Motherhood, Protection.

Titles include:	Protectress of the Kings of Upper Egypt, Lady of the South.
Relationships:	Daughter of Ra; wife of Hapi.
Images:	She is depicted as a vulture or a woman wearing the white crown of Upper Egypt or a vulture headdress.
Sacred animal:	Vulture.
Direction:	She represents the direction South.

Nephthys (Nebet Het) **(nef'this)**
Goddess of Dark Magick, Dreams,
Enchantments, Intuition, Life and Death,
Mysticism, Peace, Prophecy, Protection.

Titles include: Protectress of the Dead,
Mistress of the Palace,
Lady of the House,
The Revealer.

Relationships: Sister/wife of Set;
mother of Anubis by
her brother Osiris.

Sacred animals: Among others, the ape,
dog, hawk, horse, kite,
snake, sphinx, vulture.

Sacred gemstones: Crystal, pearl, ruby,
star sapphire.

Sacred plant: Lily.

Direction: She represents the direction West.

Nut **(noot)**
Goddess of Night, Reincarnation, the Sky, Weather.

Titles include: Mother of the Gods, Life-Giver.

Relationships: Daughter of Shu and Tefnut; sister/lover of Geb;
mother of Isis, Osiris, Nephthys, Set and Horus the
Elder; sometimes identified as the wife of Ra.

Images: She is depicted as stretching
across the sky with her
feet in the East and her
head in the West.

Sacred animals: Among others, the
boar, cow, eagle,
peacock, sow.

Sacred gemstone: Turquoise.

Osiris (Asar)
Creator and Earth God, God of Abundance, Death, Dreams, Reincarnation, Rituals, Vegetation.

Titles include:	Lord of All Things, Lord of the Underworld, King of Kings.
Relationships:	Husband/brother of Isis; father of Horus, and of Anubis with his sister, Nephthys.
Images:	Usually depicted in mummy wrappings, holding the crook and flail, with green skin to signify his association with vegetation.
Sacred animals:	Among others, the ape, bennu bird, bull, crocodile, ox, pig, ram, sphinx, vulture.
Sacred colours:	Black, green.
Sacred gemstones:	Crystal, topaz.
Sacred plants:	Among others, corn, ivy.
Direction:	He represents the direction East.

Ptah (p'ta)
Creator God, God of Arts and Crafts, Beginnings, Miracles, Regeneration.

Titles include:	The Father of Beginnings, The Opener, The Divine Artificer.
Relationships:	Husband/brother of Sekhmet; father of Neferten, also identified as the husband of Bast.
Images:	A mummified man holding a sceptre, ankh and tet; the Apis bull is the living personification of Ptah.
Sacred gemstone:	Diamond.

Ra
Creator God, God of Destiny, Magick, Prosperity, Rituals, Spells, the Sun

Titles include:	Horus of the Horizon, Golden One, Bringer of Light, Ruler of the Sky, Father of the Gods.
Relationships:	Father of Shu and Tefnut; sometimes identified as the husband of Nut, daughters include Bast, Ma'at and Sekhmet.
Images:	Often depicted as a man, head topped with a solar disc, or a man with a ram or falcon head.
Sacred animals:	Among others, the bennu bird, beetle, bull, cat, cobra, falcon, goose, hawk, lion, phoenix, ram, sparrow hawk.
Sacred colour:	Gold.
Sacred gemstones:	Topaz, yellow diamond.
Direction:	He represents the direction East.

Renenet
Goddess of Children, Harvest, Justice, Luck, Prosperity.

Titles include:	Lady of the Double Granary.
Relationships:	She gives a baby its soulname (ren), personality and future fate at birth.
Images:	Often depicted as a woman with a serpent's head wearing a solar disc.

Sekhmet
Goddess of Courage, Destruction, Revenge.

Titles include:	Lady of the Flame, Lady of the Bright Red Linen, The Powerful.
Relationships:	Daughter of Ra; sister/wife of Ptah; mother of Neferten.
Images:	Most often depicted as a lioness-headed woman, crowned with a disc and coiled cobra.
Sacred animals:	Among others, the cat, lion.
Sacred colours:	Gold, red.
Direction:	She represents the direction South.

Selqet (Serqet)
Goddess of Happy Marriages, Married Sexual Love.

Relationships:	Daughter of Ra.
Images:	She is guardian of the canopic jars after death and is most often seen as a woman with a scorpion on her head, her arms extended.
Sacred animal:	Scorpion.

Seshat
Goddess of Archives, Books, Calculation, Fate, Hieroglyphics, History, Learning, Letters, the Sky, Stars, Time, Writing.

Titles include:	The Secretary, Mistress of the House of Books.
Relationships:	Wife of Thoth.
Images:	She is record-keeper of the gods and is often seen as a woman wearing on her head a star, reversed crescent and two long straight plumes.

Set (Seth)
God of Chaos, Dark Magick, Death, Destruction, Evil, Night, Retribution, Revenge, Storm, Suffering.

Titles include:	He of the Gold Town, The Red God, Lord of Storm, He Who Is Below.
Relationships:	Brother and murderer of Osiris; husband/ brother of Nephthys.
Images:	He has reddish-white skin and bright red hair, which were both hated by the Ancient Egyptians.
Sacred animals:	Among others, the antelope, ass, boar, crocodile, goat, hippopotamus, oryx, pig, red ox, scorpion, serpent.
Sacred colour:	Red.
Sacred gemstone:	Black diamond.

Sobek, Sebek
Creator God, God of Cursing, Dark Magick, Death, the Sun.

Titles include:	Lord of Death, Hidden One.
Images:	Said to live at the bottom of the Underworld and is most often seen as a crocodile with gold earrings and bracelets on his legs.
Sacred animal:	Crocodile.
Direction:	He represents the direction West.

Tauret (ta'wor'et)
Goddess of Childbirth, Darkness, Maternity, Protection, Revenge.

Images:	A female hippopotamus with pendulous breasts, holding a piece of rolled papyrus, a symbol of protection.

Thoth (Tehuti)
God of Astrology, Books, Creativity, Divination, Fate, Healing, Invention, Judgement and Justice, Knowledge, Learning, Magick, the Moon, Peace, Prophecy, Rituals, Tarot, Time, Wisdom, Writing.

Titles include:	Lord of Holy Words, Heart of Ra, Spokesman of the Gods, The Elder, Scribe of the Gods, Lord of Books and Learning.
Relationships:	Husband of Seshat; also identified as husband of Ma'at.
Images:	Most often depicted as an ibis-headed man wearing a lunar disc and crescent on his head and holding a writing reed and palette; said to be the inventor of hieroglyphs and the first and greatest of magicians.
Sacred animals:	Among others, the ape, baboon, dog, ibis, jackal.
Sacred gemstones:	Fire opal and opal.

CHAPTER 5

Egyptian Love and Passion

The gods and goddesses provide the unconditional spiritual love we all need, but we also desire physical and emotional love. You may find your one true soulmate, or you may be fortunate enough to find more than one in a lifetime – many Wiccans believe we live many lifetimes and connect with many people.

Mainstream religions tend to stress a better life in heaven or the hereafter, whereas witchcraft allows you to change your life for the better now, while you can enjoy it, yet still offering eternal rest and happiness in the afterlife. The Ancient Egyptians considered love a disease to be cured by the local priest/magician; yet love is a recurring theme in their poetry, tomb writings and paintings and pottery shards. So, although it was perceived as a disease, it seems that most of the people didn't want to be cured, but did want to be loved just as much as we all do. They were not above asking the local priest for a love-binding spell or a curse for a wayward lover.

Witches don't wish to be rich and famous – that would interfere too much with their meditation and worship – but they do want a secure life, enough money to get by, as well as someone to share their lives with. So, if you are attracted to someone, it is worth pursuing the attraction. Why not use your magickal arsenal to nudge someone into wanting you as much as you want them? You could have the lover of your dreams.

Having said that, you cannot run wild and do whatever you please. In love magick, as with all Egyptian magick, no other person must be harmed, and a love spell directed at someone in an existing relationship is, in my opinion, an absolute no-no. Common sense needs to prevail, too, since the use of binding spells, especially in love matters, may lead to obsession, which is very self-destructive. If I wanted a person badly enough to perform a love spell, I would do it only if I knew the person held some feeling for me but perhaps hadn't yet thought of me in the way I wished. Because why waste a lot of time and energy on something that will never become reality? The crucial element is that magick should always be used with the best intentions in mind, even if the 'object' you want is another person.

An it harm none, do as thou wilt

All Wiccan traditions are based on two basic tenets: 'An it harm none, do as thou wilt' and the Law of Return – 'Whatever you send out, comes back threefold'. Witches ask only for what they need and nothing more; that's the basis of any witchcraft. Many spells include the phrase 'If it is meant to be' in order to avoid bad coming back on you.

Wiccans of different traditions can perhaps be a little too serious about their work. Many question the ethics of performing love spells with a particular person in mind. Some practitioners frown upon the use of such things as binding spells, even though you find revenge magick in many books that have nothing to do with the Egyptians. I feel you need to enjoy your spirituality and always keep a sense of humour.

In my opinion, to say that some forms of magick are bad is to negate the practitioner's judgement and intent. Performing a spell with a special someone in mind may gently nudge him or her in the right direction, if it is meant to be. I do not feel that you are forcing or 'bending' that person to your command. Remember that we all have free will, and also that the deities know what is best for us, even if we do not. If you do not get the result you desire, there will be a reason for it: you may not be in the right place in your life for a loving relationship, or you may have unresolved issues with someone that need to be addressed before you can start a new love. What goes around, comes around – and in Wicca it comes back threefold!

A spell to awaken love

One of my favourite more biting spells is a Coptic incantation that goes something like this:

> May (name) pant like a bitch in heat over his desire for me
> May he have no happiness, no peace, no sleep, no
> appetite, only hunger and lust for me
> Do not let the soul of (name) rest until he comes to me.

Quite a nice little number, don't you think? It really gets to the heart of the matter, regardless of the Law of Return. Recite it a few times and you can get very caught up in the desire and the passion that the Ancient Egyptians felt. Light a red candle, anoint it with cinnamon, vetivert or jasmine oil and meditate on the object of your desire. Recite the verse over and over if you like; you'll soon find you enjoy the feeling you get, the sense of urgency, the sense of control. Egyptian poetry is passionate, sensual and, in some cases, downright explicit, which may be one of its most appealing points. There is a passion that is unmistakable: passion for life, passion for love, passion for sexual pleasure and expression.

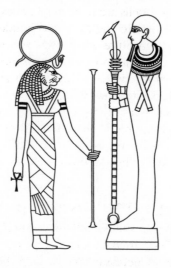

Sekhmet and Ptah

Egyptian magick walks a fine line between what has been commonly termed 'white' or 'good' magick and 'black' or 'bad' magick. I don't believe in bad magick, only bad intentions. So, in the spirit of the Ancient Egyptians, why not use all the powers at your disposal to make your love dreams a reality? If you choose to cast a love spell to capture the heart of another, that is your choice; no book is going to persuade you against your will. Try performing a spell or two, fashion a doll in the likeness of your beloved and see what happens. If nothing, wait a month or two and try again.

Magick won't cure everything, but it will give you an additional tool to use and the comfort of knowing you have tried every possible avenue before you move on and start anew. And the Ancient Egyptians also knew how to deal with a broken heart and rejection, so it can help you in that way too.

CHAPTER 6

Working with Rituals and Spells

The guidelines for each spell and ritual are just that – guidelines. These spells are to be personal expressions of your intent and devotion to the gods and goddesses. Feel free to experiment and substitute other oils, herbs or incenses if they mean more to you. If lavender oil appeals more than patchouli, go for it! I mix oils based on their scents and corresponding usage; if it is pleasing to me I write the recipe down along with its intent, so that I can repeat it another time. I keep a cotton wool ball with a drop of Passion oil (see page 162) on it in my desk. Its heady yet relaxing scent helps me to unwind during the day; it also reminds me of my most rewarding and powerful love spells.

The meaning and purpose of ritual

There is a difference between spells and rituals. Spells are based on the need or desire at hand. They are dependent upon the feelings you send out when raising the energy necessary to perform the spell. However, rituals are more formal, invoking a god or goddess to assist and are designed for celebration and thanks and are generally performed at Esbats or Sabbats. When you invoke deities, you are calling upon them to join you in your ritual, or even in spellwork, because of their ability to assist you in certain aspects of love, healing, protection and so on. Many witches like to use ritual tools, clothing, music and chanting to raise the energy needed for a successful ritual.

Rituals may be constructed to honour a specific deity, for the cleansing of ritual tools prior to use, and for dedication to the craft. However, these rituals do not require a specific day or phase of the moon, for they are personal expressions and should be deeply spiritual experiences. You may wish to write your ritual beforehand or you can express yourself straight from the heart. The Elements of Earth, Air, Fire and Water should be present at all rituals, for they sustain us and are necessary for our survival. They exert an energy that will help us connect with our selves and our deities. They correspond with the compass points, which also exert energy upon ritual work. The Ancient Egyptians believed that the Four Sons of Horus corresponded with the Elements and compass points, which is why I invoke them when I am performing rituals.

Ritual tools

Ritual tools may include your cauldron, wand, athame, chalice, pentacle and statues. These items help to direct your energy and serve to honour the deities. The wand and athame most often represent the God, or male energy and the chalice and cauldron most often represent the Goddess, or female energy. You may prefer to represent the God and Goddess with statues or candles. A gold candle for the God and a silver candle for the Goddess may be just as useful as any other items. Ritual tools and items also correspond to the Elements. So, while I perform most of my spells with just candles and incense, rituals require more effort and the tools help me to achieve satisfying spiritual experiences.

All ritual items should be cleansed before ritual use to ensure they contain no negative energy and have been dedicated to the deities (see page 63). Although I have not cleansed each of my statues, I have lit a candle and an appropriate incense to the individual deity and thanked each one for his or her image in my home.

Ritual tools should be treated with respect and reverence. You should not use them for mundane tasks, only for ritual work, and they should always be stored away when not in use. I, like many other witches, do not let others handle my ritual items because I have infused them with my energy for ritual and magickal use only. I have consecrated them to the work of the deities and feel that they are special to them. Even my closest friends and other witches have never seen my ritual tools.

It is not necessary to run out and purchase every item immediately; using a wine glass for your chalice until you find the one you want is perfectly fine, as long as you use it only for ritual work. Many items may be obtained at flea markets, thrift stores, on the internet or by mail order. Take your time to acquire the items you desire and feel comfortable with.

Ritual items, use and correspondences

Ankh
Egyptian symbol for everlasting life, often called an Egyptian Cross. It usually represents Earth.

Athame
Double-sided ritual knife, dagger, or sword. It is most often used to direct the energy raised in ritual. The athame represents masculine energy and Fire.

Book of Shadows
A record of magickal spells, recipes, rituals, poetry, dreams and any information gleaned to aid in your ritual and spellwork. Keeping a record helps you to hone your skills in magick and may provide you with valuable insight into why a spell did or didn't work.

Candles
Usually associated with the element of Fire. Candles are used in most rituals and spellwork. You might wish to use a snuffer to extinguish candles, or you can just pinch the wick with dampened fingers. Sometimes candles are left to burn out, but they are only blown out when you wish to 'blow away' the intent.

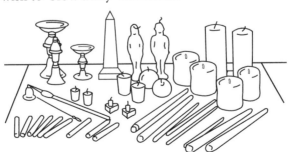

Cauldron

Used for burning incense, holding water and mixing herbs, oils and potions. The cauldron represents feminine energy and may symbolise Air or Water.

Censor

Used for burning incense to purify your ritual space and add an ambience to ritual and spellcasting. It may be used to represent Fire or Air.

Chalice

Used for holding water or wine in ritual. The chalice represents feminine energy and is usually associated with Water.

Pentacle

A flat disc inscribed with a pentagram (five-pointed star) in a circle. This represents Earth, Air, Fire, Water and Spirit – all the elements necessary for successful ritual work.

Wand

Used to direct energy, sometimes in place of the athame. It is often made of wood and adorned with crystals, metal or cord. It may be used to represent Air.

Ritual clothing

There is much debate about how necessary ritual garments and jewellery are to successful magick. I have performed spells and rituals in my everyday clothes, ritual clothing and skyclad (naked), except for my Egyptian headdress and ritual items. I would say that you should practise how you are most comfortable and feel most at ease. The deities accept you and love you as you are. You are their loving creation; how you choose to connect with them is up to you. Some witches prefer to perform rituals in a private outdoor space, depending on the weather conditions, and this may be your choice. Working skyclad outdoors is a wonderful and liberating experience, unless your neighbours catch a glimpse and call the police!

Other items

I use scarab beetles for offerings to the gods. When I'm celebrating with the cat goddess Bast, I sometimes play bells, a sistrum or finger cymbals because she loves their sound.

Preparing for rituals

Connecting with your deities to honour them for all they have provided and to seek their assistance and guidance in your life should be an exhilarating experience, approached with reverence and celebration. I prepare several days in advance by making sure I have all the ritual tools, incense, candles, music and offerings I wish to use – I wouldn't want to keep the gods and goddesses 'on hold' while I look for something in the middle of ritual. I check my schedule to make sure I don't have anything else planned for that day. Ideally a ritual should be performed on its calendar date, such as October 31 for a Samhain ritual, but a day or two either side is perfectly acceptable.

I begin the day or evening of the ritual with a final check of the items needed. Next, I take a ritual shower. Most traditional Wiccans prepare for ritual with a cleansing of some type and the Ancient Egyptians were very conscious of cleanliness (Egyptian temple priests took several ritual baths during the course of the day). I position a muslin bag filled with sea salt mixed with herbs and oils appropriate to the celebration over the shower so that they mingle with the running water. I take the time to relax and prepare my mind for the celebration, thinking of what this ritual means to me and the deities I will invoke. I sometimes burn scented candles and/or incense while I take my ritual shower; it helps me to focus my mind and relax. For additional ambience, relaxation and proper visualisation, I frequently play New Age or classical music while I prepare.

I then towel myself dry and avoid using too many chemicals such as body lotions, deodorant or perfume – unless the lotion and perfume have been created for the ritual. I apply ritual perfume and Egyptian make-up. The clothing I wear depends on the time of year; during the warmer months I prefer not to wear any. Finally I put on an Egyptian headdress and my ritual jewellery.

Next, I set up a small altar or table and lay out the ritual items I will be working with. I turn on the music I have chosen and let it enfold me. Ritual for me is a formal experience and I like to designate the boundaries of my ritual space, whether in a room or outdoors, with my canopic jars. I place a white candle in front of each of the jars, starting in the North and working clockwise. At each compass point I invoke the appropriate Son of Horus, asking for his protection and guidance while I perform my ritual, and light the candle.

When all four candles are lit, I return to my ritual altar to prepare it. The placement of my ritual items is what seems to work best for me and with which I am most comfortable. For instance, I prefer to place a silver candle and/or goddess statue on the upper left hand side of the altar and a gold candle and/or god statue on the upper right. Between them I place my censor or cauldron, depending upon the incense I will be burning or the need for a vessel for mixing herbs. I place a dish of sea salt in front of the gold candle, a small bowl of spring water in front of the silver candle and an Egyptian symbol, most often an ankh, in front of the censor or cauldron. Finally, I place my athame next to the sea salt, my chalice next to the spring water and any offering of food, flowers, or crystals between the athame and chalice.

This is how I prepare for ritual; you may find that other preparations work better for you. For instance, if you would prefer a ritual bath to a shower, you can add the sea salt and herbs or oil to the bath water. You can perform your ritual anywhere you are comfortable and will not be disturbed – the living room, bedroom, spare room or back garden. You may wish to arrange your altar in different ways until you feel you have found the placement that is right for you. Experiment and you will find what appeals to you or makes you feel most at ease. Ritual is not something that should be hurried, but if you really haven't time for a shower or bath, you can always 'smudge' yourself with incense or a sage bundle. Make sure you extinguish any candles and incense you used for your preparations; the last thing you want to do is burn the house down!

Performing your ritual

Having made all your preparations, you are ready to perform your ritual. Light the incense, breathe deeply, relax, focus your mind and prepare to connect with your deities. It is now time to invoke the god and goddess you wish to join you in your ritual. The type of ritual you are performing should lead you to the appropriate deities. If you are performing a fertility ritual, you may wish to call upon Amun, Bes or Min for your god and Bast or Heket for your goddess. When you work with your deities on a regular basis, you will instinctively know who to invoke for assistance. Creator gods and goddesses (see pages 36–53) can assist in almost any type of ritual. Light the gold candle and ask the God to protect you, guide you and celebrate this ritual with you. Next, light the silver candle and ask the Goddess for the same protection, guidance and celebration.

After the candles are lit and the deities invoked, you may then read ritual words from this or any other book, any ritual words you may have written yourself, or you can speak directly from the heart to the deities invoked. You can do whichever feels right and appropriate to the ritual, what it is for, and what you hope to accomplish.

Finally, you should thank each of the gods in turn for joining you in your ritual and then extinguish their candles.

Closing your ritual

Starting in the North and proceeding clockwise, thank each of the Four Sons of Horus for their attendance and extinguish each candle. Extinguish the incense. Gather up all the items, including any ritual clothing and jewellery, and store them until you need them again. Remove your ritual make-up, if you used it. Put on everyday clothes or nightclothes. If you have any offerings and wine left in the chalice, take them outside and return them to the Earth.

Keep in mind that it is quite normal to feel tired after raising the energy necessary to perform a spell or ritual. Eating or drinking something helps to ground that energy and brings you back to the 'real' world. I like to drink a glass of wine, which I offer up to Isis or the deity I invoked, when I have completed my work. My own final act is to record my thoughts and feelings about the ritual in my Book of Shadows.

Cleansing ritual

Whenever you obtain or receive a tool or an item of clothing or jewellery that will be used specifically for ritual work, it should be cleansed before use or before wearing. This cleansing ritual may be used at any time of the month.

Items needed
4 white pillar candles
4 canopic jars (optional)
A gold taper or pillar candle, to represent the god Osiris
A silver taper or pillar candle, to represent the goddess Isis
Spring water in a small bowl
Sea salt in a small dish
A chalice of wine or fruit juice
A slice of wholewheat bread
A censor
Sage incense
The item(s) to be cleansed
Matches
A candle snuffer

Designate your ritual area with the white candles, placing one at each compass point with the canopic jars, if you are using them. Prepare your ritual altar with the other items, arranging the bread and salt in front of the gold candle and the chalice and spring water in front of the silver. Finally, place the item(s) to be cleansed on the altar in front of you.

Go to the candle in the North, light it and recite:
> *Hapi, Son of Horus, Element of Earth, God of the North*
> *I call upon You to protect this ritual space.*

Go to the candle in the East, light it and recite:
> *Duamutef, Son of Horus, Element of Air, God of the East*
> *I call upon You to protect this ritual space.*

Go to the candle in the South, light it and recite:
> *Imsety, Son of Horus, Element of Fire, God of the South*
> *I call upon You to protect this ritual space.*

Go to the candle in the West, light it and recite:

> *Qebhsennuf, Son of Horus, Element of Water, God of the West*
> *I call upon You to protect this ritual space.*

Stand in front of the altar, light the sage incense and breathe deeply. Light the gold candle and recite:

> *Lord of Eternity, Lord of Life*
> *O Great Osiris*
> *Bless me with Your divine presence*
> *And assist Your humble servant, (magickal name).*

Next, light the silver candle and recite:

> *Mistress of Magick, Giver of Life*
> *O Great Isis*
> *Bless me with Your divine presence*
> *And assist Your humble servant, (magickal name).*

Stand quietly for as long as you wish. Feel the warmth of Osiris and Isis fill you; let the incense smoke envelop you. When you are ready, take up the first (or only) item to be cleansed and hold it high above your head. Lower your arms and sprinkle the item with some sea salt and recite:

> *Hapi, I consecrate this (name of item) with Earth*
> *To the service of Isis and Osiris*
> *And all the deities of the Beloved Land.*

Next, pass the item through the incense smoke and recite:

> *Duamutef, I consecrate this (name of item) with Air*
> *To the service of Isis and Osiris*
> *And all the deities of the Beloved Land.*

Carefully pass the item over the flames of both candles and recite:

> *Imsety, I consecrate this (name of item) with Fire*
> *To the service of Isis and Osiris*
> *And all the deities of the Beloved Land.*

Finally, sprinkle the item with some of the spring water and recite:

> *Qebhsennuf, I consecrate this (name of item) with Water*
> *To the service of Isis and Osiris*
> *And all the deities of the Beloved Land.*

Place the item back on the altar and bless any other items, one at a time, following the above actions in order. When all items have been blessed, take the slice of bread in both hands, raise it up to eye level and recite:

> *Accept this simple gift*
> *As an offering of thanks.*

Tear off a piece of the bread, eat it and place the remainder on the altar. Take up the chalice in both hands, raise it up to eye level and recite:

Accept this simple gift
As an offering of thanks.

Take a sip of wine and return the chalice to the altar. You may wish to sit quietly for a while and connect with the deities. When you are ready, pick up the candle snuffer, stand facing the silver candle and recite:

Mistress of Magick, Giver of Life
O Great Isis
Praise and thanks to You
For blessing this/these item(s) in Your name.

Snuff out the silver candle. Face the gold candle and recite:

Lord of Eternity, Lord of Life
O Great Osiris
Praise and thanks to You
For blessing this/these item(s) in Your name.

Snuff out the gold candle. Starting with the candle in the North recite:

Hapi, Son of Horus,
Element of Earth, God of the North
Praise and thanks to You
For protecting this ritual space.

Snuff out the candle, proceed to the East and recite:

Duamutef, Son of Horus,
Element of Air, God of the East
Praise and thanks to You
For protecting this ritual space.

Snuff out the candle, proceed to the South and recite:

Imsety, Son of Horus,
Element of Fire, God of the South
Praise and thanks to You
For protecting this ritual space.

Snuff out the candle, proceed to the West and recite:

Qebhsennuf, Son of Horus,
Element of Water, God of the West
Praise and thanks to You
For protecting this ritual space.

Snuff out the last candle and clear away all items except the bread and chalice of wine. You may feel a bit tired or light-headed after raising the energy necessary for the ritual. Tear off another piece of bread and eat it. Take another drink of wine to ground the energy you raised during the ritual. Take the remaining bread and wine outdoors, leave the bread and pour the wine as an offering on to the Earth. You may now wash the chalice and store it away with your other ritual items.

Jewellery Dedication ritual

I wear quite a number of items of silver jewellery as an outward sign of my religious beliefs, some of which I never remove. Those I wear for religious reasons have each been cleansed and offered to the deities. The pieces I wear simply because I like them have not been blessed, though I do wear them with the cleansed jewellery.

This ritual may be performed any time you obtain or receive a new jewellery item you wish to wear in the mundane world and is not specifically for ritual use only.

Items needed
4 white pillar candles
4 canopic jars (optional)
A gold taper or pillar candle, to represent the god Osiris
A silver taper or pillar candle, to represent the goddess Isis
Spring water in a small bowl
Sea salt in a small dish
A chalice of wine or fruit juice
A slice of wholewheat bread
A censor
Sage incense
The jewellery item(s) to be cleansed
Matches
A candle snuffer

Designate your ritual area with the white candles, placing one at each compass point with the canopic jars, if you are using them. Prepare your ritual altar with the other items, arranging the bread and salt in front of the gold candle and the spring water and chalice in front of the silver. Finally, place the item(s) to be cleansed on the altar in front of you.

Go to the candle in the North, light it and recite:

> *Hapi, Son of Horus, Element of Earth, God of the North*
> *I call upon You to protect this ritual space.*

Go to the candle in the East, light it and recite:

> *Duamutef, Son of Horus, Element of Air, God of the East*
> *I call upon You to protect this ritual space.*

Go to the candle in the South, light it and recite:

> *Imsety, Son of Horus, Element of Fire, God of the South*
> *I call upon You to protect this ritual space.*

Go to the candle in the West, light it and recite:

> *Qebhsennuf, Son of Horus, Element of Water, God of the*
> *West*
> *I call upon You to protect this ritual space.*

Stand in front of the altar, light the sage incense and breathe deeply. Light the gold candle and recite:

> *Lord of Eternity, Lord of Life*
> *O Great Osiris*
> *Bless me with Your divine presence*
> *And assist Your humble servant, (magickal name).*

Next, light the silver candle and recite:

> *Mistress of Magick, Giver of Life*
> *O Great Isis*
> *Bless me with Your divine presence*
> *And assist Your humble servant, (magickal name).*

Stand quietly for as long as you wish. Feel the warmth of Osiris and Isis fill you; let the incense smoke envelop you. When you are ready, take up the first (or only) item to be cleansed and dedicated in your hands and hold it high above your head. Lower your arms and sprinkle the item with some sea salt and recite:

> *Hapi, I consecrate this (name of item) with Earth*
> *To the service of Isis and Osiris*
> *And all the deities of the Beloved Land*
> *May this item serve*
> *As an outward sign of my faith*
> *And devotion to my chosen path.*

Next, pass the item through the incense smoke and recite:

> *Duamutef, I consecrate this (name of item) with Air*
> *To the service of Isis and Osiris*
> *And all the deities of the Beloved Land*
> *May this item serve*

> *As an outward sign of my faith*
> *And devotion to my chosen path.*

Carefully pass the item over the flames of both candles and recite:

> *Imsety, I consecrate this (name of item) with Fire*
> *To the service of Isis and Osiris*
> *And all the deities of the Beloved Land*
> *May this item serve*
> *As an outward sign of my faith*
> *And devotion to my chosen path.*

Finally, sprinkle the item with some of the spring water and recite:

> *Qebhsennuf, I consecrate this (name of item) with Water*
> *To the service of Isis and Osiris*
> *And all the deities of the Beloved Land*
> *May this item serve*
> *As an outward sign of my faith*
> *And devotion to my chosen path.*

Place the item back on the altar and bless any other items you have, one at a time, following the previous actions in order. When all items have been blessed, you may put them on and wear them always with pride and devotion.

Next, take the slice of bread in both hands, raise it up to eye level and recite:

> *Accept this simple gift*
> *As an offering of thanks.*

Tear off a piece of the bread, eat it and place the remainder on the altar. Take up the chalice in both hands, raise it up to eye level and recite:

> *Accept this simple gift*
> *As an offering of thanks.*

Take a sip of wine and return the chalice to the altar. You may wish to sit quietly for a while and connect with the deities.

When you are ready, pick up the candle snuffer, stand facing the silver candle and recite:

> *Mistress of Magick, Giver of Life*
> *O Great Isis*
> *Praise and thanks to You*
> *For blessing this/these item(s) in Your name*
> *I shall wear it/them proudly*
> *In the service of the Ancient Ways.*

Snuff out the silver candle. Face the gold candle and recite:

> *Lord of Eternity, Lord of Life*

O Great Osiris
Praise and thanks to You
For blessing this/these item(s) in Your name
I shall wear it/them proudly
In the service of the Ancient Ways.

Snuff out the gold candle. Starting with the candle in the North recite:

Hapi, Son of Horus,
Element of Earth, God of the North
Praise and thanks to You
For protecting this ritual space.

Snuff out the candle, proceed to the East and recite:

Duamutef, Son of Horus,
Element of Air, God of the East
Praise and thanks to You
For protecting this ritual space.

Snuff out the candle, proceed to the South and recite:

Imsety, Son of Horus,
Element of Fire, God of the South
Praise and thanks to You
For protecting this ritual space.

Snuff out the candle, proceed to the West and recite:

Qebhsennuf, Son of Horus,
Element of Water, God of the West
Praise and thanks to You
For protecting this ritual space.

Snuff out the last candle. You may feel a bit tired or light-headed after raising the energy necessary for the ritual and that is to be expected. Tear off another piece of bread and eat it. Take another drink of wine to ground the energy you raised during the ritual. Take the remaining bread and wine outdoors, leave the bread and pour the wine as an offering on to the Earth. You may now wash the chalice and store it away with your other ritual items.

Spellwork

When you approach spellwork, your only thought should be the task at hand. True change cannot occur if you are thinking of an overdue phone bill or if your child is coming down with the flu – unless you are doing a fast money spell or healing spell to deal with those very issues. You need to train your mind to concentrate on connecting with your needs, your desires and your deities. A simple spell may require only ten minutes to perform, but if your heart and mind are elsewhere, or if you are feeling tired or unwell, it won't be effective. Your spells will be the most rewarding and effective when you take the time to relax, concentrate your mind and connect with the cosmic energy.

Some spells demand more time and effort and that should be taken into account before you begin. You may wish to perform a candle spell requiring the candle to burn one hour each day until it has burned out. Plan in advance so that you have the time you need or the results will not manifest. Enjoy your experience; this is your time to commune with the gods and goddesses and you are the only person who matters.

A spell will not be effective if you just say the words and do nothing else. You may want to get a new job and think that casting a spell is the answer. You make all the preparations, cast the spell and sit back and wait. But nothing happens. What went wrong? Magick is not a cure-all: it is an additional 'tool' at your disposal, to aid you and give you an advantage. You still have to put in an effort for the change to occur. You still have to make the effort of sending out resumés, going to the hated interviews and possibly posting on the internet. A job won't fall into your lap simply because you cast a spell.

Being specific

Another thing to note is that you should be specific about what you ask for. The deities have a sense of humour. If you want to bring a gorgeous redhead into your life, don't phrase it like that – you might end up with an Irish Setter on your doorstep! If the man or woman of your dreams is a tall blonde, give the gods as much additional information as possible. You may wish to compose a list of all the traits you are looking for in a lover or friend before you start. Be as specific as you want and I mean this sincerely and in all respects, for you are communicating with your deities. No one need ever know what it is you truly want. Do you want a wealthy partner? Ask for it. Do you want a curvaceous woman or a well-built man? Ask for it. You are looking for what is going to make you happy. You may want someone for a lifetime, or just one night. But be clear with your intent; I can't stress that enough.

If a spell 'fails'

With magick, anything is possible. However, the gods may not grant your request, though there will be a reason so don't get discouraged. Some things may not be beneficial for us and it's good to remember the old adage 'Be careful what you wish for for it may come true'. For example, I applied for a job that I truly wanted and asked for help from the gods. I was disappointed not to get my wish and had to stay in a job that I despised. Less than a month later the position was advertised in the paper, and again several months later. I began to wonder if this was a sign that there was something wrong with the job or the company. Soon afterwards I was fortunate to find another job that suited me perfectly – very low stress, great hours, more flexibility and within walking distance of my home. Maybe the gods were trying to tell me something, but at the time of my initial search I just didn't see it. So be patient, for not all magick works the way you may think it should. It works the way that is best for you.

Preparing for spellwork

The 'personal' spells I perform have had a tremendous effect on me and have brought me closer to the gods and goddesses. I have discovered how to release some very powerful emotions through spellwork; release is good for the soul and your well-being, not just physical, but mental and emotional as well.

The preparation for spellwork is less intensive and time-consuming than it is for rituals. Spells, as I mentioned before, can be performed almost anywhere, with few if any ritual tools, and lend themselves easily to our fast-paced world. A simple spell may take only a few minutes out of your busy day.

I prepare for spellwork by listening to music to relax and thinking of what I wish to accomplish. I usually slip on my ritual jewellery for spellwork, but I don't always feel the need to wear ritual clothing. To me, spells are less formal; it is my time to connect to a particular god or goddess on a personal level for a specific intention. I know what I want to accomplish, what oils, incense, herbs and candle correspondences I wish to use and which deity can assist me. So I frequently speak to my deities from the heart, pouring out my soul and asking for guidance, rather than writing a spell in advance.

As I said earlier, there is no right or wrong way to perform magick; just follow your heart and your instincts. As with anything, the more you do it, the better you become at it. A word of warning, however – don't perform too many spells in a short period of time. You need to focus your mind for each intent and casting too many spells lessens your ability to do that. A spell a day would be excessive; one a week is not unreasonable but may be taxing. If an emergency arises that needs to be dealt with immediately, it will be difficult to focus your energy if you have already overextended yourself. You may prefer to cast one spell a month until you feel comfortable with spellwork and communicating with the deities. Don't rush it; good things come to those who wait and knowing when to cast a spell and when not to will come in time and with practice.

There may be times when you perform spells that you would like to invoke a particular god or goddess, depending on the importance and type of spell and/or the affinity you feel for a special deity. When you invoke a deity you are asking directly for that god's or goddess's assistance and guidance. You should address any deity with respect and dignity and, when you have completed your magickal work, you should always thank the deity you invoked for joining you. They are your elders and they love you: treat them as you yourself wish to be treated – with kindness, caring and respect. Make offerings of food, wine, crystals or incense to them and observe their festival days, as you might if you practised any other religion. Common courtesy aside, the deities are powerful, ancient beings who command respect and should not be treated in a shoddy manner; if you do not treat them with respect you may find you have more problems than before.

Get to know your deities – you will find some are more special to you than others and that is all part of your ongoing knowledge and exploration of Egyptian magick. Work with each deity at least once to get to know and understand what each one represents, so that you may know how to call upon them if and when you need them. Call upon them to give you insight into their nature and special 'talents'. Bring them into every facet of your life and their gifts to you will be joy, happiness, peace and love.

General invocation and thanks

This general invocation and thanks may be used in conjunction with any of the spells in this book. It may be used for any deity and can easily be adapted to include the deity name and titles for specific intentions. You may wish to write your own invocations in due course; I feel that everyone should try writing at least one invocation, spell, or ritual. You are the only one who knows what you want or require for your happiness and quality of life. Some spells are beautifully written, with rhyming lines and cadences. I prefer to speak from my heart when I express my devotion to my gods and goddesses, and certainly without worrying about whether or not it rhymes.

God invocation

> O Great (name of god)
> Eternal and powerful God
> I call upon You
> To join me in my work
> Keep me in Your protection
> And guide my words
> May I always please You
> And give praise to Your name.

Goddess invocation

> O Great (name of goddess)
> Eternal and powerful Goddess
> I call upon You
> To join me in my work
> My heart and soul are pure
> May You offer me Your protection
> That I may serve You well
> And praise Your name forever.

General thanks

> O Great (name of deity)
> Lady and Mistress/Lord and Master
> To whom I have pledged
> My eternal devotion
> I pray that I have pleased You
> With my words and actions
> Keep me safe from harm
> Hear and grant my petition.

CHAPTER 7

Correspondences in Spellcasting

Correspondences are the many factors that influence a candle spell – the candle colour, moon phase and day of the week, and any crystals, essential oils, herbs or spices and incense used.

Correspondences help to boost the energy of a spell and make the magick more potent. The more you can incorporate into spellwork, the better the chances of success for your spell. The Elements, crystals and colours emit energies that may be harnessed to aid in magickal workings. Days of the week and phases of the moon can be consulted for the most favourable time to work magick. Herbs and oils have been identified throughout the ages for their healing and magickal properties, which make them another tool for spellwork. Incense and music help to set the mood of your intent and help to pull together all the various energies used to perform a spell or ritual.

Some Wiccans wear ritual clothing, jewellery, make-up and fragrances and listen to music to set the proper mood. I have items that I wear only during spellwork or rituals; these symbols of my devotion help to put me in the right frame of mind. I may also play some New Age, classical or Arabic music.

However, correspondences are only tools, not necessities, to be used to increase the effectiveness of spellwork. Don't get too worked up if you need help from Hathor in a love matter and it is not the right day of the week. It is still your intent that matters most; the deities are always available.

If you can co-ordinate several factors together, you will get a quicker result. But remember that some spells take longer to manifest than others. Be patient – once you have performed your spell, sit back, relax and forget about it. Your intent will manifest, if it is meant to be, and it may be when you least expect it.

Elemental correspondences

The following are the correspondences I employ to designate the compass points. I have found them to be most effective, although some reference sources may have other correspondences. The Elements correspond to the Four Sons of Horus, whose heads are the stoppers on the canopic jars found in most Ancient Egyptian burial chambers. Obviously, other correspondences exist in other Wiccan traditions and you should try to find the ones that suit you best.

Earth

Direction:	North.
Symbols:	Acorns, grain, salt, sand, soil, sphinx, stones.
Tools:	Ankh, pentacle.
Crystals:	Carnelian, emerald, jasper, malachite, moss agate, peridot, smoky quartz, tiger's eye, tourmaline.
Time:	Midnight.
Season:	Winter.
Colours:	Black, blue, brown, green, silver, white.
Gods:	Hapi, baboon-headed son of Horus; Osiris.
Goddess:	Nephthys.
Body organ:	The lungs were placed in this canopic jar.
Incense:	Benzoin, styrax.
Herbs:	Barley, hops, patchouli, vetivert.
Spells:	Employment, fertility, money, prosperity.

Air

Direction:	East.
Symbols:	Balloons, bells, birds, bubbles, fans, feathers, flutes, hawk, kites.
Tools:	Censor, wand.
Crystals:	Amethyst, azurite, citrine, sapphire, topaz.
Time:	Dawn.
Season:	Spring.
Colours:	Blue, bright yellow, grey, pastels, silver, white.
God:	Duamutef, jackal-headed son of Horus; Horus.
Goddess:	Neith.
Body organ:	The stomach was placed in this canopic jar.
Incense:	Frankincense, galbanum, myrrh.

Herbs:	Almond, clover, dill, lavender, primrose, vervain, violet, yarrow.
Spells:	Finding lost items, knowledge, psychic work, study, travel.

Fire

Direction:	South.
Symbols:	Candles, lamps, lanterns, serpents, the Sun.
Tools:	Athame, sword.
Crystals:	Bloodstone, diamond, fire opal, flint, garnet, jasper, quartz crystal, ruby.
Time:	Noon.
Season:	Summer.
Colours:	Amber, gold, orange, red, white.
God:	Imsety, man-headed son of Horus; Ra.
Goddess:	Isis.
Body organ:	The liver was placed in this canopic jar.
Incense:	Copal, frankincense, rose.
Herbs:	Basil, chilli peppers, ginger, hibiscus, orange.
Spells:	Courage, healing, protection, purification, sex.

Water

Direction:	West.
Symbols:	Bells, crocodile, cymbals, the Moon, shells, sistrum.
Tools:	Cauldron, chalice.
Crystals:	Amethyst, aquamarine, blue tourmaline, coral, crystal, jade, moonstone, mother-of-pearl, pearl.
Time:	Sunset.
Season:	Autumn.
Colours:	Black, blue, green, turquoise, white.
God:	Qebhsennuf, falcon-headed son of Horus; Thoth.
Goddess:	Selqet.
Body organ:	The intestines were placed in this canopic jar.
Incense:	Lily, lotus, myrrh.
Herbs:	Gardenia, lettuce, lily, lotus, rose.
Spells:	Dream work, fertility, friendship, healing, love, marriage.

Colour correspondences

Colours vibrate with energy; blue seems to have a calming effect and red seems to energise. All colours affect us in some way and they can also have an effect in spells. A purple candle may be called for in a spell for divination, but a blue candle has the same correspondence. Which to use? Use whichever one appeals to you. Or, for added 'kick', why not try using one of each? There is no right or wrong way to perform magick; magick is experimentation, celebration, devotion, true desire and intent. Spells should resonate with your energy and that which is pleasing to you and the deities. Just because I suggest using a pink candle for a love spell doesn't mean it can't be another colour. Gold, green, orange, peach, purple, red, white or yellow could also be used, depending on what type of love you are trying to attract.

Black
Absorption, banishing, binding, breaking bad habits, closure, death, divination, eliminating negativity, endings of any kind, mourning, protection, retribution, secrets, separation, stopping gossip, wisdom. To the Ancient Egyptians, black symbolised resurrection and eternal life.

Brown
Animal magick, balance, centring, common sense, confidence, decisiveness, earth magick, environment, grounding, healing the earth, hearth and home, home magick, increase, stability, telepathy.

Copper
Money.

Dark blue
Fertility, justice.

Dark green
Counteracting ambition, greed and jealousy.

Emerald green
Attraction, fertility.

Gold
Attraction, employment, energy/stamina, financial prosperity, God designator, God magick, happiness, luck, money, physical healing, protection, royalty, security, strength, the Sun, success, vitality, wealth.

Green

Acceptance, ambition, balance, beauty, courage, earth spells, eco-magick, emotional healing, employment, envy, fertility, fruition, growth, harmony, healing, independence, intuition, love, luck, money, nature spirits, peace, personal appearance, prosperity, renewal, spells for children, success, wealth. To the Ancient Egyptians, green symbolised youth, new life and vegetation.

Grey

Loneliness, neutralisation, sorrow.

Indigo

Dignity, healing, inner harmony, meditation, organisation, psychic and mental healing, sleep, structure, wisdom.

Lavender

Inner beauty, intellect, knowledge, relief of tension and stress.

Light blue

Beauty, meditation, peace, spirituality, tranquillity.

Mauve

Co-operation, intuition, psychic powers, self-confidence, self-trust.

Mid-blue

Calmness, communication, divination, dreams, Goddess magick, happiness, healing, hope, inner peace, inspiration, loyalty/fidelity, meditation, music magick, past-life work, patience, peace, protection, psychic work, serenity, sleep, spirituality, study/learning, success, tranquillity, truth, water magick, wisdom.

Olive

Cowardice, illness, uncertainty.

Orange

Ambition, attraction, balance, business projects/proposals, communication, creativity, emotional stability, energy, fire magick, friendship, healing relationships, health, intellect, justice/law, love, material success, personal motivation, romance, strength, travel.

Peach
Empathy, friendship, gentleness, kindness, nurturing, sympathy, well-wishing.

Pink
Affection, beauty, compassion, creativity, emotional healing, femininity, fidelity, friendship, gentleness, happiness, harmony, innocence, love, peace, relaxation, romance, self-love.

Purple/violet
Ambition, clarity, connection to other entities, dignity, divination, enchantment, healing, independence, insight, intuition, meditation, power, prophetic dreams, protection, psychic and mental healing, psychic work, respect, spirituality, success, wisdom.

Red
Action, activity, anger, attraction, courage, energy, God magick, health, intensity, lust, passion, power, protection, romance, sex magick, sexual desire, sexual potency, strength, vitality. To the Ancient Egyptians, red symbolised fire and rage.

Rose
Love, youth.

Royal blue
Joviality, loyalty.

Silver
Banishing, divination, dream magick, Goddess designator, Goddess magick, money, the Moon, mysticism, negativity, peace, prosperity, protection, psychic powers, relief of inner turmoil, serenity, stability.

Teal
Balance, decision-making, practicality, spirituality, trust.

Turquoise
Knowledge, logic, stress relief, study.

White
Calm, chastity, clarity, cleansing, creativity, ecstasy, enlightenment, exorcism, healing, innocence, joy, justice, learning, love, meditation,

Moon magick, protection, purity/purification, relief of tension, spiritual protection, spirituality, stopping gossip, truth. White may be used in spellwork as a substitute for any colour.

Yellow

Air magick, attraction, communication, concentration, confidence, creative endeavours, divination, eloquence, happiness, hope, intellect, jealousy, joy, knowledge, mental magick, power, rejuvenation, success, travel, unity, vitality, wisdom.

Moon phases

The Moon exerts an energy over all of us: cats and dogs howl at the Moon, hospitals and the police notice more activity around the Full Moon and the tides rise and fall due to its influence. I have always been drawn to the Moon – I can sit for hours, looking up at the stars and the Moon, feeling so connected with my deities and nature. Obviously, the Moon can also have a profound effect on spellwork; the Full Moon is the best time for any type of magick, as it adds extra energy to any spell, but each Moon phase has a specific quality so, if you time your spells to coincide with the most sympathetic Moon phase, you are likely to gain the best results.

Before you start any rituals or spells, you might want to study the Moon each evening, watching how it changes over the course of the month and taking note of any feelings you may have as it waxes and wanes. If possible, study the Moon in different places: the beach, the mountains, the city, the country. Are your feelings affected by being in different places? Try to record what you discover in your Book of Shadows.

Magick is a journey that can deeply affect us. It 'forces' us to get in tune with ourselves, the world around us and the subtleties that we tend to miss far too often. Slow down, relax and attune yourself to the primitive, primal forces that energise us all. Open your heart, mind and soul and don't let that nagging voice in your head stop you. You know that voice: 'How silly do I look standing out here staring at the Moon? The neighbours will think I'm crazy!' Who cares what the neighbours think. And, anyway, aren't witches perceived as being a bit eccentric? Stick with it and enjoy the experience, the silence, the forces that guide us.

New Moon
Divination, new beginnings, past-life work, rest, spiritual pursuits, truth.

Waxing Moon
Attraction, clarity, growth, financial prosperity, healing, increase, inspiration, new beginnings, new love/friendship, physical stamina.

Full Moon
Aiding difficult situations, boosting spellwork, creativity, fertility, insight, power, wisdom.

Waning Moon
Banishing negative energy, breaking bad habits, dieting, elimination, endings, lessening, losses, mourning, relieving stress and depression.

Monthly Full Moons

There are twelve Full Moons in most years but in some there are thirteen. The thirteenth is referred to as the Blue Moon (blue was a lucky colour to the Ancient Egyptians). Each monthly Moon resonates with an energy you might wish to tap into. I have included common names for each Full Moon and correspondences to aid you in your spellwork.

January Full Moon
Common names: Chaste Moon, Cold Moon, Disting Moon, Guardian Moon, Moon of Little Winter, Quiet Moon, Snow Moon, Wolf Moon.
Correspondences: Beginning, planning, personal problems, protection, reversing spells.

February Full Moon
Common names: Big Winter Moon, Horning Moon, Hunger Moon, Ice Moon, Quickening Moon, Red and Cleansing Moon, Storm Moon, Wild Moon.
Correspondences: Growth, healing, plans for the future, purification, self-forgiveness, self-love.

March Full Moon
Common names: Chaste Moon, Crow Moon, Dwarf Moon, Lenting Moon, Moon of the Snowblind, Moon of the Winds, Nymph Moon,

Plough Moon, Sap Moon, Seed Moon, Storm Moon, Worm Moon.
Correspondences: Balance, growth, exploration, new beginnings, prosperity, truth.

April Full Moon
Common names: Baby Moon, Budding Trees Moon, Green Grass Moon, Growing Moon, Hare Moon, Pink Moon, Planter's Moon, Seed/Planting Moon.
Correspondences: Balance, chances, change, controlling temper, creation, production, self-confidence, self-reliance, temper.

May Full Moon
Common names: Bright Moon, Dyad Moon, Flower Moon, Frog's Return Moon, Hare Moon, Lovers' Moon, Merry Moon, Moon When The Ponies Shed, Planting Moon.
Correspondences: Communication, creativity, empathy, intuition, propagation, psychic energy.

June Full Moon
Common names: Dyad Moon, Lovers' Moon, Mead or Honey Moon, Marriage Moon, Moon of Horses, Moon of Making Fat, Strawberry Moon, Strong Sun Moon.
Correspondences: Decision-making, positive action, prevention, protection, responsibility, strength.

July Full Moon
Common names: Blessing Moon, Buck Moon, Fallow Moon, Festive Moon, Hay Moon, Maiden Moon, Mead Moon, Moon of Blood, Moon of Claiming, Thunder Moon, Wort Moon.
Correspondences: Divination, dream work, meditation, preparation, relaxation, success.

August Full Moon
Common names: Barley Moon, Bay Moon, Corn Moon, Dispute Moon, Harvest Moon, Moon When Cherries Turn Black, Poet's Moon, Ripening Moon.
Correspondences: Appreciation, friendship, harvest, health, vitality.

September Full Moon

Common names: Autumn Moon, Barley Moon, Fire Moon, Moon When Deer Paw the Earth, Singing Moon, Sturgeon Moon, Wine or Harvest Moon.

Correspondences: Balance, clearing physical, mental, emotional and spiritual confusion, organisation, resting.

October Full Moon

Common names: Blood Moon, Falling Leaf Moon, Hallow Moon, Harvest Moon, Moon of the Changing Seasons, Shedding Moon, Ten Colds Moon.

Correspondences: Balance, inner cleansing, inner harmony, justice, karma, letting go, rebirth, reincarnation.

November Full Moon

Common names: Beaver Moon, Dark Moon, Dead Moon, Fog Moon, Frost Moon, Hunter's Moon, Mad Moon, Moon of Storms, Moon When Deer Shed Antlers, Mourning Moon, Snow Moon, Winter Moon.

Correspondences: Communication, preparation, transformation.

December Full Moon

Common names: Big Winter Moon, Cold Moon, Laughing Moon, Moon of Long Nights, Moon of Popping Trees, Oak Moon, Pepper Moon, Wolf Moon, Yule Moon.

Correspondences: Darkness, endings, endurance, personal magick, rebirth, spiritual path.

Blue Moon

Correspondences: Communication with the dead, letting go of negative energy, miracles, prophecy, releasing/remembering the past, unexpected blessings.

Days of the week

If you've been paying attention, you will see that the days of the week also resonate with energy that can effect spellwork.

Ideally, love spells should begin or be performed on Tuesdays (for lust) or Fridays (for love and friendship). Some Wiccans would never attempt a love spell on any day but Friday – in my opinion this is just a helpful hint. Life does not always follow correspondences and some issues, like the illness of a loved one or the need for fast cash, cannot be planned for in advance. If you cannot wait until one of those relevant days, the deities will nevertheless hear your prayer.

Sunday
Colour correspondences: Gold, orange, yellow.
Spell correspondences: Advancement, ambition, business partnerships/ventures, children, creativity, employment, exorcism, friendships, fun, goals, God mysteries, healing, hope, joy, law, leadership, men, mental and physical health, money, personal power, physical self-defence, promotion, prosperity, protection, purification, self-confidence, strength, success.
Ruled by: The Sun.

Monday
Colour correspondences: Grey, pearl, silver, white.
Spell correspondences: Animals, beauty, childbirth, children, divination, emotions, family, fertility, garden medicine, Goddess mysteries, growth, hearth and home, imagination, initiation, intuition, life cycles, magick, motherhood, New Age pursuits, peace, private matters, prophetic dreaming, psychic development, reincarnation, spirituality, tranquillity, women.
Ruled by: The Moon.

Tuesday
Colour correspondences: Pink, orange, red.
Spell correspondences: Action, anger, banishing, beginnings, business, competition, conflict, construction, courage, destiny, disagreement, fear, gardening, group strength, hunting, lust, medicine, men, partnerships, passion, physical endurance/strength, political ventures, power, sex and sexuality, sports, surgery, war/combat.
Ruled by: Mars.

Wednesday
Colour correspondences: Magenta, purple, silver.
Spell correspondences: Actors, books, communication, computers, correspondence, diplomacy, fickleness, healing, herbalism, hiring employees, inspiration, intellect, learning, legal appointments, memory, mental prowess, messages, music, neighbours, poets, reading, self-improvement, siblings, signing contracts, spiritual pursuits, study

and students, teaching and teachers, travel, understanding, visiting friends, visual arts, wisdom, writers, written/spoken word.
Ruled by: Mercury.

Thursday
Colour correspondences: Blue, metallic colours.
Spell correspondences: Accomplishments, ambition, attraction, awards, business, education, employment, expansion, financial wealth, foreign interests, friendship, gambling, good fortune, growth, guardians, honours, investments, legal issues, logic, long-distance travel, luck, material gain, philosophy, political power, prosperity, research, self-improvement, social events, sports, success.
Ruled by: Jupiter.

Friday
Colour correspondences: Green, pink, white.
Spell correspondences: Acts of kindness/generosity, affection, aromatherapy, arts, beauty, close friendships, comfort, courtship, divination, dreams, emotions, family, fertility, fidelity, friendship, fulfilment, gardening, growth, harmony, heart, husbands/wives, income, intimate social gatherings, intuition, love, luxury, marriage, music, new projects, peace, pets, pleasure, poetry, psychic efforts, romance, sea travel, sensuality, soulmates, sweethearts.
Ruled by: Venus.

Saturday
Colour correspondences: Black, grey, red, white.
Spell correspondences: Accepting/changing bad situations, banishing, binding, completion, death, debts, discovery, the elderly, endurance, justice, karmic lessons, lies, losses, manifestation, meditation, mental and emotional distress, morality, mysteries, neutralisation, obstacles, past lives, protection, reality, rebirth, reincarnation, sacrifice, separation, spirit communications, stalkers, transformation, wisdom.
Ruled by: Saturn.

CHAPTER 8

Crystals, Oils, Herbs and Incense in Egyptian Love Magick

Crystals and gemstones are useful in the performance of spells and rituals. Their energy can be a focus in meditation, or they may be an aid in raising additional energy in love spells. They may also be used as an offering to a particular deity, or to represent the deity itself. The Ancient Egyptians wore many items of jewellery, decorated with gemstones, for personal adornment and in ritual use.

Oils, whether essential or blends, are useful in anointing candles for additional energy, especially in love spells. Try visualising what you wish to accomplish while working an oil into a candle.

In everyday Egyptian life, herbs, flowers and oils were used in cosmetics and toiletries, not only for their pleasant fragrances (the Ancient Egyptians were very aware of personal hygiene). Many women wore cones of wax prepared with fragrant oils and herbs on their heads, which would slowly melt and keep them well-perfumed throughout the day. Herbs and incense were used on a daily basis in their worship of the deities. Myrrh was burned in the temples at noon every day.

Crystals and gems

Crystals and gems resonate with energies that may be used for several magickal and therapeutic purposes. They are used extensively in vibrational medicine, when they are applied to various parts of the body to heal aches, pains and illness. They are appropriate offerings to the deities (amulets, often of carnelian, malachite, turquoise or lapis lazuli, were inserted in the layers of mummification bandages in the belief that these would speed the soul of the deceased to the afterlife). They may be added to oils and incense to infuse them with additional magickal power.

Crystals and gems are also great tools at your disposal for a favourable outcome to any ritual or spell. You can use a particular crystal to represent a person, idea or desire, or use the colour of the stone to represent the type of spell you are performing. Crystals can be used over and over again, as long as they are cleansed after each use.

I have included crystals and gems that are associated with individual deities on pages 36–53 and you may wish to use those for offerings or as representations of the deity in spellwork or rituals.

Happiness
Amethyst, aquamarine, cat's eye, chrysoprase, lapis lazuli, rose quartz, ruby, sardonyx, turquoise, yellow zircon.

Love
Agate, alexandrite, amber, amethyst, beryl, chrysocolla, coral, emerald, herkimer diamond, jade, lapis lazuli, lepidolite, malachite, moonstone, pearl, peridot, pink calcite, pink tourmaline, rhodocrosite, rose quartz, sapphire, sard, sardonyx, topaz, turquoise, watermelon tourmaline, yellow zircon.

Lust
Amber, carnelian, diamond, star sapphire, staurolite, sunstone, yellow zircon.

Oils

I'm a very fragrance-oriented person and love to experiment with oils, herbs and spices. I sometimes think I must resemble a mad scientist in films when I'm mixing potions and concoctions just for the sheer pleasure of it.

I use only unscented candles, which I anoint with an oil blend or an essential oil and then often roll in herbs and spices that correspond to the spellwork. The only time I would ever use just an unscented base oil would be if the candle was scented; then I would roll the candle in herbs or spices for additional fragrance but I wouldn't use an essential oil on a scented candle. However, if you wanted to use a scented candle and the candle colour and fragrance coincide with the spell you wish to perform, you could certainly try it and see if it works. Before starting a spell, you could, as I would, hold the scented candle in your dominant hand (the hand with which you write) and envision your desire and what you hope to accomplish.

I have tried to keep the recipes in this book as simple as possible to make them a good starting point for any spellwork (see pages 121–4). You are free to experiment and use your instincts to lead you in directions you never thought possible.

A hymn to Neferten for creating potions and oils

This invocation may be used whenever you are mixing a batch of potions or anointing oils for magickal use. It is not necessary to perform any formal ritual – just repeating the words during your work and concentrating on your intent will add energy to your potion.

Great Neferten
God of Fragrance and Perfume
Guide my hands and work in Your service
Help me to make a pleasing scent
The potion I am creating
Is a potion for (purpose)
My intention is genuine
My heart and soul are pure
Great Neferten
God of Fragrance and Perfume
Guide my hands and work
And assist Your humble servant.

Mixing oils

When mixing oils for anointing candles or for sensual massage, you should follow some basics. I read many books on aromatherapy before I attempted to mix my first potion and I was glad I did.

A carrier (or base) oil has little or no fragrance; it adds longevity to essential oils and helps minimise or eliminate any skin reaction from undiluted essential oils. I generally start with a small amount of carrier oil and then add essential oils. For example, if you wish to mix coconut, rose and vanilla essential oils to a carrier of almond oil, start by placing 2.5 ml/½ tsp of almond oil in a light-blocking bottle (see below). Then add 1 drop of coconut oil and mix thoroughly, then 1 drop of rose oil and mix again. Finally, add 1 drop of vanilla, mix well and inhale to check the fragrance. If one scent seems stronger than the others you may wish to add more of the other essential oils, drop by drop, until you have the fragrance you desire. When using essential oils, less is better: you don't want a potion with an overpowering scent – not to mention the fact that some essential oils are very costly.

Anointing and massage oils should not be made in large quantities in advance because all oils have a shelf life, which will vary from potion to potion. I recommend using any oil blends within one year. You may have to experiment a little and keep a record to determine how long your blends can be kept. Obviously, you should always label your potions with their constituents and the date you made them. Essential oils should be stored in light-blocking (amber, green or blue) glass bottles in a cool, dark and dry area since some may lose their potency when exposed to sunlight.

Carrier oils may be found in New Age and magickal shops, in natural food stores and on the internet. Essential oils are carried by some New Age and magickal shops and independent booksellers and can also be bought by mail order and on the internet. Buy in small quantities at first and buy only what you need for a particular spell or ritual. Make sure you are purchasing true essential oils and not synthetics or diluted oils. Having said that, synthetics should be used if the pure oil is extracted from animals, and some essences cannot be extracted with pure results or may be poisonous and in those cases a blend will work just as well. You may have to try several avenues before you find a reputable dealer and then later on you could purchase a variety of oils to keep on hand for any eventuality. (See Suppliers on pages 248–52.)

Any of the recipes for anointing oils may be used for massage, as long as they are in a carrier oil as some essential oils are too harsh to be used undiluted on sensitive skin. You should carry out a skin test in advance; put just a drop of the mixture on the inside of your arm and that of the person you will be massaging and check over the next few hours for any adverse reaction. Experiment with different fragrances for the pleasure of you and your partner. You may wish to start with just one essential oil mixed with a carrier oil and then try a mix of many oils for maximum effect. In the list of oils to use to attract love, lust and happiness to ease mourning, I have included other oils that I have found mix well with them, which I hope will be a good basis for when you try creating your own blends.

Many of the oils listed for attracting love or lust also have aphrodisiac qualities, which will heighten sensual or sexual encounters. The oil blends you create may also be infused with your personal essence, meaning any bodily fluid such as blood, tears and saliva. Using your own bodily fluids in an oil blend will obviously enhance the magickal power but I should add a word of extreme caution: to avoid the risk of blood-borne diseases, it is safer to use these blends only for anointing candles.

Sensual massage

Sensual massage may be incorporated into a love spell or ritual to re-ignite the passion in an existing relationship or you may wish to share it with a new lover. The oil should be warmed slightly for comfort and to release more fragrance, thus adding to your sexual experience. I very rarely, if ever, use essential oil blends on sensitive areas of the body, unless you know you will not have an adverse reaction. Some essential oils should never be taken internally, so real care should be taken where you use your sensual blends.

Sexual magick between consenting adults can be wonderfully liberating and erotic. Since I became a witch, every encounter has not only been an exhilarating sexual experience, it has also been an offering to the deities. But I cannot say strongly enough that you must practise safe sex: some oils and lubricants may affect a condom adversely, so be very careful. You can incorporate putting on a condom as part of your love play; it can be very exciting and stimulating for a man to have his partner slip it on him. If a new partner refuses to wear a condom, then that person, in my opinion, does not have your welfare at heart.

Love-making should be spontaneous and enjoyable, but I do encourage common sense and would never advocate sex with strangers or with multiple partners. No one cares about you more than the deities but you have to be sensible and protect yourself. Think before you act and don't let your passions get the better of you: the consequences of one unprotected encounter could be deadly for you and your partner years from now.

Oils to attract love

B = Blend; S = Synthetic

Absinthe (B)
Associated with: Horus, Isis.
Mixes with: Amber, basil, bay, carnation, cinnamon, clove, coriander (cilantro), geranium, ginger, juniper, lavender, lemon, lime, neroli, nutmeg, orange, peppermint, rosemary, sandalwood.

Acacia
Associated with: Osiris, Ra.
Mixes with: Almond, amber, bay, carnation, cinnamon, civet, clover, honey, juniper, lavender, lemon, lemon verbena, marjoram, neroli, olive, orange, peppermint, rosemary, sandalwood, sesame, vanilla.

Almond
Can be used as a base or an essential oil.
Associated with: Ptah, Thoth.
Mixes with: Acacia, amber, caraway, clover, lavender, lemon, lemon verbena, magnolia, mandrake, marjoram, neroli, peppermint, vanilla.

Amber
Blends with any essential oil.

Apricot
Can be used as a base or an essential oil.
Mixes with: Amber, cardamom, chamomile, coconut, gardenia, geranium, hyacinth, jasmine, lavender, lemon, lemon balm, lotus, magnolia, myrrh, myrtle, neroli, orchid, orris, passion flower, peach, plumeria, rose, sandalwood, spearmint, sweet pea, thyme, tuberose, vanilla, violet, ylang ylang.

Aster
Mixes with: Amber, cardamom, chamomile, coconut, gardenia, geranium, hyacinth, jasmine, lavender, lemon, lemon balm, lotus,

magnolia, myrrh, myrtle, neroli, orchid, orris, passion flower, peach, plumeria, rose, sandalwood, spearmint, sweet pea, thyme, tuberose, vanilla, violet, ylang ylang.

Basil
Mixes with: Absinthe, amber, civet, coriander (cilantro), cypress, geranium, ginger, jasmine, juniper, lavender, lemon, mandrake, marjoram, myrtle, neroli, olive, orange, palmarosa, peppermint, petitgrain, rosemary, sesame, spearmint, thyme, violet.

Bay
Used extensively by the Ancient Egyptians medicinally and in worship to Ra.
Associated with: Ra.
Mixes with: Absinthe, acacia, amber, cardamom, carnation, cinnamon, civet, clove, coriander (cilantro), cypress, geranium, ginger, honey, jasmine, juniper, lavender, lemon, mandrake, myrtle, neroli, nutmeg, olive, orange, palmarosa, rose, rosemary, sandalwood, sesame, vanilla, violet, ylang ylang.

Benzoin
Can be used as a fixative or as a substitute for vanilla. It has a chocolate-vanilla fragrance.
Associated with: Apophis, Hathor, Khepera.

Caraway
Used by the Egyptians for flavouring foods; traces have been found in many burial sites.
Mixes with: Almond, amber, cardamom, clove, clover, lavender, lemon, mandrake, neroli.

Cardamom
The Ancient Egyptians used this spice in perfumes and incense and chewed the seeds to keep their teeth white.
Mixes with: Amber, apricot, aster, bay, caraway, carnation, chamomile, cherry, cinnamon, clover, coconut, coriander (cilantro), frangipani, gardenia, geranium, ginger, jasmine, lavender, lemon, lemon verbena, lime, lotus, magnolia, mimosa, myrtle, neroli, orange, orchid, orris, palmarosa, papaya, passion flower, peach, petitgrain, plumeria, poppy, primrose, raspberry, rose, rosemary, sandalwood, spearmint, strawberry, sweet pea, tulip, vanilla, vetivert, ylang ylang.

Carnation

Mixes with: Absinthe, acacia, amber, bay, cardamom, chamomile, cinnamon, civet, clove, coriander (cilantro), geranium, honey, hyacinth, jasmine, lavender, lemon, linden, mandrake, neroli, olive, orange, rose, sandalwood, sesame, ylang ylang.

Chamomile

Used by the Ancient Egyptians to cure fevers and for nervous disorders. It was used in the mummification of Ramesses II and Tutankhamun.

Mixes with: Amber, apricot, aster, cardamom, carnation, cherry, clove, coconut, cypress, frangipani, gardenia, geranium, jasmine, lavender, lemon, lime, lotus, marjoram, mimosa, myrrh, neroli, orange, orchid, orris, palmarosa, papaya, passion flower, peach, plumeria, poppy, raspberry, rose, rosemary, sandalwood, spearmint, strawberry, sweet pea, yarrow, ylang ylang.

Cherry

Mixes with: Amber, cardamom, chamomile, coconut, gardenia, geranium, hyacinth, jasmine, lavender, lemon, lemon balm, lotus, magnolia, mimosa, myrrh, myrtle, neroli, orchid, orris, passion flower, peach, plumeria, rose, sandalwood, spearmint, sweet pea, thyme, tuberose, vanilla, violet, ylang ylang.

Cinnamon

Used by the Ancient Egyptians as an oil for the feet.

Associated with: Amun, Ra.

Mixes with: Absinthe, acacia, amber, bay, cardamom, carnation, civet, clove, coriander (cilantro), cypress, geranium, ginger, honey, jasmine, lavender, lemon, lime, mandrake, myrrh, myrtle, neroli, nutmeg, olive, orange, orris, petitgrain, rose, sandalwood, sesame, thyme, vanilla, violet, ylang ylang.

Civet (S)

Associated with: Isis, Mut, Nephthys, Set.

Mixes with: Acacia, amber, basil, bay, carnation, cinnamon, clove, coriander (cilantro), geranium, juniper, lavender, lemon, lime, neroli, nutmeg, orange, peppermint, rosemary, sandalwood, vanilla.

Clove

Associated with: Amun.

Mixes with: Absinthe, amber, bay, caraway, cardamom, carnation, chamomile, cinnamon, civet, coriander (cilantro), geranium, ginger, honeysuckle, jasmine, lavender, lemon, linden, mandrake, myrtle, neroli, nutmeg, olive, orange, orris, palmarosa, petitgrain, rose, rosemary, sandalwood, sesame, vanilla, violet, ylang ylang.

Clover
Associated with: Hathor.
Mixes with: Acacia, almond, amber, caraway, cardamom, lavender, lemon, lemon verbena, marjoram, neroli, peppermint, thyme, vanilla.

Coconut
Can be used as a base or as an essential oil.
Associated with: Nut.
Mixes with: Amber, apricot, aster, cardamom, chamomile, cherry, frangipani, gardenia, hyacinth, jasmine, lavender, lemon, lemon balm, lime, lotus, mimosa, myrrh, neroli, orchid, orris, papaya, passion flower, peach, plumeria, poppy, raspberry, rose, sandalwood, spearmint, strawberry, sweet pea, thyme, vanilla, violet, ylang ylang.

Coriander (cilantro)
Used by the Ancient Egyptians as an aphrodisiac. Found in Tutankhamun's tomb.
Mixes with: Absinthe, amber, basil, bay, cardamom, carnation, cinnamon, civet, clove, cypress, geranium, ginger, jasmine, lavender, lemon, mandrake, neroli, nutmeg, olive, orange, palmarosa, petitgrain, rose, sandalwood, sesame, vanilla, vetivert, ylang ylang.

Cypress
Used to make sarcophagi and for medicinal purposes.
Associated with: Heket, Isis, Mut, Nephthys.
Mixes with: Amber, basil, bay, chamomile, cinnamon, coriander (cilantro), geranium, honey, honeysuckle, hyacinth, juniper, lavender, lemon, lemon verbena, lime, magnolia, marjoram, mimosa, musk, myrrh, myrtle, neroli, orange, orris, peppermint, petitgrain, primrose, rosemary, sandalwood, thyme, tulip, yarrow.

Frangipani
Mixes with: Amber, cardamom, chamomile, coconut, gardenia, geranium, hyacinth, jasmine, lavender, lemon, lemon balm, lotus,

magnolia, myrrh, myrtle, neroli, orchid, orris, passion flower, peach, plumeria, rose, sandalwood, spearmint, sweet pea, thyme, tuberose, vanilla, violet, ylang ylang.

Gardenia
Mixes with: Amber, apricot, aster, cardamom, chamomile, cherry, coconut, frangipani, hyacinth, jasmine, lavender, lemon, lemon balm, lime, lotus, mimosa, myrrh, neroli, orchid, orris, papaya, passion flower, peach, plumeria, poppy, raspberry, rose, sandalwood, spearmint, strawberry, sweet pea, thyme, vanilla, violet, ylang ylang.

Geranium (rose)
Associated with: Isis.
Mixes with: Absinthe, amber, aster, apricot, aster, basil, bay, cardamom, carnation, chamomile, cherry, cinnamon, civet, clove, coriander (cilantro), cypress, frangipani, ginger, hyacinth, jasmine, juniper, lavender, lemon, lemon verbena, lime, linden, magnolia, mandrake, myrrh, myrtle, neroli, nutmeg, olive, orange, orchid, orris, palmarosa, passion flower, peach, peppermint, petitgrain, plumeria, primrose, raspberry, rose, rosemary, sandalwood, sesame, spearmint, strawberry, sweet pea, thyme, tulip, vanilla, vetivert, violet, yarrow, ylang ylang.

Ginger
Mixes with: Absinthe, amber, basil, bay, cardamom, cinnamon, clove, coriander (cilantro), geranium, jasmine, juniper, lavender, lemon, lime, myrtle, neroli, orange, palmarosa, petitgrain, rose, rosemary, sandalwood, thyme, vanilla, vetivert, yarrow, ylang ylang.

Honey
Can be used as a base or an ingredient.
Mixes with: Acacia, amber, bay, carnation, cinnamon, cypress, honeysuckle, juniper, lavender, lemon, magnolia, neroli, orange, primrose, rosemary, sandalwood, vanilla, vetivert.

Honeysuckle
Mixes with: Amber, clove, cypress, honey, lavender, lemon, lemon verbena, magnolia, musk, neroli, nutmeg, primrose, tulip, vetivert.

Hyacinth
Mixes with: Amber, apricot, aster, carnation, cherry, coconut, cypress,

frangipani, gardenia, geranium, lavender, lemon, lemon verbena, lime, linden, lotus, magnolia, mimosa, neroli, orange, orchid, orris, papaya, passion flower, peach, petitgrain, plumeria, poppy, primrose, raspberry, rose, sandalwood, spearmint, strawberry, sweet pea, tuberose, tulip, violet, ylang ylang.

Jasmine
Associated with: Shu.
Mixes with: Amber, apricot, aster, basil, bay, cardamom, carnation, chamomile, cherry, cinnamon, clove, coconut, coriander (cilantro), frangipani, gardenia, geranium, ginger, lavender, lemon, lemon verbena, lime, linden, lotus, mimosa, neroli, nutmeg, orange, orchid, orris, palmarosa, papaya, passion flower, peach, petitgrain, plumeria, poppy, raspberry, rose, sandalwood, spearmint, strawberry, sweet pea, tuberose, vanilla, vetivert, violet, ylang ylang.

Juniper
Possibly used in animal mummification.
Mixes with: Absinthe, acacia, amber, basil, bay, civet, cypress, geranium, ginger, honey, lavender, lemon, mandrake, marjoram, myrrh, neroli, olive, orange, palmarosa, peppermint, petitgrain, rosemary, sandalwood, sesame, vetivert.

Lavender
Blends with any essential oil.
Associated with: Isis, Thoth.

Lemon
Used by the Ancient Egyptians to fight food poisoning and typhoid. Blends with any essential oil.

Lemon balm
Mixes with: Amber, apricot, aster, cherry, coconut, frangipani, gardenia, lavender, lemon, lime, lotus, mimosa, neroli, orchid, orris, papaya, passion flower, peach, plumeria, poppy, raspberry, spearmint, strawberry, sweet pea.

Lemon verbena
Mixes with: Acacia, almond, amber, cardamom, clover, cypress, geranium, honeysuckle, hyacinth, jasmine, lavender, lemon, magnolia,

mandrake, myrtle, neroli, orchid, orris, plumeria, primrose, rose, rosemary, sandalwood, spearmint, sweet pea, thyme, tuberose, vanilla, vetivert, violet, ylang ylang.

Lime
Mixes with: Absinthe, amber, cardamom, chamomile, cinnamon, civet, coconut, cypress, gardenia, geranium, ginger, hyacinth, jasmine, lavender, lemon, lemon balm, lotus, magnolia, mandrake, myrrh, myrtle, neroli, nutmeg, olive, orange, orchid, orris, passion flower, peach, petitgrain, plumeria, rose, sandalwood, sesame, spearmint, sweet pea, thyme, tuberose, vanilla, violet, ylang ylang.

Linden
Mixes with: Amber, carnation, clove, geranium, hyacinth, jasmine, lavender, lemon, neroli, orange, petitgrain, rose, sandalwood, tuberose, ylang ylang.

Lotus
Symbol of rebirth.
Associated with: Isis, Khepera, Neferten.
Mixes with: Amber, apricot, aster, cardamom, chamomile, cherry, coconut, frangipani, gardenia, hyacinth, jasmine, lavender, lemon, lemon balm, lime, mimosa, myrrh, neroli, orchid, orris, papaya, passion flower, peach, plumeria, poppy, raspberry, rose, sandalwood, spearmint, strawberry, sweet pea, vanilla, violet, ylang ylang.

Magnolia
Mixes with: Almond, amber, apricot, aster, cardamom, cherry, cypress, frangipani, geranium, honey, honeysuckle, hyacinth, lavender, lemon, lemon verbena, lime, musk, myrtle, neroli, orange, orchid, orris, passion flower, peach, plumeria, primrose, raspberry, rose, spearmint, strawberry, sweet pea, thyme, tuberose, tulip, vanilla, vetivert, violet, ylang ylang.

Mandrake
Associated with: Hathor, Shu.
Mixes with: Almond, amber, basil, bay, caraway, carnation, cinnamon, clove, coriander (cilantro), geranium, juniper, lavender, lemon, lemon verbena, lime, neroli, nutmeg, orange, peppermint, rosemary, spearmint, thyme.

Marjoram
Associated with: Sobek.
Mixes with: Acacia, almond, amber, basil, chamomile, clover, cypress, juniper, lavender, lemon, neroli, orange, peppermint, petitgrain, rosemary, thyme, yarrow.

Mimosa
Mixes with: Amber, cardamom, chamomile, cherry, coconut, cypress, gardenia, hyacinth, jasmine, lavender, lemon, lemon balm, lotus, myrrh, neroli, orchid, orris, passion flower, peach, plumeria, rose, sandalwood, spearmint, sweet pea, thyme, vanilla, violet, ylang ylang.

Musk (Egyptian) (S)
Associated with: Amun, Isis, Nut, Ra, Set.
Mixes with: Amber, cypress, honeysuckle, lavender, lemon, magnolia, neroli, primrose, vetivert.

Myrrh
Used in incense, unguents, cosmetics and mummification.
Associated with: Hathor, Horus, Isis, Mut, Nephthys, Osiris, Ra.
Mixes with: Amber, apricot, aster, chamomile, cherry, cinnamon, coconut, cypress, frangipani, gardenia, geranium, juniper, lavender, lemon, lime, lotus, mimosa, neroli, orchid, orris, palmarosa, papaya, passion flower, peach, plumeria, poppy, raspberry, rosemary, sandalwood, spearmint, strawberry, sweet pea, ylang ylang.

Myrtle
Used by the Ancient Egyptians in the worship of Hathor, and medicinally to treat facial tics.
Associated with: Hathor.
Mixes with: Amber, apricot, aster, basil, bay, cardamom, cherry, cinnamon, clove, cypress, frangipani, geranium, ginger, lavender, lemon, lemon verbena, lime, magnolia, neroli, orange, orchid, orris, passion flower, peach, plumeria, primrose, raspberry, rosemary, spearmint, strawberry, sweet pea, thyme, tulip, vanilla, yarrow.

Neroli
Blends with any essential oil.

Nutmeg
Used in embalming by the Ancient Egyptians.
Mixes with: Absinthe, amber, bay, cinnamon, civet, clove, coriander (cilantro), geranium, honeysuckle, jasmine, lavender, lemon, lime, mandrake, neroli, olive, orange, rose, sesame, vanilla.

Olive
Can be used as a base or as an ingredient.
Associated with: Amun, Isis, Nut, Ra.
Mixes with: Acacia, amber, basil, bay, carnation, cinnamon, clove, coriander (cilantro), geranium, juniper, lavender, lemon, lime, neroli, nutmeg, orange, peppermint, rosemary, sandalwood, vanilla.

Orange
Mixes with: Absinthe, acacia, amber, basil, bay, cardamom, carnation, chamomile, cinnamon, civet, clove, coriander (cilantro), cypress, geranium, ginger, honey, hyacinth, jasmine, juniper, lavender, lemon, lime, linden, magnolia, mandrake, marjoram, myrtle, neroli, nutmeg, olive, palmarosa, petitgrain, rose, rosemary, sandalwood, sesame, thyme, tuberose, vanilla, vetivert, ylang ylang.

Orchid
Mixes with: Amber, apricot, aster, cardamom, chamomile, cherry, coconut, frangipani, gardenia, geranium, hyacinth, jasmine, lavender, lemon, lemon balm, lemon verbena, lime, lotus, magnolia, mimosa, myrrh, myrtle, neroli, orris, papaya, passion flower, peach, plumeria, poppy, primrose, raspberry, rose, sandalwood, spearmint, strawberry, sweet pea, thyme, tuberose, tulip, vanilla, violet, ylang ylang.

Orris
Associated with: Isis, Osiris, Set.
Mixes with: Amber, apricot, aster, cardamom, chamomile, cherry, cinnamon, clove, coconut, cypress, frangipani, gardenia, geranium, hyacinth, jasmine, lavender, lemon, lemon balm, lemon verbena, lime, lotus, magnolia, mimosa, myrrh, myrtle, neroli, orchid, papaya, passion flower, peach, plumeria, poppy, primrose, raspberry, rose, sandalwood, spearmint, strawberry, sweet pea, thyme, tuberose, tulip, vanilla, violet, ylang ylang.

Palmarosa
Mixes with: Amber, basil, bay, cardamom, chamomile, clove, coriander (cilantro), geranium, ginger, jasmine, juniper, lavender, lemon, myrrh, neroli, orange, petitgrain, rose, rosemary, sandalwood, thyme, vanilla, yarrow, ylang ylang.

Papaya
Mixes with: Amber, cardamom, chamomile, coconut, gardenia, hyacinth, jasmine, lavender, lemon, lemon balm, lotus, myrrh, neroli, orchid, orris, passion flower, peach, plumeria, rose, sandalwood, spearmint, sweet pea, thyme, vanilla, violet, ylang ylang.

Passion flower
Mixes with: Amber, apricot, aster, cardamom, chamomile, cherry, coconut, frangipani, gardenia, geranium, hyacinth, jasmine, lavender, lemon, lemon balm, lime, lotus, magnolia, mimosa, myrrh, myrtle, neroli, orchid, orris, papaya, peach, plumeria, poppy, raspberry, rose, rosemary, sandalwood, spearmint, strawberry, sweet pea, thyme, tuberose, vanilla, violet, ylang ylang.

Peach
Mixes with: Amber, apricot, aster, cardamom, chamomile, cherry, coconut, frangipani, gardenia, geranium, hyacinth, jasmine, lavender, lemon, lemon balm, lime, lotus, magnolia, mimosa, myrrh, myrtle, neroli, orchid, orris, papaya, passion flower, plumeria, poppy, raspberry, rose, sandalwood, spearmint, strawberry, sweet pea, thyme, tuberose, vanilla, violet, ylang ylang.

Peppermint
Possibly used as perfume, aphrodisiac or medicine by the Ancient Egyptians.
Mixes with: Absinthe, acacia, almond, amber, basil, civet, clover, cypress, geranium, juniper, lavender, lemon, mandrake, marjoram, neroli, olive, rosemary, sesame, spearmint, yarrow.

Petitgrain
Mixes with: Amber, basil, cardamom, cinnamon, clove, coriander (cilantro), cypress, geranium, ginger, hyacinth, jasmine, juniper, lavender, lemon, lime, linden, marjoram, neroli, orange, palmarosa, rose, rosemary, sandalwood, vanilla, ylang ylang.

Plumeria
Mixes with: Amber, apricot, aster, cardamom, chamomile, cherry, coconut, frangipani, gardenia, geranium, hyacinth, jasmine, lavender, lemon, lemon balm, lemon verbena, lime, lotus, magnolia, mimosa, myrrh, myrtle, neroli, orchid, orris, papaya, passion flower, peach, poppy, primrose, raspberry, rose, sandalwood, spearmint, strawberry, sweet pea, thyme, tuberose, tulip, vanilla, violet, ylang ylang.

Poppy
Associated with: Anubis, Isis, Khepera, Mut, Nephthys.
Mixes with: Amber, cardamom, chamomile, coconut, gardenia, hyacinth, jasmine, lavender, lemon, lemon balm, lotus, myrrh, neroli, orchid, orris, passion flower, peach, plumeria, rose, sandalwood, spearmint, sweet pea, thyme, vanilla, violet, ylang ylang.

Primrose
Mixes with: Amber, cardamom, cypress, geranium, honey, honeysuckle, hyacinth, lavender, lemon, lemon verbena, magnolia, musk, myrtle, neroli, orchid, orris, plumeria, rose, spearmint, sweet pea, thyme, tuberose, vanilla, vetivert, violet, ylang ylang.

Raspberry
Mixes with: Amber, cardamom, chamomile, coconut, gardenia, geranium, hyacinth, jasmine, lavender, lemon, lemon balm, lotus, magnolia, myrrh, myrtle, neroli, orchid, orris, passion flower, peach, plumeria, rose, sandalwood, spearmint, sweet pea, thyme, tuberose, vanilla, violet, ylang ylang.

Rose
Associated with: Hathor, Isis.
Mixes with: Amber, apricot, aster, bay, cardamom, carnation, chamomile, cherry, cinnamon, clove, coconut, coriander (cilantro), frangipani, gardenia, geranium, ginger, hyacinth, jasmine, lavender, lemon, lemon verbena, lime, linden, lotus, magnolia, mimosa, neroli, nutmeg, orange, orchid, orris, palmarosa, papaya, passion flower, peach, petitgrain, plumeria, poppy, primrose, raspberry, rosemary, sandalwood, spearmint, strawberry, sweet pea, tuberose, tulip, vanilla, vetivert, violet, ylang ylang.

Rosemary

Traces have been found in Egyptian tombs.

Mixes with: Absinthe, acacia, amber, basil, bay, cardamom, chamomile, civet, clove, cypress, geranium, ginger, honey, juniper, lavender, lemon, lemon verbena, mandrake, marjoram, myrrh, myrtle, neroli, olive, orange, palmarosa, passion flower, peppermint, petitgrain, rose, sandalwood, sesame, spearmint, thyme, yarrow, ylang ylang.

Sandalwood

Used medicinally and for incense and embalming by the Ancient Egyptians.

Associated with: Hathor, Sekhmet, Shu.

Mixes with: Absinthe, acacia, amber, apricot, aster, bay, cardamom, carnation, chamomile, cherry, cinnamon, civet, clove, coconut, coriander (cilantro), cypress, frangipani, gardenia, geranium, ginger, honey, hyacinth, jasmine, juniper, lavender, lemon, lemon verbena, lime, linden, lotus, mimosa, myrrh, neroli, olive, orange, orchid, orris, palmarosa, papaya, passion flower, peach, petitgrain, plumeria, poppy, raspberry, rose, rosemary, sesame, spearmint, strawberry, sweet pea, thyme, tuberose, vanilla, vetivert, violet, ylang ylang.

Sesame

Can be used as a base or as an ingredient.

Mixes with: Acacia, amber, basil, bay, carnation, cinnamon, clove, coriander (cilantro), geranium, juniper, lavender, lemon, lime, neroli, nutmeg, orange, peppermint, rosemary, sandalwood, vanilla.

Spearmint

Mixes with: Amber, apricot, aster, basil, cardamom, chamomile, cherry, coconut, frangipani, gardenia, geranium, hyacinth, jasmine, lavender, lemon, lemon balm, lemon verbena, lime, lotus, magnolia, mandrake, mimosa, myrrh, myrtle, neroli, orchid, orris, papaya, passion flower, peach, peppermint, plumeria, poppy, primrose, raspberry, rose, rosemary, sandalwood, strawberry, sweet pea, thyme, tuberose, tulip, vanilla, violet, ylang ylang.

Strawberry

Mixes with: Amber, cardamom, chamomile, coconut, gardenia, geranium, hyacinth, jasmine, lavender, lemon, lemon balm, lotus, magnolia, myrrh, myrtle, neroli, orchid, orris, passion flower, peach, plumeria, rose, sandalwood, spearmint, sweet pea, thyme, tuberose, vanilla, violet, ylang ylang.

Sweet pea (B)
Mixes with: Amber, apricot, aster, cardamom, chamomile, cherry, coconut, frangipani, gardenia, geranium, hyacinth, jasmine, lavender, lemon, lemon balm, lemon verbena, lime, lotus, magnolia, mimosa, myrrh, myrtle, neroli, orchid, orris, papaya, passion flower, peach, plumeria, poppy, primrose, raspberry, rose, sandalwood, spearmint, strawberry, thyme, tuberose, tulip, vanilla, violet, ylang ylang.

Thyme
Used by the Ancient Egyptians in embalming.
Mixes with: Amber, apricot, aster, basil, cherry, cinnamon, clover, coconut, cypress, frangipani, gardenia, geranium, ginger, lavender, lemon, lemon verbena, lime, magnolia, mandrake, marjoram, mimosa, myrtle, neroli, orange, orchid, orris, palmarosa, papaya, passion flower, peach, plumeria, poppy, primrose, raspberry, rosemary, sandalwood, spearmint, strawberry, sweet pea, tulip.

Tuberose
Used in religious festivals.
Mixes with: Amber, apricot, aster, cherry, frangipani, hyacinth, jasmine, lavender, lemon, lemon verbena, lime, linden, magnolia, neroli, orange, orchid, orris, passion flower, peach, plumeria, primrose, raspberry, rose, sandalwood, spearmint, strawberry, sweet pea, tulip, vanilla, violet.

Tulip
Mixes with: Amber, cardamom, cypress, geranium, honeysuckle, hyacinth, lavender, lemon, magnolia, myrtle, neroli, orchid, orris, plumeria, rose, spearmint, sweet pea, thyme, tuberose, vanilla, vetivert, violet, ylang ylang.

Vanilla
Mixes with: Acacia, almond, amber, apricot, aster, bay, cardamom, cherry, cinnamon, civet, clove, clover, coconut, coriander (cilantro), frangipani, gardenia, geranium, ginger, honey, jasmine, lavender, lemon, lemon verbena, lime, lotus, magnolia, mimosa, myrtle, neroli, nutmeg, olive, orange, orchid, orris, palmarosa, papaya, passion

flower, peach, petitgrain, plumeria, poppy, primrose, raspberry, rose, sandalwood, sesame, spearmint, strawberry, sweet pea, tuberose, tulip, ylang ylang.

Vetivert
Mixes with: Amber, cardamom, coriander (cilantro), geranium, ginger, honey, honeysuckle, jasmine, juniper, lavender, lemon, lemon verbena, magnolia, musk, neroli, orange, primrose, rose, sandalwood, tulip, ylang ylang.

Violet
Mixes with: Amber, apricot, aster, basil, bay, cherry, cinnamon, clove, coconut, frangipani, gardenia, geranium, hyacinth, jasmine, lavender, lemon, lemon verbena, lime, lotus, magnolia, mimosa, neroli, orchid, orris, papaya, passion flower, peach, plumeria, poppy, primrose, raspberry, rose, sandalwood, spearmint, strawberry, sweet pea, tuberose, tulip.

Yarrow
Mixes with: Amber, chamomile, cypress, geranium, ginger, lavender, lemon, marjoram, myrtle, neroli, palmarosa, peppermint, rosemary.

Ylang ylang
Mixes with: Amber, apricot, aster, bay, cardamom, carnation, chamomile, cherry, cinnamon, clove, coconut, coriander (cilantro), frangipani, gardenia, geranium, ginger, hyacinth, jasmine, lavender, lemon, lemon verbena, lime, linden, lotus, magnolia, mimosa, myrrh, neroli, orange, orchid, orris, palmarosa, papaya, passion flower, peach, petitgrain, plumeria, poppy, primrose, raspberry, rose, rosemary, sandalwood, spearmint, strawberry, sweet pea, tulip, vanilla, vetivert.

Oils to attract lust

B = Blend; S = Synthetic

Almond
Can be used as a base or an essential oil.
Associated with: Ptah, Thoth.
Mixes with: Ambergris, lavender, lemongrass, mistletoe, peppermint, vanilla.

Ambergris (B or S)
Associated with: Anubis, Khepera, Ptah.
Mixes with: Almond, lavender, lemongrass, musk, peppermint, vanilla.

Apricot
Can be used as a base oil or as an ingredient.
Mixes with: Cardamom, coconut, geranium, jasmine, lavender, lotus, magnolia, myrrh, myrtle, orris, rose, sandalwood, tuberose, vanilla, violet, ylang ylang.

Basil
Mixes with: Black pepper, galangal, geranium, ginger, ginseng, jasmine, lavender, lemongrass, myrtle, olive, orange, peppermint, petitgrain, rosemary, saffron, sesame, tangerine, violet.

Benzoin
Can be used as a fixative or as a substitute for vanilla. It has a chocolate-vanilla fragrance.
Associated with: Apophis, Hathor, Khepera.

Black pepper
Associated with: Horus.
Mixes with: Basil, cardamom, clove, geranium, ginger, lavender, lemongrass, myrrh, orange, patchouli, peppermint, petitgrain, rosemary, sandalwood, vanilla, vetivert, ylang ylang.

Cardamom
The Ancient Egyptians used this spice in perfumes and incense and chewed the seeds to keep their teeth white.
Mixes with: Apricot, black pepper, cinnamon, coconut, cyclamen, frangipani, ginger, hibiscus, jasmine, lavender, lemongrass, lotus, magnolia, myrtle, orange, orris, patchouli, petitgrain, primrose, rose, sandalwood, vanilla, vetivert, ylang ylang.

Cassia
May be used as a substitute for cinnamon.

Cinnamon
Used by the Ancient Egyptians as an oil for the feet.
Associated with: Amun and Ra.

Mixes with: Cardamom, clove, galangal, geranium, ginger, ginseng, honey, jasmine, lavender, lemongrass, mistletoe, myrrh, myrtle, narcissus, nutmeg, olive, orange, patchouli, petitgrain, rose, saffron, sandalwood, sesame, tangerine, vanilla, violet, ylang ylang.

Clove
Associated with: Amun.
Mixes with: Black pepper, cinnamon, galangal, geranium, ginger, ginseng, honeysuckle, jasmine, lavender, lemongrass, myrtle, narcissus, nutmeg, olive, orange, orris, patchouli, petitgrain, rose, rosemary, saffron, sandalwood, sesame, tangerine, vanilla, violet, ylang ylang.

Coconut
Can be used as a base or as an essential oil.
Associated with: Nut.
Mixes with: Apricot, cardamom, cyclamen, frangipani, hibiscus, jasmine, lavender, lotus, myrrh, orris, rose, sandalwood, vanilla, violet, ylang ylang.

Cyclamen
Mixes with: Cardamom, coconut, geranium, jasmine, lavender, lotus, magnolia, myrrh, orris, rose, sandalwood, tuberose, vanilla, violet, ylang ylang.

Frangipani
Mixes with: Cardamom, coconut, geranium, jasmine, lavender, lotus, magnolia, myrrh, orris, rose, sandalwood, tuberose, vanilla, violet, ylang ylang.

Galangal
Mixes with: Basil, cinnamon, clove, geranium, ginger, ginseng, lavender, nutmeg, olive, orange, peppermint, rosemary, saffron, sesame, tangerine.

Geranium (rose)
Associated with: Isis.
Mixes with: Apricot, basil, black pepper, cinnamon, clove, cyclamen, frangipani, galangal, ginger, ginseng, hibiscus, jasmine, lavender, lemongrass, magnolia, myrrh, myrtle, nutmeg, olive, orange, orris, patchouli, peppermint, petitgrain, primrose, rose, rosemary, saffron, sandalwood, sesame, tangerine, vanilla, vetivert, violet, ylang ylang.

Ginger
Mixes with: Basil, black pepper, cardamom, cinnamon, clove, galangal, geranium, jasmine, lavender, myrtle, orange, patchouli, petitgrain, rose, rosemary, sandalwood, vanilla, vetivert, ylang ylang.

Ginseng
Associated with: Shu.
Mixes with: Basil, cinnamon, clove, galangal, geranium, lavender, mistletoe, nutmeg, orange, peppermint, rosemary, sandalwood, tangerine, vanilla.

Hibiscus
Mixes with: Cardamom, coconut, geranium, jasmine, lavender, lotus, magnolia, myrrh, myrtle, orris, rose, sandalwood, tuberose, vanilla, violet, ylang ylang.

Honey
Can be used as a base or an ingredient.
Mixes with: Cinnamon, honeysuckle, lavender, magnolia, mistletoe, narcissus, orange, patchouli, primrose, rosemary, sandalwood, tangerine, vanilla, vetivert.

Honeysuckle
Mixes with: Clove, honey, lavender, magnolia, musk, narcissus, nutmeg, patchouli, primrose, vetivert.

Jasmine
Associated with: Shu.
Mixes with: Apricot, basil, cardamom, cinnamon, clove, coconut, cyclamen, frangipani, geranium, ginger, hibiscus, lavender, lotus, narcissus, nutmeg, orange, orris, patchouli, petitgrain, rose, sandalwood, tuberose, vanilla, vetivert, violet, ylang ylang.

Lavender
Blends with any essential oil.
Associated with: Isis, Thoth.

Lemongrass
Mixes with: Almond, ambergris, basil, black pepper, cardamom, cinnamon, clove, geranium, lavender, mistletoe, nutmeg, orange, patchouli, petitgrain, rosemary, vetivert.

Lotus
Associated with: Isis, Khepera, Neferten.
Mixes with: Apricot, cardamom, coconut, cyclamen, frangipani, hibiscus, jasmine, lavender, myrrh, orris, rose, sandalwood, vanilla, violet, ylang ylang.

Magnolia
Mixes with: Apricot, cardamom, cyclamen, frangipani, geranium, hibiscus, honey, honeysuckle, lavender, musk, myrtle, narcissus, orris, patchouli, primrose, rose, tuberose, vanilla, vetivert, violet, ylang ylang.

Mistletoe
Mixes with: Almond, cinnamon, ginseng, honey, lavender, lemongrass, olive, orange, peppermint, rosemary, saffron, sandalwood, sesame, tangerine, vanilla.

Musk (Egyptian) (S)
Associated with: Amun, Isis, Nut, Ra, Set.
Mixes with: Ambergris, honeysuckle, lavender, magnolia, narcissus, patchouli, primrose, vetivert.

Myrrh
Used in incense, unguents, cosmetics and mummification.
Associated with: Hathor, Horus, Isis, Mut, Nephthys, Osiris, Ra.
Mixes with: Apricot, black pepper, cinnamon, coconut, cyclamen, frangipani, geranium, hibiscus, lavender, lotus, orris, patchouli, rosemary, sandalwood, ylang ylang.

Myrtle
Used by the Ancient Egyptians in the worship of Hathor, and medicinally to treat facial tics.
Associated with: Hathor.
Mixes with: Apricot, basil, cardamom, cinnamon, clove, geranium, ginger, hibiscus, lavender, magnolia, orange, orris, primrose, rosemary, vanilla.

Narcissus
The Ancient Egyptians fashioned funeral wreaths with these flowers.
Associated with: Isis.

Mixes with: Cinnamon, clove, honey, honeysuckle, jasmine, lavender, magnolia, musk, orange, primrose, sandalwood, tuberose, ylang ylang.

Nutmeg
Used in embalming by the Ancient Egyptians.
Mixes with: Cinnamon, clove, galangal, geranium, ginseng, honeysuckle, jasmine, lavender, lemongrass, olive, orange, rose, saffron, sesame, tangerine, vanilla.

Olive
Can be used as a base or as an ingredient.
Associated with: Amun, Isis, Nut, Ra.
Mixes with: Basil, cinnamon, clove, galangal, geranium, lavender, mistletoe, nutmeg, orange, peppermint, rosemary, sandalwood, tangerine, vanilla.

Orange
Mixes with: Basil, black pepper, cardamom, cinnamon, clove, galangal, geranium, ginger, ginseng, honey, jasmine, lavender, lemongrass, mistletoe, myrtle, narcissus, nutmeg, olive, patchouli, petitgrain, rose, rosemary, saffron, sandalwood, sesame, tangerine, tuberose, vanilla, vetivert, ylang ylang.

Orris
Associated with: Isis, Osiris, Set.
Mixes with: Apricot, cardamom, clove, coconut, cyclamen, frangipani, geranium, hibiscus, jasmine, lavender, lotus, magnolia, myrrh, myrtle, primrose, rose, sandalwood, tuberose, vanilla, violet, ylang ylang.

Patchouli
Associated with: Hathor.
Mixes with: Black pepper, cardamom, cinnamon, clove, geranium, ginger, honey, honeysuckle, jasmine, lavender, lemongrass, magnolia, musk, myrrh, orange, petitgrain, primrose, rose, sandalwood, vanilla, ylang ylang.

Peppermint
Possibly used as perfume, aphrodisiac or medicine by the Ancient Egyptians.
Mixes with: Almond, ambergris, basil, black pepper, galangal,

geranium, ginseng, lavender, mistletoe, olive, rosemary, saffron, sesame, tangerine.

Petitgrain
Mixes with: Basil, black pepper, cardamom, cinnamon, clove, geranium, ginger, jasmine, lavender, lemongrass, orange, patchouli, rose, rosemary, sandalwood, vanilla, ylang ylang.

Primrose
Mixes with: Cardamom, geranium, honey, honeysuckle, lavender, magnolia, musk, myrtle, narcissus, orris, patchouli, rose, tuberose, vanilla, vetivert, violet, ylang ylang.

Rose
Associated with: Hathor, Isis.
Mixes with: Apricot, cardamom, cinnamon, clove, coconut, cyclamen, frangipani, geranium, ginger, hibiscus, jasmine, lavender, lotus, magnolia, nutmeg, orange, orris, patchouli, petitgrain, primrose, rosemary, sandalwood, tuberose, vanilla, vetivert, violet, ylang ylang.

Rosemary
Traces have been found in Egyptian tombs.
Mixes with: Basil, black pepper, clove, galangal, geranium, ginger, ginseng, honey, lavender, lemongrass, mistletoe, myrrh, myrtle, olive, orange, peppermint, petitgrain, rose, saffron, sesame, tangerine.

Saffron
Associated with: Amun.
Mixes with: Basil, cinnamon, clove, galangal, geranium, lavender, mistletoe, nutmeg, orange, peppermint, rosemary, sandalwood, tangerine, vanilla.

Sandalwood
Used medicinally and for incense and embalming by the Ancient Egyptians.
Associated with: Hathor, Sekhmet, Shu.
Mixes with: Apricot, black pepper, cardamom, cinnamon, clove, coconut, cyclamen, frangipani, geranium, ginger, ginseng, hibiscus, honey, jasmine, lavender, lotus, mistletoe, myrrh, narcissus, olive, orange, orris, patchouli, petitgrain, rose, saffron, sesame, tangerine, tuberose, vanilla, vetivert, violet, ylang ylang.

Sesame

Can be used as a base or as an ingredient.

Mixes with: Basil, cinnamon, clove, galangal, geranium, lavender, mistletoe, nutmeg, orange, peppermint, rosemary, sandalwood, tangerine, vanilla.

Tangerine

Mixes with: Basil, cinnamon, clove, galangal, geranium, ginseng, honey, lavender, mistletoe, nutmeg, olive, orange, peppermint, rosemary, saffron, sandalwood, sesame, vanilla, violet.

Tuberose

Used in religious festivals.

Mixes with: Apricot, cyclamen, frangipani, hibiscus, jasmine, lavender, magnolia, narcissus, orange, orris, primrose, rose, sandalwood, vanilla, violet.

Vanilla

Mixes with: Almond, ambergris, apricot, black pepper, cardamom, cinnamon, clove, coconut, cyclamen, frangipani, geranium, ginger, ginseng, hibiscus, honey, jasmine, lavender, lotus, magnolia, mistletoe, myrtle, nutmeg, olive, orange, orris, patchouli, petitgrain, primrose, rose, saffron, sandalwood, sesame, tangerine, tuberose, ylang ylang.

Vetivert

Mixes with: Black pepper, cardamom, geranium, ginger, honey, honeysuckle, jasmine, lavender, lemongrass, magnolia, musk, orange, primrose, rose, sandalwood, ylang ylang.

Violet

Mixes with: Apricot, basil, cinnamon, clove, coconut, cyclamen, frangipani, geranium, hibiscus, jasmine, lavender, lotus, magnolia, orris, primrose, rose, sandalwood, tangerine, tuberose.

Ylang ylang

Mixes with: Apricot, black pepper, cardamom, cinnamon, clove, coconut, cyclamen, frangipani, geranium, ginger, hibiscus, jasmine, lavender, lotus, magnolia, myrrh, narcissus, orange, orris, patchouli, petitgrain, primrose, rose, sandalwood, vanilla, vetivert.

Oils to attract happiness

B = Blend

Almond
Can be used as a base or an essential oil.
Associated with: Ptah, Thoth.
Mixes with: Amber, lavender, lily of the valley, marjoram, vanilla.

Amber
Blends with any essential oil.

Apple blossom
Mixes with: Amber, apricot, cherry, coconut, hyacinth, lavender, lilac, lily of the valley, sweet pea, vanilla.

Apricot
Can be used as a base or an essential oil.
Mixes with: Amber, apple blossom, cherry, coconut, hyacinth, lavender, lilac, lily of the valley, sweet pea.

Benzoin
Can be used as a fixative or as a substitute for vanilla. It has a chocolate-vanilla fragrance.
Associated with: Apophis, Hathor, Khepera.

Cherry
Mixes with: Amber, apple blossom, apricot, coconut, hyacinth, lavender, lilac, lily of the valley, sweet pea.

Coconut
Can be used as a base or as an essential oil.
Associated with: Nut.
Mixes with: Amber, apple blossom, apricot, cherry, hyacinth, lavender, lilac, lily of the valley, sweet pea.

Honey
Can be used as a base or an ingredient.
Mixes with: Amber, lavender, orange, vanilla.

Hyacinth
Mixes with: Amber, apple blossom, apricot, cherry, coconut, lavender, lilac, lily of the valley, orange, sweet pea, vanilla.

Lavender
Blends with any essential oil.
Associated with: Isis, Thoth.

Lilac
Mixes with: Amber, apple blossom, apricot, cherry, coconut, hyacinth, lavender, sweet pea, vanilla.

Lily of the valley
Associated with: Isis, Nut, Osiris.
Mixes with: Almond, amber, apple blossom, apricot, cherry, coconut, hyacinth, lavender, marjoram, orange, sweet pea, vanilla.

Marjoram
Associated with: Sobek.
Mixes with: Almond, amber, lavender, lily of the valley, orange, vanilla.

Olive
Can be used as a base or as an ingredient.
Associated with: Amun, Isis, Nut, Ra.
Mixes with: Amber, lavender, orange, vanilla.

Orange
Mixes with: Amber, honey, hyacinth, lavender, lily of the valley, marjoram, olive, saffron, sesame, vanilla.

Saffron
Associated with: Amun.
Mixes with: Amber, lavender, orange, vanilla.

Sesame
Can be used as a base or as an ingredient.
Mixes with: Amber, lavender, orange, vanilla.

Sweet pea (B)
Mixes with: Amber, apple blossom, apricot, cherry, coconut, hyacinth, lavender, lilac, lily of the valley, vanilla.

Vanilla
Mixes with: Almond, amber, apple blossom, honey, hyacinth, lavender, lilac, lily of the valley, marjoram, olive, orange, saffron, sesame, sweet pea.

Oils for mourning

Almond
Can be used as a base or an essential oil.
Associated with: Ptah, Thoth.
Mixes with: Lavender, vanilla.

Apricot
Can be used as a base or an essential oil.
Mixes with: Coconut, geranium, lavender, vanilla.

Benzoin
Can be used as a fixative or as a substitute for vanilla. It has a chocolate-vanilla fragrance.
Associated with: Apophis, Hathor, Khepera.

Coconut
Can be used as a base or as an essential oil.
Associated with: Nut.
Mixes with: Apricot, geranium, lavender, narcissus, vanilla.

Cypress
Used to make sarcophagi and for medicinal purposes.
Associated with: Heket, Isis, Mut, Nephthys.
Mixes with: Frankincense, galbanum, geranium, honey, lavender, narcissus.

Frankincense
Used by the Ancient Egyptians as an offering to the Gods, for meditation, in cosmetics and to soothe aching limbs.
Associated with: Amun, Ra.
Mixes with: Cypress, galbanum, geranium, honey, lavender, marigold, olive, sesame, vanilla.

Galbanum
Used for embalming by the Ancient Egyptians.

Associated with: Ma'at, Mut, Nut.
Mixes with: Cypress, frankincense, geranium, lavender, vanilla.

Geranium (rose)
Associated with: Isis.
Mixes with: Apricot, coconut, cypress, frankincense, galbanum, lavender, vanilla.

Honey
Can be used as a base or an ingredient.
Mixes with: Cypress, frankincense, lavender, narcissus, vanilla.

Lavender
Blends with any essential oil.
Associated with: Isis, Thoth.

Marigold
Used to bless the departed.
Mixes with: Frankincense, lavender, olive, sesame.

Narcissus
The Ancient Egyptians fashioned funeral wreaths with these flowers.
Associated with: Isis.
Mixes with: Coconut, cypress, honey, lavender, vanilla.

Olive
Can be used as a base or as an ingredient.
Associated with: Amun, Isis, Nut, Ra.
Mixes with: Frankincense, lavender, marigold, vanilla.

Sesame
Can be used as a base or as an ingredient.
Mixes with: Frankincense, lavender, marigold, vanilla.

Vanilla
Mixes with: Almond, apricot, coconut, frankincense, galbanum, geranium, honey, lavender, narcissus, olive, sesame.

Incenses and resins

Some commercially produced incenses are natural, others are not. I have used both with great success. Incense comes in sticks, cones and resins and also in a loose form. The loose variety and resins are specifically for use on charcoal discs. Resins are a sticky sap-like substance formed in plants, especially fir and pine trees, which emit a fragrance when burned.

See which types of incense suit you best. I use all types: cones burn quicker than sticks and are perfect for simple spells, as are resins and loose incense. Sticks burn longer for use with more time-consuming spells or ritual work. Loose incense and resins are perfect for any magickal work since you control the amount used and it can be mixed on the spot for maximum effect and fragrance. When using loose incense and resins, always light the charcoal disc first and wait for it to stop sparking before placing anything on it.

I have included some recipes for you to experiment with if you feel adventurous and want to make your own incense (see pages 119–20).

R = Resin

Love
Almond, apple blossom, basil, blue Nile, caraway, carob, catnip (associated with Bast), cinnamon, cinquefoil, clove, coriander (cilantro), dill, dragon's blood (R – associated with Horus and Isis), Egyptian musk, frankincense, gardenia, geranium, hyacinth, jasmine, juniper, lavender, lotus blossom, meadowsweet, myrrh, myrtle, orange, orris, pansy, patchouli, rose, rosemary, rue (to ease a painful love), spearmint, valerian (associated with Thoth), vanilla, vervain (associated with Isis), violet, white copal (R), yarrow, ylang ylang.

Lust
Amber (R), blue Nile, caraway, carob, catnip, cinnamon, cinquefoil, clove, dragon's blood (R), Egyptian musk, frankincense, gardenia, lavender, lotus blossom, myrtle, oak, patchouli, rose, vanilla, vervain, white copal (R).

Purification and mourning
Acacia, anise, bay, camphor (to banish a lover), cedarwood (associated with Amun and Isis), chamomile, cinnamon, copal (R), Egyptian musk, frankincense, myrrh, peppermint, pine, sage, sandalwood.

Herbs and spices

Burning herbs and spices for incense is a traditional practice. Obviously, the actual dried plant material carries a stronger essence than commercially produced incense for ritual and spellwork. However, not all plants smell pleasing when burned on charcoal discs and may need to be mixed with an essential oil, other herbs or sawdust. After all, if the scent is unpleasant to you, the gods probably won't enjoy it either. Spend a day trying just a pinch of different herbs and spices on burning charcoal to check the fragrance it emits. You could even make this a celebration to the gods and goddesses. Be creative – that's what magick is all about.

Rolling an anointed candle in herbs and spices is another way to get the energy of the herbs and a hint of their fragrance and it allows you to burn incense as well, if you wish. The more you put into a ritual or spell, the more powerful it will be and the more apt to manifest the desired result. I find that spices rolled on an anointed candle add extra power and a lovely soft fragrance when burned at the same time as incense. You can mix and grind the herbs together using a pestle and mortar, or a peppermill, nutmeg or citrus grater or food processor will grind herbs to a fine powder. My favourite method for applying the powdered herbs and spices is to place them on aluminium foil and roll the candle to get complete and maximum coverage. Another way is to sprinkle the herbs on to the candle, making sure you have some foil underneath to catch any extra herbs. With trial and error you will find a method that suits your needs.

Many of us associate chocolate with love – we often give our lover a box of chocolates on Valentine's Day and on special occasions. Chocolate body paints and body frostings are on the market, which may also be used in erotic spells and rituals. However, chocolate was unknown to the Ancient Egyptians, though they were acquainted with carob, an evergreen tree that produces pods containing a sweetish pulp. Some people use carob in place of chocolate. If you or your lover/spouse wish, carob powder may be mixed with spices and used in love spells. If you prefer to use the real thing, always use the best and richest dark chocolate you can obtain. Melt the chocolate in a double boiler or the microwave (we modern witches use electrical appliances for speed) and spread it on a candle or dip the candle in the chocolate before you begin your spell. You may wish to add a herb or spice to the chocolate – ground mint leaves, for instance, would add a nice fresh hint while the candle burns.

Happiness
Anise, apple blossom, carob, catnip, heliotrope, hyacinth, lavender, lilac, lily of the valley, marjoram, meadowsweet, saffron, St John's wort, sesame.

Love
Apple blossom, balm of Gilead, basil, caraway, cardamom, carob, catnip, chamomile, chickweed, cinnamon, clove, coriander (cilantro), cumin, dill, gardenia, geranium (rose), ginger, grape root (associated with Hathor), hibiscus, honeysuckle, jasmine, juniper, lavender, lemon, lemon balm, lemon verbena, linden, lime, marigold, marjoram, meadowsweet, mimosa, mistletoe, myrtle, nutmeg, orange, orchid, orris, patchouli, peppermint, plumeria, raspberry, rose, rosemary, sarsaparilla, spearmint, strawberry, thyme, tonka, tuberose, valerian, vanilla, vervain, vetivert, violet, yarrow.

Lust
Caraway, carob, chilli pepper, cinnamon, clove, deerstongue, ginger, ginseng, hibiscus, lemongrass, nettle, nutmeg, olive, parsley, patchouli, peppermint, rosemary, saffron, sesame, tuberose, vanilla, violet.

Purification
Anise, benzoin, betony, cinnamon, cinquefoil, clove, fennel, hyssop, lavender, lemon, oak leaves, pine, rosemary, rue, sandalwood, thyme, valerian, vervain.

Incense recipes

The loose incenses you can make with these recipes are to be used with charcoal discs. Amber oil, resin or a tumbled stone may be added to increase the effectiveness of any incense.

Altar incense*
1 part ground cinnamon
3 parts frankincense resin
2 parts myrrh resin

Egyptian incense*
1 part ground calamus
1 part ground cedar
1 part ground cinnamon
4 parts frankincense resin
3 parts gum arabic resin
1 part ground juniper berries
2 parts myrrh resin

Isis incense*
1 part frankincense resin
3 parts myrrh resin
1 part ground rose petals
2 parts ground sandalwood
A few drops lotus bouquet

Sandalwood and calamus kyphi incense*
1 part ground red sandalwood
½ part frankincense resin
¼ part myrrh resin
1 part ground galangal
¼ part ground juniper berries
¼ part dragon's blood resin
1 part ground calamus root
1 part ground bay laurel
¼ part ground orris root
¼ part henna powder
¼ part ground cinnamon
¼ part ground balm of Gilead
¼ part ground styrax bark
Add oils of amber, acacia, honey, lotus, musk, orris and styrax to personal taste.

Frankincense kyphi incense*
3 parts frankincense resin
2 parts benzoin resin
2 parts myrrh resin
1 part ground juniper berries
½ part ground galangal
½ part ground cinnamon
½ part ground cedar
2 drops lotus bouquet
2 drops wine
2 drops honey
A few raisins
Mix together thoroughly and grind to a fine powder.

Temple incense*
3 parts frankincense resin
2 part myrrh resin
A few drops lavender oil
A few drops sandalwood oil

*Cunningham, Scott. *The Complete Book of Incense, Oils and Brews.* Llewellyn Worldwide, PO Box 64383, St Paul, MN 55164. All rights reserved.

Love fest

The following recipes may be used to anoint candles for an all-out love fest with the one you love or to summon a lover.

You will need 20 candles, each of which you inscribe with your name and the name of your lover. Then anoint one candle with each one of the oils. Roll every candle in carob powder and set them all in candle holders. Because of the carob powder, the candles may flare like torches so you have to be vigilant; make sure they are on a sturdy, fire-safe surface and not liable to tip over, and check on them from time to time.

The multiple fragrances are very invigorating and the entire process really puts you in the mood to bring love into your life. Any of the incantations in this book to call love, celebrate love, or for reconciliation may be used when you light each candle, or you may wish to create your own.

Almond and peppermint love fest oil
2.5 ml/½ tsp olive oil
1 drop essential almond oil
1 drop peppermint oil

Almond and spearmint love fest oil
2.5 ml/½ tsp olive oil
1 drop essential almond oil
1 drop spearmint oil

Almond and vanilla love fest oil
2.5 ml/½ tsp coconut oil
1 drop essential almond oil
1 drop vanilla oil

Apple and cinnamon love fest oil
2.5 ml/½ tsp avocado oil
1 drop apple oil
1 drop cinnamon oil

Apple and jasmine love fest oil
2.5 ml/½ tsp almond oil (base)
2 drops apple oil
1 drop jasmine oil

Apple and lilac love fest oil
2.5 ml/½ tsp rose hip oil
1 drop apple oil
1 drop lilac oil

Cinnamon and Egyptian musk love fest oil
2.5 ml/½ tsp coconut oil
1 drop cinnamon oil
1 drop Egyptian musk oil

Cinnamon and orange love fest oil
2.5 ml/½ tsp grapeseed oil
1 drop cinnamon oil
1 drop orange oil

Cinnamon and patchouli love fest oil
2.5 ml/½ tsp hemp seed oil
2 drops cinnamon oil
1 drop patchouli oil

Cinnamon and peppermint love fest oil
2.5 ml/½ tsp almond oil (base)
1 drop cinnamon oil
1 drop peppermint oil

Cinnamon and vanilla love fest oil
2.5 ml/½ tsp hazelnut (filbert) oil
1 drop cinnamon oil
1 drop vanilla oil

Coconut and orange love fest oil
2.5 ml/½ tsp jojoba oil
1 drop essential coconut oil
1 drop orange oil

Egyptian musk and spearmint love fest oil
2.5 ml/¹/₂ tsp avocado oil
1 drop Egyptian musk oil
1 drop spearmint oil

Frangipani and vanilla love fest oil
2.5 ml/¹/₂ tsp almond oil (base)
1 drop frangipani oil
2 drops vanilla oil

Frangipani and vetivert love fest oil
2.5 ml/¹/₂ tsp hazelnut (filbert) oil
1 drop frangipani oil
1 drop vetivert oil

Heliotrope and vanilla love fest oil
2.5 ml/¹/₂ tsp rose hip oil
1 drop heliotrope oil
1 drop vanilla oil

Honeysuckle and lilac love fest oil
2.5 ml/¹/₂ tsp sesame oil
1 drop honeysuckle oil
1 drop lilac oil

Jasmine and patchouli love fest oil
2.5 ml/¹/₂ tsp hemp seed oil
1 drop jasmine oil
1 drop patchouli oil

Patchouli and vetivert love fest oil
2.5 ml/¹/₂ tsp sesame oil
1 drop patchouli oil
1 drop vetivert oil

Spearmint and vanilla love fest oil
2.5 ml/¹/₂ tsp apricot oil
1 drop spearmint oil
1 drop vanilla oil

Love/lust oil recipes

These can be used for any love candle spell in this book. You may prefer to try your hand at your own recipes or you may just want to use one essential oil to anoint a candle. Amber oil, resin or a tumbled stone may be added to increase the effectiveness of any oil.

Benzoin, frankincense and myrrh love/lust oil
2.5 ml/¹/₂ tsp olive oil
1 drop benzoin
2 drops frankincense oil
1 drop myrrh oil

Benzoin and lavender love/lust oil
2.5 ml/¹/₂ tsp almond oil
2 drops benzoin
2 drops lavender oil

Benzoin, lavender and orange love/lust oil
2.5 ml/½ tsp apricot oil
3 drops benzoin
2 drops lavender oil
1 drop orange oil

Benzoin and peppermint love/lust oil
2.5 ml/½ tsp jojoba oil
3 drops benzoin
2 drops peppermint oil

Benzoin and sandalwood love/lust oil
2.5 ml/½ tsp apricot oil
2 drops benzoin
3 drops sandalwood oil

Cinnamon, almond and coconut love/lust oil
2.5 ml/½ tsp jojoba oil
2 drops cinnamon oil
1 drop essential almond oil
2 drops essential coconut oil

Cinnamon, coconut and orange love/lust oil
2.5 ml/½ tsp apricot oil
2 drops cinnamon oil
2 drops essential coconut oil
1 drop orange oil

Cinnamon, coconut and vanilla love/lust oil
2.5 ml/½ tsp olive oil
1 drop cinnamon oil
2 drops essential coconut oil
1 drop vanilla oil

Cinnamon, orange and vanilla love/lust oil
2.5 ml/½ tsp jojoba oil
2 drops cinnamon oil
1 drop orange oil
2 drops vanilla oil

Coconut, almond and vanilla love/lust oil
2.5 ml/½ tsp olive oil
2 drops essential coconut oil
1 drop essential almond oil
2 drops vanilla oil

Coconut, clove and orange love/lust oil
2.5 ml/½ tsp almond oil
2 drops essential coconut oil
1 drop clove bud oil
1 drop orange oil

Coconut, orange and vanilla love/lust oil
2.5 ml/½ tsp jojoba oil
2 drops essential coconut oil
1 drop orange oil
2 drops vanilla oil

Frangipani and sandalwood love/lust oil
2.5 ml/½ tsp almond oil
2 drops frangipani oil
5 drops sandalwood oil

Gardenia and ginger love/lust oil
2.5 ml/½ tsp apricot oil
3 drops gardenia oil
4 drops ginger oil

Myrrh and ylang ylang love/lust oil
2.5 ml/½ tsp almond oil
1 drop myrrh oil
3 drops ylang ylang oil

Spearmint and ylang ylang love/lust oil
2.5 ml/½ tsp olive oil
1 drop spearmint oil
4 drops ylang ylang oil

Spearmint and tangerine love/lust oil
2.5 ml/½ tsp jojoba oil
1 drop spearmint oil
1 drop tangerine oil

Other oils

The following oils may be used in conjunction with any spell or ritual, for anointing candles, as ritual perfumes or in a diffuser in place of incense. They all have an Egyptian flavour, which is why I have included them here.

*Altar oil**
30 ml/2 tbsp base oil
1 drop cedar oil
4 drops frankincense oil
2 drops myrrh oil

*Initiation oil**
30 ml/2 tbsp base oil
3 drops frankincense oil
3 drops myrrh oil
1 drop sandalwood oil

*Temple oil**
30 ml/2 tbsp base oil
1 drop bay oil
4 drops frankincense oil
2 drops rosemary oil
1 drop sandalwood oil

*Lotus bouquet**
Rose oil
Jasmine oil
White (or light) musk oil
Ylang ylang oil
Mix one drop of each at a time, adjusting to personal taste, until the scent is heavy, floral and warm.

*Cunningham, Scott. *The Complete Book of Incense, Oils and Brews.* Llewellyn Worldwide, PO Box 64383, St Paul, MN 55164. All rights reserved.

CHAPTER 9

The Essence of Egyptian Love Spells

Spells are designed for a specific need, desire or concern. The most common spells are for love, money, healing, assistance in finding and/or keeping a job, or protection.

The simplicity or complexity of a spell should depend on the nature of your need, how important that need is to you and the time you are willing to devote to manifest your desire. Lighting a candle to a deity and speaking from your heart about a difficult situation may be just as effective as a more elaborate spell; the final outcome always depends upon your intent and your ability to focus your mind to cause the change you desire. If you are looking for love in general, you may feel that a simple spell will do the trick: if finding your soulmate is of primary importance, you may wish to perform a more elaborate spell.

I like to use candles in all my spellwork, but they are not essential – spells may consist of only an incantation, coupled with your desire to cause change in your life and visualisation of your goal. Magick is change: change of perception, change of energy, change of mindset. Your mind is a powerful tool and, with the proper use of meditation and visualisation, all things are possible.

A very simple spell for love

Find a dandelion that has turned to white seed. Think of your lover, or the person you would like as your lover, ask the help of a special god or goddess that you feel an affinity for, or perhaps Bast (sexual pleasure) or Hathor (love), and blow the seeds to the winds. You have released the energy of your intent to the heavens, which hopefully will bring about the change you desire.

Performing spells for other people

This is really a question of ethics. Personally, I wouldn't want the responsibility of performing a spell for someone else, especially in matters of the heart. And I would never work magick for someone without their permission and knowledge.

There are exceptions, however. A friend once told me that she had a loved one who was seriously ill. She did not know my religious beliefs, and I did not know hers, but when I asked if she would like me to burn a candle for her she said yes and seemed genuinely touched that I would even care enough to do so. Witches are *very* caring people. My intent, when I performed the spell, was to assist my friend and her loved one. I asked the gods and goddesses for their guidance and their healing, if that was meant to be. The loved one passed away quietly and painlessly, which is all one can hope for at the end of our days. My friend told me that my kindness helped her to accept the passing. In my mind, the spell had done its work.

Candle spells

Candle spells can be fairly simple affairs. When you are ready to use it, charge the unlit candle with your energy and intention by holding it in your dominant hand and visualising your intent. Put the candle down and write what you wish to accomplish on a piece of paper. Kiss the paper and anoint it with oil, if you desire. Anoint the candle, light it and think of your intention. Hold that image for as long as you feel the need to. Read aloud what you have written on the paper, as if you were speaking to the person you desire, light the paper with the candle flame and let it burn completely in your cauldron or other fire-safe container. You have now released your wish to the deities. Snuff out the candle with a snuffer or dampen your fingers with water and pinch it out (candle flames are only blown out in a spell or ritual when you wish to blow away the intent). Collect the paper ashes and scatter them to the winds.

A more elaborate spell might be performed in the following manner. First, charge the candle by carving love symbols on the candle, such as the hieroglyphs for love, beloved, heart and so forth (see pages 20–1 for some of the most relevant hieroglyphs). You could also carve the name of the person you want to attract. Anoint the candle with one or more essential oils, from wick to base, while visualising your intent. Next, roll the candle in a mixture of herbs, spices, magick powders and/or glitter, such as ground cinnamon, ground rose petals and red glitter. The candle is now ready to be lit and you may begin your spell.

I burn the candle for one hour each evening (or day if it is more convenient) while I visualise my desire. When the candle is completely burned down, I take whatever candle remains are left and bury them or throw them into a moving body of water, thus releasing my spell.

Basic spell altars

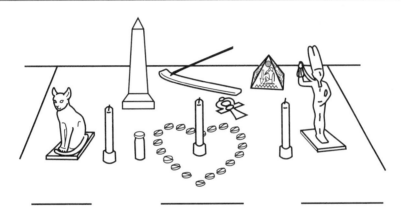

Most traditional Wiccans work in a circle composed of sea salt and designated by candles at the compass points. The circle, actually more of a sphere of power, is cast to delineate the spell or ritual area and for protection from negative influences that might affect the outcome. Ancient Egyptian priests worked in a temple and did not cast circles for their magickal spells and rituals. The average Ancient Egyptian performed his or her spells at home, also without casting a circle. This might feel a little strange to experienced Wiccan practitioners at first, but the end results can be just as rewarding.

I'm not suggesting you need to set up a temple in your home or apartment. I have worked some spells in my living room, kitchen, bedroom and even walking by the lake near my home. If I am performing a particularly important spell, I generally designate the compass points of my working area with canopic jars and/or white pillar candles, but I do not cast a circle. The success of a spell depends on your intent and having the tools you feel you need to accomplish the task at hand.

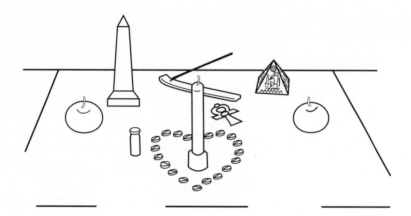

Binding and banishing spells

Binding spells (to tie someone to you) and banishing spells (to rid yourself of someone) were practised extensively by the Ancient Egyptians. As I know that they used this kind of magic, I have chosen to include them here, even though both of these types of spell may be approached by some with less than honourable intentions. Witchcraft is not based on revenge or retribution; it seeks to change through positive energy, not destructive energy. I use magick for positive change, not for revenge or to have power over someone, even if they have hurt me or failed to return my affections. Thus, binding or banishing should be approached with positive intentions, to bind someone from seriously harming themselves or others or to banish some negative influence from your life.

Binding spells should be approached responsibly and with care. Love should be given freely between two people, not forced upon someone; if you do a binding spell to tie someone to you, will you ever be sure that the person truly loves you or was he or she just bewitched by you? Also, if you do a binding spell to keep someone or to draw someone to you, you may find you can't get rid of them again. I have a few ethical dilemmas with binding spells, for even one done with the best intentions may not manifest the result you desire. I have, however, included two binding spells as examples and each has been tried with varying degrees of success (see pages 156 and 158).

A true banishing spell in the Ancient Egyptian sense is very destructive, seeking to destroy the person or render him or her helpless, as with the binding spells. I have no interest in exploring what might almost be the realm of 'dark' magick, nor any need to take such extreme measures. I am sure you also feel that true magick is not destructive or dangerous. However, banishing spells are valuable in our times to rid ourselves of unwanted behaviour, such as smoking, self-abuse, abuse by others or eating disorders and, since I have included two binding spells, I have also given you two examples of banishing spells (see pages 190 and 192). To seek to improve your life with positive intent is acceptable: to improve your life for purely selfish gains is not.

For example, you and your partner have been together for many years and you feel that you have grown apart; you no longer share the same interests and you argue more. In your heart you still love your partner, but you also know that the relationship is in trouble. My advice is to always try to work out the problems first through traditional means. Try to spark some romance back into the relationship. But if you've done that without any apparent improvement, you may need to turn to magick. I have also included some spells to help the people involved deal with the end of relationships, which happens to all of us at some point in our lives (see pages 185–9 and 193–203).

I have been in two abusive relationships – one physical and the other emotional. I attempted to get help for the abusive partner but eventually realised I was being destroyed so I got out of both situations and put my life back together. I silently wished each of my former lovers would find the help they so desperately needed and hoped for only positive things for them; this was not an easy task, but it was a necessary one for me to move on with my life. I have been fortunate and have learned to trust again. I now know that I am a person of worth and have broken out of the cycle of abuse that can follow you relationship after relationship.

Love is based on mutual trust, respect, friendship and affection: abuse is not a form of love. A binding spell to stop destructive behaviour or a banishing spell to dispel the negative effect it has on your life would be appropriate. A protection spell might help to stop the abuse, but you must think first of your well-being. To stay with an abusive lover can only end badly for all concerned. Heal yourself and bring only positive energy into your life.

Self-dedication ritual

This could be the most important ritual you ever perform. You should take special care in the preparation and spend many hours meditating on your decision. If you have any reservations or self-doubt, then witchcraft may not be for you, or you may not be ready for it yet. Don't feel you have to dedicate yourself to Egyptian magick in order to perform any spell in this book. Test the waters, see how the preparation and performance of the spell make you feel and wait to see if the spell works for your intention. As I have mentioned earlier, witchcraft is not an easy path, but I have never doubted my decision to embrace Egyptian magick and have found much comfort in the Old Ways and my devotion to the Egyptian deities.

This ritual is designed for you to dedicate your life to the gods and goddesses of Ancient Egypt, when you are ready to take that step. I also use much of this ritual as a rededication whenever I feel the desire for a deeply moving experience with my deities to thank them for their guidance and protection.

Items needed
4 white pillar candles
4 canopic jars (optional)
A gold pillar candle, to represent the god Osiris
A silver pillar candle, to represent the goddess Isis
A white taper candle
Frankincense or sandalwood incense
A censor
Spring water in a small bowl
Sea salt in a small dish
A chalice of wine or fruit juice

An athame or wand (optional)
Ritual clothing and/or jewellery
Matches
A candle snuffer

Designate your ritual space with the white pillar candles and the
canopic jars, if you are using them. Place all the other items on your
altar or another flat surface. The gold candle should be on the right side
of the altar, the silver candle on the left, with the censor of incense
between them. Place the dish of sea salt and the athame in front of the
gold candle and the bowl of spring water and the chalice of wine in
front of the silver. The ritual clothing to be cleansed may be placed next
to the altar and the jewellery on the altar, along with the candle snuffer.
The white taper candle should be placed in front of the censor. Sit,
stand, or kneel in front of your altar, close your eyes and take several
deep breaths. Take your time and relax. When you feel ready, open your
eyes and begin the ritual.

First light the incense, breathe deeply and relax. Go to the candle in
the North, light it and recite:

> *I call upon Hapi, Son of Horus*
> *Element of Earth, God of the North*
> *Protect me and guide my path of dedication*
> *To the Ancient Ways.*

Go to the candle in the East, light it and recite:

> *I call upon Duamutef, Son of Horus*
> *Element of Air, God of the East*
> *Protect me and guide my path of dedication*
> *To the Ancient Ways.*

Go to the candle in the South, light it and recite:

> *I call upon Imsety, Son of Horus*
> *Element of Fire, God of the South*
> *Protect me and guide my path of dedication*
> *To the Ancient Ways.*

Go to the candle in the West, light it and recite:

> *I call upon Qebhsennuf, Son of Horus*
> *Element of Water, God of the West*
> *Protect me and guide my path of dedication*
> *To the Ancient Ways.*

Light the gold, silver and white candles on the altar, in that order. Close
your eyes and feel the presence of the god and goddess. When you are
ready, open your eyes and invite them to join you by saying:

> *I ask Isis and Osiris to be with me*
> *And I welcome You both*
> *With an open heart and an open soul*
> *Fill me with Your love and protection*
> *As I pledge myself to Your service*
> *I, (your legal name)*
> *Call upon the Gods and Goddesses of Egypt*
> *Witness my dedication to the Ancient Magick*
> *Which I have chosen to follow*
> *Of my own free will*
> *I offer myself, Your humble servant*
> *And all my works of ritual and magick*
> *To the service of Isis and Osiris*
> *And all the deities of the Beloved Land*
> *I promise not to misuse*
> *My power and knowledge*
> *I promise to keep unto myself*
> *The secrets of my craft*
> *I further promise to strive always*
> *To greater knowledge and understanding*
> *Of the path I have chosen*
> *I know this path may be a difficult one*
> *But, in my heart*
> *I carry the Ancient Ones with me always*
> *As a symbol of my promise*
> *I take the name of (magickal name)*
> *May the Gods and Goddesses*
> *Know me by this name*
> *And may I always serve it well.*

If you wish to consecrate any ritual clothing or jewellery you may do so now by reciting:

> *I consecrate this (item)*
> *To the service of my Gods and my magick.*

Sprinkle it with a little salt and recite:

> *Hapi, I dedicate it with Earth.*

Pass it through the incense smoke and recite:

> *Duamutef, I dedicate it with Air.*

Pass it carefully over the candle flame and recite:

> *Imsety, I dedicate it with Fire.*

Sprinkle it with a little water and recite:
> *Qebhsennuf, I dedicate it with Water.*

Finally, hold the item aloft and recite:
> *My Mother and Father, Isis and Osiris*
> *I dedicate this (item)*
> *To You and Your service*
> *With all my love and devotion.*

You may now put the item on and wear it any time you perform any ritual or magick. If you have other items to dedicate you may repeat the actions for each one in turn.

Next, take the chalice of wine in both hands, raise it to eye level and recite:
> *This is the chalice*
> *Symbol of Isis, the Great Mother*
> *Who brings love and life*
> *To all who believe.*

Place the chalice on your altar and take up the athame in both hands with the point facing up (if you do not yet have an athame, you may use your wand or the index finger of your dominant hand). Recite:
> *This is the athame*
> *Symbol of Osiris, the Great Father*
> *Who brings love and renewal*
> *To all who believe.*

Holding the athame in your dominant hand, point down, take the chalice in your other hand, insert the tip of the athame into the wine and recite:
> *Joined together*
> *May Isis and Osiris*
> *Bring forth life eternal.*

Remove the athame from the chalice and place it back on the altar. Take a small sip of wine and recite:
> *Praise to Thee*
> *Great Isis and Osiris*
> *With this wine*
> *Consecrated by my Lord and Lady*
> *I have dedicated myself*
> *To Your service*
> *Protect me and guide my way*
> *For I am Your humble servant*
> *Your handmaiden/manservant*
> *Your beloved daughter/son, (magickal name).*

Take another sip of wine and sit for a time while you reflect upon your promise to the gods.

When you are ready, hold your hands high above you and thank the gods for their attendance:

> *I, (magickal name)*
> *Give thanks to Thee, Isis and Osiris*
> *And all the Ancient Ones*
> *For bearing witness to my dedication*
> *Though my work is now done*
> *I will carry with me always*
> *Your love, protection and guidance.*

Snuff out the white, gold and silver candles on the altar with the candle snuffer. Go to the candle in the North, extinguish it with the snuffer and recite:

> *I give thanks to Thee, Hapi, Son of Horus*
> *Element of Earth, God of the North*
> *For bearing witness to my dedication*
> *Though my work is now done*
> *I will carry with me always*
> *Your love, protection and guidance.*

Go to the candle in the East, extinguish it with the snuffer and recite:

> *I give thanks to Thee, Duamutef, Son of Horus*
> *Element of Air, God of the East*
> *For bearing witness to my dedication*
> *Though my work is now done*
> *I will carry with me always*
> *Your love, protection and guidance.*

Go to the candle in the South, extinguish it with the snuffer and recite:

> *I give thanks to Thee, Imsety, Son of Horus*
> *Element of Fire, God of the South*
> *For bearing witness to my dedication*
> *Though my work is now done*
> *I will carry with me always*
> *Your love, protection and guidance.*

Go to the candle in West, extinguish it with the candle snuffer and recite:

> *I give thanks to Thee, Qebhsennuf, Son of Horus*
> *Element of Water, God of the West*
> *For bearing witness to my dedication*
> *Though my work is now done*

I will carry with me always
Your love, protection and guidance.

You may now remove any ritual clothing and jewellery and clear away and store all your ritual items. Take the chalice outside and pour some of the consecrated wine on the ground as an offering to the Earth. You should eat or drink something to ground the energy you raised during this ritual.

CHAPTER 10

Egyptian Spells to Bring Love into Your Life

Some of the spells in this section are designed for two approaches: one is a simple spell, the other a bit more involved and time-consuming. As I have explained earlier, the success of your spells will depend on how much they mean to you, how strong your intent is and how much time you are willing to devote to manifest your desire. I am not saying that if you do a simple version of the spell your desire won't manifest – sometimes the simplest spells are the best. But, I do know that love can be an all-powerful force and, when in the grip of unrequited or unreciprocated love, we may want to infuse our desire with more power, more energy and more intent. All the simple versions follow the same format with variations only in candle colour and incense used.

Always look within for your true intention in performing a love spell. A spell to bring love into your life is beneficial; we all need love and to deny yourself something so basic is not wise or healthy. But your motives must be positive: spells are not designed to take someone away from another person, to discard a lover the way some people discard last year's fashion, or to trick someone. Always give careful consideration to any spell you perform. It sometimes happens that if you write down what it is you desire, think about it for a few days and then read what you have written, you then decide that a spell is not the best option at the moment. Take a look at your life – are you ready to devote time and energy to another? If your career is very important to you right now, then this may not be the right time to enter into a relationship.

Take your time and know what it is you truly want. If you feel that a spell to bring love is the correct choice for you, meditate on your intent so it is clear in your mind. Then you may begin.

Some of these spells call for you to burn paper completely to ash. The Ancient Egyptians wrote on papyrus, a form of paper. I don't have the ability to create my own paper and making papyrus for spells seems to me to be a waste of good plant material. To simulate papyrus I use paper from brown paper bags, which can be obtained almost anywhere. I have performed spells in the past that required the use of ashes as a component of the spell so you may wish to collect up the ashes from previous spellwork or from the burning of incense and store them in an airtight container. Always be practical and don't dispose of anything from the spell altars that you might need another time.

The recipes for the anointing oils used for each of these spells can be found on pages 161–2, or you may choose to use just one essential oil that corresponds to your particular desire.

Call a lover spell

This spell is designed to bring love to you. It might be a new lover or someone special being nudged into seeing you in a different light. It may be performed at any time, though maximum effect would occur on a Tuesday or Friday during the Waxing Moon, or on the night of the Full Moon.

Items needed
3 gold 10 cm/4 in taper or votive candles
3 silver 10 cm/4 in taper or votive candles
Amun oil (see page 161)
Bast oil (see page 161)
Hathor oil (see page 161)
Imhotep oil (see page 161)
Isis oil (see page 162)
Osiris oil (see page 162)
Combined frankincense and myrrh incense
A censor
Matches

Light the incense, breathe deeply and relax. Take one of the gold candles and anoint it, wick to base, with Amun oil while you recite:

> *Amun, God of Spells*
> *I call upon You*
> *To bless my magick*
> *Hidden One*
> *Bring a lover to me.*

Light the candle and place it in front of you and to the right. Next, take one of the silver candles and anoint it, wick to base, with Bast oil while you recite:

> Bast, Goddess of Pleasure
> I call upon You
> To bless my desire
> Lady of the East
> Bring a lover to me.

Light the candle and place it in front of you to the left of the gold candle. Take another silver candle and anoint it, wick to base, with Hathor oil while you recite:

> Hathor, Goddess of Joy and Love
> I call upon You
> To bless my heart
> Mistress of Heaven
> Bring a lover to me.

Light the candle and place it in front of you to the left of the silver candle. Take another of the gold candles and anoint it, wick to base, with Imhotep oil while you recite:

> Imhotep, God of Magick
> I call upon You
> To bless my intent
> He Who Comes in Peace
> Bring a lover to me.

Light the candle and place it in front of you to the left of the second silver candle. Take the remaining silver candle and anoint it, wick to base, with Isis oil; then take the remaining gold candle and anoint it, wick to base, with Osiris oil. As you light the candles recite:

> Isis, Great Mother
> Osiris, Great Father
> I call upon You both
> To bless my request
> Giver of Life
> Lord of All Things
> Bring a lover to me.

Place the silver candle in front of you to the left of the gold candle and place the last gold candle to the left of the last silver candle. Speak to your deities from the heart and tell them your wish. Remain with the candles until all have burned out of their own accord. If a lover does not appear in your life, wait a month before repeating this spell. The one you seek may be right in front of you.

Come to me spell (simple)

This spell is designed for when you are attracted to someone who doesn't seem to be reading your signals. The best time to perform it is on a Tuesday or Friday during the Waxing Moon or on the night of the Full Moon.

Items needed
A red 10 cm/4 in taper or votive candle
Come to Me oil (see page 161)
Catnip incense
A censor
A red pen
Paper from a brown paper bag
Tweezers
A cauldron or other fire-safe container
Matches

Light the incense, breathe deeply and relax. Anoint the candle, wick to base, with Come to Me oil and recite as you visualise your intent:

> Come to me, my beloved
> Open your mind to me
> And know that I love you
> Open your eyes to me
> And see that I am for you
> Open your heart to me
> And feel my desire
> Open your ears to me
> And hear my plea
> Come to me, my beloved
> Feel my passion
> Burning like the temple fire
> I come to you in my dreams
> And lie beside you
> This is my only solace
> Sleep has become my salvation
> Come to me, my beloved.

Place the candle in front of you and light it. Using the red pen, write the above incantation once on the piece of brown paper. When you have finished, read it aloud once, kiss the paper once and anoint it with one drop of Come to Me oil. Fold the paper twice, hold it with the tweezers and light it from the candle flame. Drop it into the cauldron and make sure it burns completely to ash. Remain with the candle until it burns out of its own accord, while thinking of your desire and how you wish for it to manifest.

Come to me spell (expanded)

This spell is designed for when you are attracted to someone who doesn't seem to be reading your signals. The best time to begin it is on a Tuesday or Friday on the night of the New Moon or during the Waxing Moon. If you don't have a statue of Bast, use a silver candle or a picture of a cat instead.

Items needed
A red taper or pillar candle
Come to Me oil (see page 161)
Catnip incense
A censor
A statue of Bast
Ground cinnamon, ginger and nutmeg
Mortar and pestle
Fresh red rose petals
Red and silver glitter
A nail
Paper from a brown paper bag
A red pen
A picture of your intended or a list of his/her qualities
A candle snuffer
A square of red cotton fabric
Red thread or ribbon
Matches

Light the catnip incense, breathe deeply and relax. You may wish to invoke Bast, Goddess of Pleasure, to assist you in your endeavour; this is not essential, but every little bit helps. With the nail, carve your name and the name of your intended on the candle. If you do not have a particular person in mind, you may carve 'My Beloved' or 'My Brother'/'My Sister' instead. Carve the hieroglyph for love at the end of both names.

Place the cinnamon in your mortar, add the ginger and finally the nutmeg and grind them a bit with the pestle to mix and combine them while you visualise your intent. Anoint the candle, wick to base, with Come to Me oil, reciting the following incantation as many times as you feel the desire:

Come to me, my beloved
Open your mind to me
And know that I love you
Open your eyes to me
And see that I am for you
Open your heart to me
And feel my desire
Open your ears to me
And hear my plea
Come to me, my beloved
Feel my passion
Burning like the temple fire
I come to you in my dreams
And lie beside you
This is my only solace
Sleep has become my salvation
Come to me, my beloved.

Roll the candle in the spice mixture until it is well covered. Place the candle in front of you, but do not light it yet.

If you have a picture of your intended, look deep into his or her eyes and speak to the picture as if the person were there with you. Tell your intended what is in your heart, what is your desire, how you feel and what you want from him or her. If you have a list of qualities instead, read the list aloud, slowly and 'feeling' each quality that you are looking for in a lover. Kiss the picture or list once, anoint it with one drop of Come to Me oil and place it to the right of the candle.

Using the red pen, write the above incantation once on the brown paper. When you have finished, read the incantation aloud to the picture or list. Kiss the paper once, anoint it with one drop of Come to Me oil and place it over the picture or list so the writing is facing the picture.

Take the candle and place it on top of the paper and picture. Sprinkle the rose petals in a clockwise direction in a circle around the candle. Next, again in a clockwise direction, sprinkle the red glitter over the rose petals and finally the silver glitter in a similar manner. Don't use so much glitter that you cannot see the rose petals – just a little sprinkle will do. Light the candle, again reciting the incantation aloud as you do so.

Sit for an hour and think of your intention. You may wish to speak directly to Bast during this time and ask for her guidance and help in this matter. Speak to her from your heart and know that she is with you. When the candle has burned for an hour, thank Bast for coming to join you in this important work, snuff out the candle with the candle snuffer and leave everything where it is.

For the next seven days or evenings, recite the incantation as you light the candle and let it burn for one hour. If you wish, you may invoke Bast each time; just remember to thank her each time before you snuff out the candle.

On the seventh day, let the candle burn for one hour, then snuff it out. Gather up the remains of the candle, the rose petals, glitter, the picture or list and the paper with the incantation on it. Place all of these items in the fabric and tie it up securely with the red thread or ribbon. Place this little love packet in a dresser drawer, perhaps the one with your nightgowns, pyjamas or underwear, and leave it undisturbed for one full cycle of the Moon. At the end of that time, bury it in the earth or throw it into a body of water, thus releasing your intent. Sit back and relax; your wish should manifest if it is meant to be.

Have you another? spell (simple)

This spell is designed to make someone you are attracted to notice you. The best time to perform it is on a Tuesday or Friday during the Waxing Moon or on the night of the Full Moon.

Items needed
A pink 10 cm/4 in taper or votive candle
Have You Another? oil (see page 161)
Rose incense
A censor
Paper from a brown paper bag
A red pen
Tweezers
A cauldron or other fire-safe container
Matches

Light the incense, breathe deeply and relax. Anoint the candle, wick to base, with Have You Another? oil and recite the following once as you visualise your intent:

My love for you is as endless
As the Nile
Why do you not see me?
I cannot eat or sleep
Without a thought of you
Yet you do not speak to me
I pass you each day going
To the river
I brush your tunic and yet
You do not meet my gaze
Have you another who has
Captured your heart?

Place the candle in front of you and light it. Using the red pen, write the above incantation once on the piece of brown paper. When you have finished, read it aloud once, kiss the paper once and anoint it with one drop of Have You Another? oil. Fold the paper twice, hold it with the tweezers and light it from the candle flame. Drop it into the cauldron and make sure it burns completely to ash. Remain with the candle until it burns out of its own accord, while thinking of your desire and how you wish for it to manifest.

Have you another? spell (expanded)

This spell is designed to make someone you are attracted to notice you. The best time to perform it is whenever you will be seeing that special someone.

Items needed
A pink 10 cm/4 in taper candle
Have You Another oil? (see page 161)
Rose incense
A censor
A mirror
Matches

Light the incense, breathe deeply and relax. Anoint the candle, wick to base, with Have You Another? oil and recite the following once as you visualise your intent:

My love for you is as endless
As the Nile

Why do you not see me?
I cannot eat or sleep
Without a thought of you
Yet you do not speak to me
I pass you each day going
To the river
I brush your tunic and yet
You do not meet my gaze
Have you another who has
Captured your heart?

Place the candle in front of you and light it. Take up the mirror and look at your reflection. Speak to yourself of how you are special and worthy of love. Recite the above incantation again, as if you were speaking to the person you desire. Anoint your forehead, nape of the neck, breasts and directly above your genitals with the Have You Another? oil. Prepare yourself as you normally would for a date, put on make-up or any special clothing and jewellery.

Remain with the candle until it burns out of its own accord. Look in the mirror once more and speak lovingly to yourself; be prepared for anything because you are ready to invite love into your life.

Hymn to Amun spell

This spell is designed to cause a special someone to think of you and, hopefully, return your affections. It may be done at any time during the month but for added energy it is best performed during the Waxing Moon or on the night of the Full Moon. Choose the candle colour that best suits your intention: gold to make a dream come true, green or pink to draw affection, or yellow to cause someone to think about you.

Items needed
A 10 cm/4 in taper candle
Hymn to Amun oil (see page 161)
Frankincense incense
A censor
Paper from a brown paper bag
A red pen
A cauldron or other fire-safe container
Tweezers
Matches

Light the incense, breathe deeply and relax. Using the red pen, write on the brown paper your reasons for wanting to bring this person into your life. Be specific, and also write the reasons you feel this person is the person you desire and what you hope to accomplish with this spell. Anoint the candle, wick to base, with Hymn to Amun oil and recite:

> O Great Amun
> Hear the plea of Your humble servant, (your legal or magickal name)
> I anoint this candle in Your name
> Bring to me the one whom I desire most
> Bring (name of intended) to me
> O Great Amun
> You have the power to make it so
> Hear my plea
> Great Amun, Hidden One
> He Who hears all prayers
> Bring (name of intended) to me now
> So that I may share my life with him
> Forever and all eternity
> Watch over him, protect him
> Keep him safe
> Until I can hold him in my arms
> O Great Amun, hear my prayer and answer me.

Kiss the paper once, anoint it with a drop of Hymn to Amun oil and fold it twice. Light the candle and silently ask Amun for his assistance in this matter. Using the tweezers, hold the piece of paper to the candle flame to light it, drop it into the cauldron and let it burn completely to ash.

Remain with the candle until it burns out of its own accord and think positive thoughts of how much you desire this to manifest. When the candle burns out, thank Amun for hearing your prayer.

Hymn to Hathor spell

This spell is intended to call a loved one to you. The best time to begin it is a Tuesday or Friday evening during the Waxing Moon.

Items needed

A red or pink taper or pillar candle
Passion or Hathor oil (see pages 162 and 161)
Cinnamon incense

A censor
A nail
Matches

Light the incense and breathe deeply several times to relax and concentrate your mind on the task at hand. Carve your intended's name, or 'My Soulmate' or 'Someone Special' on the candle, along with the hieroglyphs for love, beloved, heart etc. or any other symbols of love. Anoint the candle, from wick to base, with Passion or Hathor oil, reciting the following over and over again and all the while imbuing the candle with your intent and visualising you and that special someone together:

> *Great Hathor, the Golden One*
> *Goddess of Joy and Love*
> *I anoint this candle in Your name*
> *Hear my prayer*
> *Help me to obtain the love of (name of intended)*
> *I love him more than life itself*
> *I must have him*
> *Thoughts of him consume me night and day*
> *I crave the sound of his voice*
> *My heart aches for his love*
> *My body longs for his touch*
> *My lips yearn to feel his kiss*
> *My loins are aflame with desire*
> *Great Hathor, Mistress of Heaven*
> *Hear my prayer*
> *Bring (name of intended) to me now*
> *So that I may share my love with him*
> *Forever and all Eternity.*

Light the candle and recite the above incantation seven times, changing the word 'anoint' to 'light' or 'burn'. The number seven is very magickal and also represents the Seven Hathors (Holy Midwives); they were the Goddesses of Fate who determined the destiny of a child at birth and helped to protect the body from harm. Focus your mind on your intent while you recite the incantation. Hold that feeling as long as you desire. You may also wish to speak to Hathor straight from the heart about any other feelings you have about this person.

When you feel ready, snuff out the candle. Light the candle each evening, reciting the incantation seven times, until the candle is completely burned out. Dispose of any candle remains by burying them in the earth or throwing them into a moving body of water. Thank Hathor for hearing your prayer and know that she has your best interests at heart. Love works in mysterious ways – the one you seek may find you when you least expect it.

Ignite your passion spell (simple)

This spell is designed to start a fire in the heart of the one you desire. The best time to perform it is on a Tuesday or Friday during the Waxing Moon or on the night of the Full Moon.

Items needed
A gold or green 10 cm/4 in taper or votive candle
Ignite Your Passion oil (see page 161)
Musk incense
A censor
Paper from a brown paper bag
A red pen
Tweezers
A cauldron or other fire-safe container
Matches

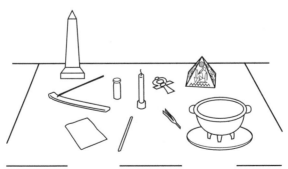

Light the incense, breathe deeply and relax. Anoint the candle, wick to base, with Ignite Your Passion oil and recite the following once as you visualise your intent:

> *I shall have you, my brother*
> *For you are my destiny*
> *And I am yours*
> *Come to me, I command you*
> *Come, embrace your sister*
> *Your fairest one*
> *Come to me, I command you*
> *For you have been chosen for me*
> *By the Mistress of Heaven*
> *I shall have you, my brother*
> *I would give my life for you*
> *Come, kiss your sister*
> *I shall ignite in you a passion*
> *You have never known*
> *And a desire that only I can satisfy*
> *I shall love you like no other*
> *For Great Hathor has decreed it so*
> *Come, embrace your destiny.*

Place the candle in front of you and light it. Using the red pen, write the above incantation once on the brown paper. When you have finished writing the incantation, read it aloud once, kiss the paper once and anoint it with one drop of Ignite Your Passion oil. Fold the paper twice, hold it with the tweezers and light it from the candle flame. Drop it into the cauldron and make sure it burns completely to ash.

Remain with the candle until it burns out of its own accord, while thinking of your desire and how you wish for it to manifest.

Ignite your passion spell (expanded)

This spell is designed to start a fire in the heart of the one you desire. The best time to start its seven-day course is on a Tuesday or Friday during the Waxing Moon; try to have the spell end on the night of the Full Moon.

Items needed
A gold or green taper or pillar candle
Ignite Your Passion oil (see page 161)

Musk incense
A censor
A nail
Orris root powder
Dried patchouli flowers
Chilli powder
A mortar and pestle
A picture of your lover (or write his name on a piece of paper with red ink)
A candle snuffer
Matches

Light the incense, breathe deeply and relax. Using the nail, inscribe the candle with the name of your lover/intended and recite the following while you anoint the candle, wick to base, with Ignite Your Passion oil:

> *I shall have you, my brother*
> *For you are my destiny*
> *And I am yours*
> *Come to me, I command you*
> *Come, embrace your sister*
> *Your fairest one*
> *Come to me, I command you*
> *For you have been chosen for me*
> *By the Mistress of Heaven*
> *I shall have you, my brother*
> *I would give my life for you*
> *Come, kiss your sister*
> *I shall ignite in you a passion*
> *You have never known*
> *And a desire that only I can satisfy*
> *I shall love you like no other*
> *For Great Hathor has decreed it so*
> *Come, embrace your destiny.*

Place the orris root powder, patchouli flowers and chilli powder in the mortar and mix and grind well with the pestle. Take up the picture or paper and recite the incantation once to it. Set the picture or paper underneath the candle and sprinkle the contents of the mortar in a heart shape around it and the base of the candle. Light the candle and speak directly to your lover as if he or she were there with you – tell him or her of your love. You may also wish to invoke Hathor's help; speak directly to her and ask for her help and guidance. After an hour, snuff out the candle and leave everything as it is. Don't forget to thank Hathor if you asked her to join in your endeavour.

Each evening, light the candle, recite the incantation and let the candle burn for one hour as you think of your intention. On the seventh evening, allow the candle to burn down completely. Gather up the spices, place them on the picture or paper, fold it into a packet and keep it in a safe place (or you may wish to carry it with you). When you know you may see your intended, take a pinch of the spices out of the packet and discreetly sprinkle them where he or she will walk on them. If you are able to place a pinch in his or her pocket, all the better but, again, you need to do this unobserved. Sit back, relax and wait for your desire to manifest, if it is meant to be.

Lay with me spell (simple)

This spell is designed to cause a special someone to think of you as a love interest. The best time to perform it is on a Tuesday or Friday during the Waxing Moon or on the night of the Full Moon.

Items needed
A yellow 10 cm/4 in taper or votive candle
Lay With Me oil (see page 162)
Meadowsweet incense
A censor
Paper from a brown paper bag
A red pen
Tweezers
A cauldron or other fire-safe container
Matches

Light the incense, breathe deeply and relax. Anoint the candle, wick to base, with Lay With Me oil and recite the following once as you visualise your intent:

> *I long to lay with you, my brother*
> *By the banks of the Nile*
> *I long to feel your strong arms*
> *Hold me safe and secure*
> *I long to rest my head*
> *On your bare chest*
> *Speed to your sister, your beloved*

So I may kiss your lips
That taste like pomegranate wine
My soul cries out to you
But you do not seem to hear
I long to lay with you, my brother
By the banks of the Nile.

Place the candle in front of you and light it. With the red pen, write the above incantation once on the piece of brown paper. When you have finished writing the incantation, read it aloud once, kiss the paper once and anoint it with one drop of Lay With Me oil. Fold the paper twice, hold it with the tweezers and light it from the candle flame. Drop it into the cauldron and make sure it burns completely to ash. Remain with the candle until it burns out of its own accord, while thinking of your desire and how you wish for it to manifest.

Lay with me spell (expanded)

This spell is designed to cause a special someone to think of you as a love interest. The best time to begin it is on a Tuesday or Friday, between the New Moon and the Full Moon, trying to make the last day of the spell coincide with the night before the Full Moon. If you don't have a statue of Hathor, use a silver candle instead.

Items needed
A yellow taper or pillar candle
Lay With Me oil (see page 162)
Meadowsweet incense
A censor
A statue of Hathor
Dried myrtle leaves
Dried spearmint leaves
2 drops red or white wine
A mortar and pestle
Flat yellow marbles
A candle snuffer
A cauldron or other fire-safe container
Matches

Light the incense, breathe deeply and relax. You may wish to invoke Hathor to assist you in your endeavour; this is not essential, but every little helps. Place some, but not all, of the dried myrtle and dried

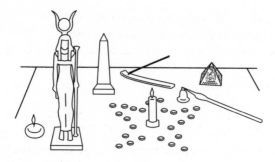

spearmint leaves in the mortar and grind them to a powder with the pestle. Add the wine and mix well while reciting the following:

> *I long to lay with you, my brother*
> *By the banks of the Nile*
> *I long to feel your strong arms*
> *Hold me safe and secure*
> *I long to rest my head*
> *On your bare chest*
> *Speed to your sister, your beloved*
> *So I may kiss your lips*
> *That taste like pomegranate wine*
> *My soul cries out to you*
> *But you do not seem to hear*
> *I long to lay with you, my brother*
> *By the banks of the Nile.*

Anoint the candle, wick to base, with Lay With Me oil and roll the candle in the leaf and wine mixture. Place the candle in front of you and arrange the flat yellow marbles around the base in the shape of a star. Light the candle and recite the incantation three times. Sit for an hour and think of your intention; you may wish to speak to Hathor directly and ask for her guidance and assistance. Always speak from your heart and know that she will hear you.

When the candle has burned for an hour, thank Hathor for coming to join you in this important matter, snuff out the candle with the candle snuffer and leave everything where it is.

For the next seven days or evenings, light the candle, recite the incantation three times and let the candle burn for one hour. If you invoke Hathor each time, remember to thank her before you snuff out the candle. On the seventh day, let the candle burn for one hour and snuff it out. Gather up the remains of the candle and place it in your cauldron. Sprinkle it with the remaining dried myrtle and spearmint leaves while you recite the incantation one last time. Light the cauldron and sit with it until the leaves and candle have burned completely, thus releasing your intent. Sit back, relax and wait for your desire to manifest, if it is meant to be.

Tremble with desire spell (simple)

This spell is designed to give you the courage to approach the object of your interest to make your intentions known. The best time to perform it is on a Tuesday or Friday during the Waxing Moon or on the night of the Full Moon.

Items needed
A pink 10 cm/4 in taper or votive candle
Tremble With Desire oil (see page 162)
Myrtle incense
A censor
Paper from a brown paper bag
A red pen
Tweezers
A cauldron or other fire-safe container
Matches

Light the incense, breathe deeply and relax. Anoint the candle, wick to base, with Tremble With Desire oil and recite the following once as you visualise your intent:

I love you with every fibre of my being
Thoughts of you consume me
If you should touch me
I would tremble with desire
My love for you
Would then be known to you
I despair that you do not feel as I do
I could not bear your rejection
My need is great yet
I suffer in silence
Kiss your sister and still my mind
I desire you more than life itself.

Place the candle in front of you and light it. Using the red pen, write the above incantation on the piece of brown paper. When you have finished writing, read it aloud once, kiss the paper once and anoint it with one drop of Tremble With Desire oil. Fold the paper twice, hold it with the tweezers and light it from the candle flame. Drop it into the cauldron and make sure it burns completely to ash.

Remain with the candle until it burns out of its own accord, while thinking of your desire and how you wish for it to manifest.

Tremble with desire spell (expanded)

This spell is designed to give you the courage to approach the object of your interest to make your intentions known. It should begin during the Waxing Moon and ideally should end on the night of the Full Moon.

Items needed
2 pink 10 cm/4 in taper or votive candles
1 red 10 cm/4 in taper or votive candle
1 orange 10 cm/4 in taper or votive candle
1 yellow 10 cm/4 in taper or votive candle
1 green 10 cm/4 in taper or votive candle
1 white 10 cm/4 in taper or votive candle
Tremble With Desire oil (see page 162)
Myrtle incense
Dried lavender flowers
Ground ginger
Dried yarrow flowers
Dried jasmine flowers
Dried violet flowers
Orris root powder
Dried lilac flowers
A nail
A censor
Matches
A small muslin drawstring bag

On the first night, light the incense and inscribe one of the pink candles with your name and the name of your beloved. Anoint the candle from wick to base with Tremble With Desire oil, place it on the altar and sprinkle the lavender flowers around the base. Light the candle and recite the following:

> *I love you with every fibre of my being*
> *Thoughts of you consume me*

If you should touch me
I would tremble with desire
My love for you
Would then be known to you
I despair that you do not feel as I do
I could not bear your rejection
My need is great yet
I suffer in silence
Kiss your sister and still my mind
I desire you more than life itself.

Let the candle burn out of its own accord and leave the remains of the candle and the lavender where it is.

On the second night, light the incense and inscribe the red candle with both your names. Anoint the candle from wick to base with the oil and place it on the altar to the right of the previous night's candle. Sprinkle the ginger around the base, light the candle and recite the incantation. Again, let the candle burn out of its own accord and leave everything where it is.

On the third night, light the incense and inscribe the orange candle with both your names. Anoint the candle from wick to base with the oil and place it on the altar to the right of the red candle. Sprinkle the yarrow flowers around the base, light the candle and recite the incantation. Let the candle burn out as before.

On the fourth night, light the incense and inscribe the yellow candle. Anoint it from wick to base with the oil and place it on the altar to the right of the orange candle. Sprinkle the jasmine flowers around the base, light the candle and recite the incantation. Let the candle burn out as before.

On the fifth night, light the incense and inscribe the green candle. Anoint it from wick to base with the oil and place it on the altar to the right of the yellow candle. Sprinkle the violet flowers round the base, light the candle and recite the incantation. Let the candle burn out.

On the sixth night, light the incense and inscribe the white candle. Anoint it from wick to base with the oil and place it on the altar to the right of the green candle. Sprinkle the orris root powder around the base, light the candle and recite the incantation. Let the candle burn out.

On the seventh and final night, light the incense and inscribe the second pink candle. Anoint it from wick to base with the oil and place it on the altar to the right of the white candle. Sprinkle the base with the lilac flowers, light the candle and recite the incantation. Let the candle burn out.

Now you may gather up any remains of the candles and the herbs and dried flowers and place them all in the muslin bag. Carry the bag for one full cycle of the Moon and then bury the bag in the earth, thus releasing your desire.

A tied binding spell

Remember when you perform binding spells to be careful what you wish for. Be very sure that this is what you really want because you may not be able to get rid of your intended once you have him or her.

Items needed
A black 10 cm/4 in taper candle
A red 10 cm/4 in taper candle
Combined frankincense and myrrh incense
Binding oil (see page 161)
A censor
An orange cloth
Love or lust herbs, spices and flowers (your choice)
Hair and/or nail clippings or personal items (optional)
A needle and thread
A length of cord or a leather strip
A clothing marker (colour of your choice)
Matches

Make a poppet (doll) of orange cloth in the sex of your intended. You can be as creative as you wish. If you can obtain a lock of hair, nail clippings, or anything he or she has touched, you should incorporate it into the poppet. Stuff the poppet with herbs, spices and flowers that resonate with your love or lust. Stitch the poppet to close it securely. Draw a face on the poppet that resembles your intended, with characteristics such as eye colour and glasses. Draw a heart in the right position on the chest. Place the poppet on your table or altar and place your hands over it as you recite:

> *I have fashioned you*
> *Just for me*
> *You shall desire no other*
> *You shall have eyes only for me*
> *Your heart shall beat only for me*
> *You shall dream only of me*

> *When I command*
> *You shall come to me*
> *For you cannot escape my snare*
> *You shall be my captive*
> *For I have fashioned you*
> *Just for me.*

Kiss the poppet on the forehead, lips, heart and genitals and then anoint those areas with Binding oil. As you do so, recite:

> *As I kiss you*
> *So shall you kiss me*
> *As I touch you*
> *So shall you touch me*
> *As I burn for you*
> *So shall you burn for me*
> *You are my captive*
> *I shall have you for my own*
> *My need for you is great*
> *And my will is strong.*

Take the length of cord or leather strip and, starting at the feet, wrap the cord around the poppet closely, but not too tight. Think of your intended and what your desires for him or her are. Continue wrapping up to the neck and secure the end under the wrapped cord. Holding the poppet in your non-dominant hand, place your dominant hand over it and recite:

> *Come to me, my beloved*
> *I am your mistress*
> *You cannot escape my grasp*
> *You are powerless against me*
> *Your only thoughts*
> *Shall be thoughts of me*
> *I am your mistress*
> *And you shall be my humble servant.*

Light the frankincense and myrrh incense and pass the poppet through the smoke. Next, carve your name on the red candle and your intended's name on the black candle. Anoint them both with Binding oil and light them. Take each candle and drip some wax on the poppet where the heart is. Place the candles side by side so that they are touching each other and pass the poppet over the flames, being careful not to singe it. As you pass it again through the incense smoke and over the flames, recite:

You are bound to me
Forever and all Eternity
My love for you is endless
I consecrate our love with
Smoke and fire
You are now bound to me
Forever and all Eternity.

Place the poppet on the altar in front of the candles. As the candles burn down and their wax begins to mingle recite:

As these candles melt together
So shall your heart melt for me
As these candles become one
So shall we join
One body, one heart, one love
Bound together
Forever and all Eternity.

Stay with the candles until they burn themselves out. Take the poppet and place it in a safe place where it will not be disturbed – a box in the back of a closet, a dresser drawer, or any other out-of-the-way area. Relax and wait for your spell to manifest, if it is meant to be.

Alternatively, for the 'creatively challenged', this spell may be performed with a doll bought from a toy store. Try to get a doll that resembles the person you are trying to attract – if he or she has brown hair, get a doll with brown hair. You can always paste a picture of the person's face on the doll, if you have one. Cleanse the doll as you would any ritual tool before you use it and, instead of stuffing the doll with herbs, you can sprinkle them on the doll the day before and let it sit overnight on your altar until you are ready to begin the spell. Place the herbs in a muslin bag and keep the bag with the bound doll in a safe place.

A pierced binding spell

Again, you must use common sense when performing a binding spell. You may get what you thought you desired and then find that it is not really what it seemed.

Items needed
A black taper or pillar candle
Copal resin incense
A charcoal disc

A censor
Binding oil (see page 161)
Air-drying modelling clay
A nail
13 straight pins
Hair and/or nail clippings (optional)
A candle snuffer
Matches

Using the nail, carve your name and your intended's name on the candle and anoint it, wick to base, with Binding oil. Light the candle, light the charcoal disc and place the copal resin incense on the disc after it stops sparking. Fashion a representation of your intended with the clay, making the figure as anatomically correct as possible. If you want, you could fashion it with the hands and feet bound behind the figure, as the Ancient Egyptians did. If you can obtain hair or finger nail clippings, you can press them into the clay.

When the figure is complete, use the nail to carve the face, a heart on the chest and your intended's initials on the back. Kiss the forehead, heart, initials and genitals and then anoint the same areas with Binding oil. Place the figure on the altar, hold your hands over it and recite:

> As Khnum fashioned mankind
> On his potter's wheel
> I have fashioned you from Earth
> You are my creation
> You shall desire no other
> When I command
> You shall come to me
> For I have created you
> Just for my pleasure.

Take each pin, kiss it and anoint it with Binding oil. Stick one anointed pin in the following areas to 'activate' them with your energy and recite at the appropriate areas:

> As I pierce your forehead (one pin)
> You shall think only of me
> As I pierce your eyes (one pin in each eye)
> You shall see only me
> As I pierce your ears (one pin in each ear)
> You shall hear only my voice
> As I pierce your mouth (one pin)

> *You shall kiss only me*
> *As I pierce your heart (one pin)*
> *You shall love only me*
> *As I pierce your genitals (one pin)*
> *You shall desire only me*
> *As I pierce your arms (one pin in each arm)*
> *They shall ache to hold me*
> *As I pierce your legs (one pin in each leg)*
> *They shall speed you to me*
> *With this final pin*
> *I pierce again your heart (one pin)*
> *To complete my spell*
> *And bind your heart to mine.*

Pick up the figure and pass it through the incense smoke and carefully over the candle flame as you recite:

> *You are bound to me*
> *Forever and all Eternity*
> *My love for you is endless*
> *I consecrate our love with*
> *Smoke and fire*
> *You are now bound to me*
> *Forever and all Eternity.*

Place the figure back on the altar in front of the candle. Snuff out the candle with the snuffer and leave everything where it is. Each day or evening, for at least seven days or until the candle has burned completely, allow the candle to burn for one hour, anoint the initials with Binding oil and recite as you light the candle:

> *I have pierced your forehead*
> *So you shall think only of me*
> *I have pierced your eyes*
> *So you shall see only me*
> *I have pierced your ears*
> *So you shall hear only my voice*
> *I have pierced your mouth*
> *So you shall kiss only me*
> *I have pierced your heart*
> *So you shall love only me*
> *I have pierced your genitals*
> *So you shall desire only me*
> *I have pierced your arms*

So they shall ache to hold me
I have pierced your legs
So they shall speed you to me
You are bound to me
Until I release you
From your captivity.

When the candle has burned down completely, place any candle remains with the figure and put them in a safe place where no one will disturb them.

Love initiating oils

Amun oil
2.5 ml/½ tsp olive oil
2 drops cinnamon oil
1 drop Egyptian musk oil
1 drop frankincense oil
1 drop essential saffron oil

Bast oil
2.5 ml/½ tsp almond oil
1 drop frankincense oil
1 drop myrrh oil
1 drop tuberose oil

Binding oil
5 ml/1 tsp apricot oil
4 drops cinnamon oil
3 drops ginger oil
3 drops nutmeg oil
3 drops peppermint oil

Come to Me oil
2.5 ml/½ tsp olive oil
2 drops clove bud oil
3 drops tangerine oil

Hathor oil
2.5 ml/½ tsp avocado oil
1 drop mandrake oil
1 drop patchouli oil
1 drop red myrtle oil
2 drops sandalwood oil

Have You Another? oil
2.5 ml/½ tsp jojoba oil
2 drops essential almond oil
2 drops vanilla oil

Hymn to Amun oil
2.5 ml/½ tsp almond oil
5 drops cinnamon oil
2 drops clove bud oil

Ignite Your Passion oil
2.5 ml/½ tsp sesame oil
1 drop cinnamon oil
3 drops ginseng oil

Imhotep oil
2.5 ml/½ tsp sesame oil
1 drop lemon oil
1 drop nutmeg oil
1 drop peppermint oil

Isis oil
2.5 ml/½ tsp olive oil
1 drop Egyptian musk oil
3 drops lily of the valley oil
2 drops lotus oil
1 drop myrrh oil
1 drop orris root oil

Lay With Me oil
2.5 ml/½ tsp almond oil
1 drop gardenia oil
3 drops mimosa oil

Osiris oil
2.5 ml/½ tsp sesame oil
2 drops acacia oil
1 drop lily of the valley oil
1 drop myrrh oil
1 drop orris root oil

Passion oil
5 ml/1 tsp coconut oil
1 drop gardenia oil
2 drops hyacinth oil
1 drop jasmine oil
2 drops poppy oil
1 drop sandalwood oil
1 drop violet oil

Tremble With Desire oil
2.5 ml/½ tsp apricot oil
2 drops orange oil
5 drops vanilla oil

CHAPTER 11

Egyptian Spells to Celebrate and Deepen Love

You have him or her – now what to do? Enjoy your new lover, explore your relationship and keep it fresh and vital. Anyone who invests time and energy to entice love also needs to invest the time necessary to share with another. Our daily lives are hectic: job concerns take time away from our loved ones; family crises may arise. I have a dear friend who works full time, has a part-time job, takes two evening classes a week and wonders why she has no time for herself. You need to set priorities, and set limits on how much time you need to devote to other issues in your life and how much to spend on intimacy and relaxation.

Over time, we get comfortable with our partner and tend to forget the little things we enjoyed during the 'courting and mating dance'. Keeping love alive is just as, if not more, important than finding love. If a plant is not watered, cared for and nourished, it will wither and die – and so will our love for one another. Love takes time, attention, compassion, strength and understanding. Life is not always easy, but it is much more manageable when you have someone with whom to share the burden. The test of true love usually occurs during a crisis such as losing a job, illness, financial problems or bereavement. Share your fears and anxieties and open up to the tremendous possibilities of love. You might have to risk getting hurt once or twice before you have what could be the most incredibly passionate experience of your life.

For those who have the time, the following incantations are for you. They may be used as spells for one, for when the relationship seems to have hit a snag, or as joint activities to keep your love for each other burning as brightly as when you first met. This is not only for new lovers; everyone in a relationship sometimes feels neglected or questions their heart. Spend time with your partner and share one of the incantations. I have designed them for multiple use: the guidelines for each incantation may be used interchangeably so, if the 'activities' for one spell appeal to you and the incantation from another is just what you are looking for, put them together and make your own magick.

For each of the following activities, prepare a day or two in advance so you and your lover can spend all of your time together. Take the phone off the hook, have someone watch the kids for the evening and, most importantly, turn off the television or computers. This is the time to explore your relationship and your love for one another; there should be no distractions and no interruptions. If it would be easier to book a night or weekend at a hotel or bed and breakfast, do it. Everything in these spells is portable – just make sure you are careful with the candles and ask permission to burn them.

Most of the activities are designed to culminate in sexual intercourse. Some of the activities are explicit: this is not meant to shock or to be lewd, since sexual relations between consenting adults is nothing to be ashamed of. The Ancient Egyptians understood very well that true loving, sexual contact should be enjoyed and be a celebration to the gods and goddesses. Read on and enjoy; the deities want you to be happy and satisfied.

Aflame with desire spell

This activity is designed for the times when you are apart, such as when one of you is away on business. I would choose to play soft and sensual music, but any music that means something to the two of you would be appropriate.

Items needed
A yellow pillar candle
Aflame with Desire oil (see page 173)
Violet incense
Additional candles in any colours
A censor
Matches
Music
A telephone

Write the incantation below on a piece of paper, kiss it and anoint it with a drop of Aflame With Desire oil. Place the paper in an envelope and slip it into your lover's suitcase before the trip if you are the one that is staying, or put it somewhere in the house where your partner is bound to find it if you are the one who is going away. Arrange for him or her to call you at a specific time when both of you can spend time together on the telephone. Prior to the appointed time, the partner at home should place the additional candles around the room and put a drop or two of Aflame With Desire oil on each one before lighting. If it is feasible for the away partner to do the same, all the better. Start the music, light the violet incense and begin the activity.

Anoint the yellow pillar candle, wick to base, with Aflame With Desire oil, light it and recite:

> My brother, I wish to lay down
> Beside you
> My heart is aflame with desire
> For your love
> My body aches for your touch
> I long to feel your lips
> Pressed to mine
> My torment is great when we are apart
> Come to me, my brother
> Put an end to my torment
> With just a word
> A glance
> And I shall be satisfied.

When the call comes through, ask your partner to open the envelope and read the incantation. Speak to each other of your love and how much you miss each other when apart. You can be as explicit as you wish but, since you are not physically together, you do not want to make either of you uncomfortable – unless you have agreed on a mutually satisfactory outlet for your desires. Some people have been made to feel that masturbation is wrong: I feel that sex, whether with the person you love or through personal gratification, is a choice to be made on your own. You need to determine what you and your partner are comfortable with before you get to a point in the conversation where there may be no turning back. And who better to 'talk dirty' to your partner than you? You know what his desires and fantasies are and what will get his attention. When you and your partner have completed your 'love call', make sure that all candles and incense are extinguished before turning in for the evening.

Glow like honey spell

This activity is designed to foster trust between lovers. I like to play classical or New Age music during this spell but the choice is yours. Always be mindful of each other's comfort and have a safe 'stop now' word or signal that either of you can use to let the other know if you feel the activity is getting out of hand. This spell is for trust and sensitivity, not for pain.

Items needed
A red pillar candle
Additional candles in any colours
Glow Like Honey oil (see page 173)
Myrrh incense
A censor
Matches
Music
Feathers
A variety of fragrant flowers
An assortment of essential oils
Ice cubes
Food or beverages (optional)
A blindfold

Place the additional candles around the room. You may wish to put a drop or two of Glow Like Honey oil on each one prior to lighting. Place the red pillar candle and the censor on one table and the other items on another. Start the music, light the incense and begin the activity.

Both of you should anoint the red pillar candle, wick to base, with Glow Like Honey oil and then light it. The man then recites:

> *My sister*
> *Your skin glows like honey*
> *I see your tunic slip from your shoulder*
> *And I glimpse your milky white breasts*
> *I wish to place my kiss there*
> *As you approach*
> *I catch the scent of your perfume*
> *You smell of cinnamon and myrrh*
> *And I am intoxicated*
> *My desire rises in me*
> *And I can barely contain myself*

Tonight I shall meet you at the river
I shall bathe with you
And we shall lie together
I wish to bury my face in your hair
And taste your sun-kissed lips.

Both of you undress until completely naked and then the man blindfolds the woman. Experiment by lightly stroking the blindfolded partner with the feathers on various parts of the body. Place a flower under the blindfolded person's nose, then another. When using the oils, see which ones, when inhaled, have an effect on the 'blind' partner. Use an ice cube on various parts of the body, but don't leave it on too long. If you have food or beverages, apply them to the blindfolded partner's body and then gently lick them off.

You may wish to switch roles and let the woman blindfold the man and do the same to him. When you have completed the activity, you could shower together before turning in for the evening. Make sure all candles and incense have been extinguished.

Love no other spell

This activity is designed for when one of you is a little under the weather – it's always good to have someone tend to us when we are ill, especially the one we love. The music should be soothing to the ailing partner; I would want to hear light classical.

Items needed
A pink or green pillar candle
Additional candles in any colours
Love No Other oil (see page 173)
Cedarwood incense
A censor
Matches
Beverages
Music

Place the additional candles around the room for ambience and put a drop or two of Love No Other oil on each one before lighting. Start the music, light the incense and begin the activity.

The ill person should be tucked in for the evening with an appropriate beverage, such as hot tea with honey and lemon, hot mulled cider or plain fruit juice. The person performing the activity should anoint the pink or green pillar candle, wick to base, with Love No Other oil, light it and recite:

> *Let me hold you in my arms*
> *Let me anoint you with oils and unguent*
> *Let me soothe your pain*
> *Let me cool your fevered brow*
> *Let me restore you to health*
> *For you possess my heart and soul*
> *And I can love no other but you.*

Cuddle with your partner and cater to his or her every need. One activity that may be soothing, along with the music, is reading to your partner. Ask their preference of reading material and snuggle up for a nice quiet evening together. Check your partner's temperature from time to time and if there is a fever apply a cold compress to the forehead. Relax together and let your partner know that he or she is the most important person in your life. Make sure all candles and incense are extinguished before turning in for the evening.

My sister's loveliness spell

This activity is designed for the man to show his woman how much she means to him. I think that soft and sensuous classical music would be ideal for this spell.

Items needed
A purple pillar candle
Additional candles in any colours
My Sister's Loveliness oil (see page 173)
Lotus incense
A censor
Matches
Music
Her favourite meal
Her favourite massage oil

Write the following incantation on a piece of paper:

> *My sister's loveliness revives me*
> *All the priests spells and charms cannot cure me*
> *Only the sight of my sister*

Can make me well
She is my health and life
Her embrace soothes me
Her voice comforts me
Her kiss rejuvenates me
She nourishes me with her love
Bring my sister, my beloved, to me
And I shall be well again.

Slip this paper, along with an invitation to dinner at home, into her briefcase or handbag, or leave it where she will find it before work.

Now, men, the work is all yours! Prepare or buy her favourite meal so that it can be ready for her when she comes back. If she is lucky enough not to work, make sure she is out for the day so you can arrange everything. Place the additional candles around the room for a soft, sensual setting and put one or two drops of My Sister's Loveliness oil on each before lighting. When she gets home, give her the time to change and make herself comfortable. Then start the music, light the incense and begin the activity.

Anoint the purple pillar candle, wick to base, with My Sister's Loveliness oil, light it and place it on the table where dinner will be served. When she is seated, recite the incantation you wrote out earlier. Serve her dinner and wait on her like she is a queen. You may want to massage her feet to relax her after her busy day. This is your chance to tell her how much she means to you and to thank her for everything she does for you. Take the activity as far as you both wish and make sure you extinguish all candles and incense before retiring for the evening.

Quench your desire spell

This activity is designed for the woman to wait on her man and to show him just how much he excites and arouses her. The music should be sensitive and seductive – and arousing too!

Items needed
A red pillar candle
Additional candles in any colours
Quench Your Desire oil (see page 173)
Musk incense
A censor
Matches

His favourite beverage
His favourite foods (optional)
Quench Your Desire massage oil (see page 174)
Music

Anoint the red pillar candle, wick to base, in advance, so it is ready to light. Place the additional candles around the room and put one or two drops of Quench Your Desire oil on each one before lighting. All food and beverage items, along with the Quench Your Desire massage oil, should be on one table and the anointed candle and the censor with the incense should be on another. Dress in something sexy (red, black and white are always good colour choices) and have your partner sit in a comfortable chair or on the couch. Start the music, light the incense and begin the activity.

Light the red pillar candle and recite to your partner:

> Your voice is like honey
> Your touch intoxicates me like date wine
> The flame of love burns within me
> Draw me close to you, my brother
> My heart leaps in my breast
> At the thought of lying with you tonight
> I see the desire in your eyes
> For your sister
> And I shall quench your desire, my beloved
> For I am your humble servant
> Your handmaiden
> Your lover
> My only desire is your pleasure
> Let me please you, my brother.

Dance for your partner and slowly strip for him, but let him know that he is allowed to watch but not touch yet. Feed him some of the food and dance some more, this time more provocatively. Ask him if he would like you to massage his feet or back. If he says yes, use the Quench Your Desire massage oil. Remember, you are his servant, to wait on him and indulge him in whatever he desires. When you feel it is appropriate, tell him he may touch you now. Take the activity as far as you both desire – hopefully you will have a wonderfully erotic sexual experience. Make sure you extinguish all candles and incense before turning in for the evening.

Remain with me forever spell

This activity is designed for the man to wait on his woman to show her how much she means to him. Try playing New Age or light classical music for this spell. The foods I have listed are just suggestions: any of her favourites will do but they should be associated with feeling good or sensuous activity.

Items needed
A red pillar candle
Additional candles in any colours
Remain With Me Forever oil (see page 173)
Blue Nile incense
A censor
Matches
Wine, champagne or beer
Whipped cream
Chocolate sauce
Honey
Sliced fruits such as apples, bananas, cherries and strawberries
Music

Place the additional candles around the room ready for lighting. You may wish to place a drop or two of Remain With Me Forever oil on each one. All the food and drink items should be on one table and the red pillar candle and the censor with the incense on another. Start the music, light the incense and begin the activity.

Both partners anoint the candle, wick to base, with Remain With Me Forever oil while the man recites:

> *Fairest One*
> *Let me devour you with my eyes*
> *I am hungry for your love*
> *To me, you are like Menqet*
> *Goddess of Beer*
> *When I drink from you*
> *I am intoxicated with your love*
> *I cannot free myself from your snare*
> *Your body entices me to remain*
> *With you forever.*

The man lights the candle and looks deeply at his partner. Pamper her by feeding her the food. Try dipping a strawberry in the chocolate sauce, whipped cream, honey, or champagne before you feed it to her. If she wants, let her feed you also. Make this a feast to your partner and let her know how important she is to you. You may wish to recite the above incantation to her again, or as many times as you desire.

Use the foods and alcohol to anoint various parts of her body and slowly and gently lick them off. She may wish to do the same – remember that this is a feast for her so let her do whatever you are both comfortable with. When you have completed your 'feast' you may wish to shower before retiring for the evening. Make sure all candles and the incense are extinguished.

Soul on fire spell

This activity is designed for your mutual pleasure and maximum satisfaction.

Items needed
A pink pillar candle
Additional candles in any colours
Soul on Fire oil (see page 174)
Cinnamon incense
A censor
Matches
Flower petals (preferably roses; red and pink are best)
Soul on Fire massage oil (see page 174)
Music

Place the additional candles around the room for soft lighting and place a drop or two of Soul on Fire oil on each one before lighting. Sprinkle the flower petals on the bed or floor. Place the censor with the incense on a table with the pink pillar candle and ensure that the Soul on Fire massage oil will be handy at all times. Start the music, light the cinnamon incense and begin the activity.

Both of you anoint the pink pillar candle, wick to base, with the Soul on Fire oil and recite in unison:

> *You have set my soul on fire*
> *I burn with desire for you*
> *All the waters of the Nile*
> *Cannot extinguish my need for you*
> *Your touch will only fan the flame*

Your kiss consumes me
I long to drown in your caress
Being with you tonight
I am ablaze with passion
Only your love can ease the fire
In my heart
My soul
My body.

Light the candle, look deeply into each other's eyes and speak the incantation again with intensity and feeling; you may wish to recite it together or individually to each other. Listen to what your partner is saying and feel the love between the two of you. Undress each other slowly and gently. Take the Soul on Fire massage oil and, starting at the feet, massage your partner. If things start to heat up too fast, slow down and switch places so your partner can massage you from the feet up.

This activity is sure to spark passion between the two of you and should be prolonged as long as possible for maximum enjoyment. You may wish to finish the evening with a shower together and then extinguish all candles and incense before retiring.

Love deepening oils

Aflame With Desire oil
2.5 ml/½ tsp grapeseed oil
2 drops cherry blossom oil
3 drops lilac oil

Glow Like Honey oil
2.5 ml/½ tsp olive oil
1 drop cinnamon oil
3 drops myrrh oil

Love No Other oil
2.5 ml/½ tsp hemp seed oil
3 drops apple oil
1 drop essential coconut oil

My Sister's Loveliness oil
2.5 ml/½ tsp coconut oil
1 drop clove bud oil
3 drops nutmeg oil

Quench Your Desire oil
2.5 ml/½ tsp almond oil
1 drop jasmine oil
2 drops patchouli oil

Remain With Me Forever oil
2.5 ml/½ tsp hazelnut (filbert) oil
2 drops Egyptian musk oil
2 drops honeysuckle oil

Soul on Fire oil
2.5 ml/½ tsp grapeseed oil
2 drops black pepper oil
2 drops lemongrass oil

Quench Your Desire massage oil
60 ml/4 tbsp unscented massage oil
4 drops cinnamon oil
5 drops clove bud oil
3 drops orange oil
5 drops sandalwood oil
2 drops ylang ylang oil

Soul on Fire massage oil
60 ml/4 tbsp unscented massage oil
2 drops essential almond oil
1 drop lemongrass oil
2 drops orange oil
3 drops patchouli oil
3 drops vetivert oil

CHAPTER 12

Egyptian Spells for Reconciliation

Although we all do our best to keep the peace, at some time or another our lover may get on our nerves, or worse. Tempers flare and words are said in the heat of the moment that we wish we had never said. Stress can make even the happiest couple do and say things that they don't mean. Sometimes it is beneficial to get things off your chest, but remember to do it responsibly. So often, when we are angry or hurt, we lash out at the very person we love the most. We 'dump' on them for all indiscretions, real or imaginary, past or present.

Since we all have human failings, we need to try to temper our words and not bring past wounds into current relationships. Having said this, I know this is easier said than done. If you have a problem with a current lover or spouse, speak only of the issues between you, not about what has happened in the past. Keep your focus on the present, unless these problems have been brewing for some time. Address only the issue at hand; don't bring up the fact that he forgot your birthday five years ago. Try to establish what the problem is in a calm, rational manner, then take a deep breath, relax and meditate before you approach the situation.

The spells in this section are meant to aid in bringing the two of you together after a disagreement. Ideally both partners will participate in these activities, though if your partner is not of the same religious persuasion this may not be possible. As the witch in the relationship, you should take the initiative and work the spell you feel best suits the situation. I do not advocate that one partner should always apologise; in any disagreement, there must be a mutual understanding. But for your peace of mind, a spell for reconciliation might be just the thing to nudge your partner or you in the right direction. Even witches can learn to say sorry; we aren't always right and should be adult enough to admit it when we make a mistake.

Some indiscretions may take longer to resolve than others. We all make choices in life, good or bad, for our own reasons. If your lover or spouse is less than honourable in your relationship, reconciliation may just be prolonging the inevitable. Take a long, hard look at the reason for the disagreement and make an impartial evaluation. Love is wonderful, love can solve many things, but love must be mutual in order for it to survive. When approaching spells of this type, be honest with yourself and be honest about your partner and the relationship you share. Some people argue just to make up and that seems a bit dysfunctional to me. Arguments and fighting expend too much negative energy; a relationship should be based on love, trust, understanding and honesty. Reconciling with a partner who does not share your values is inviting trouble.

All the spells in this section may be performed on any day of the week, though Thursday is more of a day for activity rather than personal issues such as reconciliation. All beverages in this section should be non-alcoholic (alcohol can lead to more heated discussions and both of you should be level-headed when reconciling) unless otherwise noted. Any of these spells may lead to sexual encounters, but you should only engage in such activity after a disagreement if it feels appropriate for both partners. No one should ever feel pressured to engage in sexual activity against their will or better judgement and you should not rush into a reconciliation just for the sake of great sex. Only the two of you will know if the time is right to resume your relationship as before.

If, at the conclusion of the spell, both partners do not feel an acceptable resolution has been reached, you may wish to wait a day or two and try again.

Another day spell

This spell is designed to foster communication after a disagreement. The food and non-alcoholic beverages should be your choice.

Items needed
A purple pillar candle
Amber oil
Bay incense
A censor
Matches
Beverages
Comfort foods

One partner anoints the candle, wick to base, with the amber oil. The other partner then lights the candle, followed by the incense. Both should breathe deeply and relax. Face each other and speak the following to each other in turn:

> I cannot bear
> Another day apart from you
> My heart and soul
> Cry out to you
> Yet you seem not to hear
> I want to feel
> Your arms around me
> I long to hear your voice
> Come back to me
> For I cannot bear
> Another day apart from you.

Speak to each other honestly about the disagreement and how best to resolve it. Share some food and drink. Try to get beyond the disagreement so that you can share intimacy again. If you wish to engage in sexual activity, that is a decision for the two of you to agree upon mutually. Extinguish the candle when both agree a resolution has been achieved.

Be still my heart spell

This spell is designed to clear the air over a misunderstanding, be it real or imaginary. Start the music before you begin the activity; soft classical is a good choice.

Items needed
A blue pillar candle
Rose oil
Myrrh resin incense
A charcoal disc
A censor
Matches
Music

One partner anoints the candle, wick to base, with the rose oil. The other partner lights the candle, then the charcoal disc. When the disc stops sparking, the first partner places some myrrh resin incense on it.

Both should relax and breathe deeply, then face each other and speak the following incantation, either in unison or one at a time:

> Be still my heart
> Do not let doubt cloud my mind
> For our love is a true love
> An eternal love
> Be still my heart
> Your touch soothes my soul
> I know you are mine alone
> No other can take you from me
> Be still my heart
> Your words comfort me
> And all my fears take flight
> Like a lapwing bird
> Be still my heart.

Speak honestly of the doubts, fears and anxieties that have caused this misunderstanding. Listen to what your partner has to say and don't interrupt. Each partner should allow the other to speak in turn. Really listen to each other and both of you should discuss any doubts you have so you may re-establish a comfortable intimacy. Remember that all relationships must be based on mutual trust and understanding. Extinguish the candle when both of you agree that a resolution has been reached to your mutual satisfaction.

Do not deny me spell

This spell is designed for one partner to apologise to the other for having said strong words in the heat of a disagreement.

Items needed
An orange pillar candle
Primrose oil
Benzoin resin incense
A charcoal disc
A censor
Matches
Comfort foods
Your favourite flower(s)

One partner anoints the candle, wick to base, with the primrose oil. The other partner lights the candle, then the charcoal disc. When the disc stops sparking, the first partner places some benzoin resin incense on the charcoal. Both partners should breathe deeply and relax. The partner who spoke harsh words should speak the following to his or her partner:

> *Do not deny me, my beloved*
> *I said hurtful words*
> *And I see the pain in your eyes*
> *Let me kiss away the tears*
> *Speak loving words to me*
> *Quell the torment in my heart*
> *Put an end to my suffering*
> *For you are my beloved*
> *I would surely die without your love.*

If the other partner also said harsh words, he or she should also speak the incantation. The partner who 'started the disagreement' should present the other with his or her favourite flower; if you wish to exchange flowers, that is perfectly acceptable. An exchange of tokens of affection will help the healing. Speak from the heart – be adult enough to admit you were wrong in speaking so harshly. The other partner needs to be gracious and accept the apology – forgiveness helps to foster intimacy. Share some food and feed each other if it feels appropriate. Extinguish the candle when both of you agree that a resolution has been reached.

Flame of desire spell

This spell is designed to re-establish a loving relationship after the successful resolution of a problem. Start the soft and sensuous music before you begin the activity.

Items needed
A red pillar candle
Cinnamon oil
Musk incense
A censor
Matches
Music
Your favourite foods
Favourite beverages, which may be alcoholic
Massage oil (if appropriate)

One partner anoints the candle, wick to base, with the cinnamon oil. The other partner lights the candle and the incense. Both should breathe deeply and relax. Each partner should speak the following to the other in turn:

> *I see the flame of desire in your heart*
> *Yet still you punish me*
> *You will not draw me close*
> *You keep your distance*
> *But I know it is only a façade*
> *For I see the flame of desire in your heart*
> *My arms ache to hold you*
> *My body begs for your touch*
> *Come to me, my beloved*
> *And I shall never again cause you torment.*

This is the time to rebuild your relationship. Share your feelings and be totally honest with each other. Share the food and beverages and feed each other to establish the trust you once felt for one another. If it feels appropriate, massage each other's shoulders, back or feet. Do not rush the activity, but see what develops and take the activity as far as you both agree upon, even to a sexual encounter. Extinguish the candle when both of you agree that a mutually satisfactory conclusion has been achieved.

Hymn to Isis spell

This spell is designed to heal a couple that have been through a separation. Until you have worked a bit harder at a reconciliation, this activity should not be consummated with sexual activity. Falling into bed with each other after an estrangement may not be the best solution to your problems. Start the music before you begin the activity.

Items needed
A green pillar candle
Lavender oil
Frankincense resin incense
A charcoal disc
A censor
Matches
Music

Your favourite foods
Your favourite beverages, preferably non-alcoholic

One partner anoints the candle, wick to base, with the lavender oil. The other lights the candle and the charcoal disc. When the disc stops sparking, the first partner places some frankincense resin incense on it. Both should breathe deeply and relax. Both speak the following incantation, one after the other:

> *I implore you, Great Mother*
> *Bring peace and serenity*
> *To reside in his/her heart*
> *Show me what I must do*
> *So I may ignite the flame of his/her passion*
> *Isis, Mistress of Magick*
> *Guide my words and actions*
> *Open up his/her heart to me*
> *Make him/her return to my waiting arms.*

Partake of the food and beverages while you discuss your estrangement. Talk openly and honestly with each other to comfort and heal any hurt. Try to determine the best way forward to strengthen your relationship. Let the incense smoke envelop the two of you and feel the presence of Isis. You both may wish to silently ask her to show you what must be done to heal the relationship, if that is meant to be. This activity should conclude with some loving action between the two of you, perhaps a kiss or a hug.

When you feel you have resolved some or all of the issues involved, one of you may extinguish the candle. You might want to perform this particular activity together more than once and over the course of several days or weeks, depending on how difficult the situation may be.

Your cruel words spell

This spell is designed to open up all avenues of communication. It is ideal for when there has been only a minor misunderstanding that may easily be remedied with a little quiet time together and some loving attention.

Items needed
A pink pillar candle
Violet oil

Amber resin incense
A charcoal disc
A censor
Matches
Your favourite massage oil
Feathers

One partner anoints the candle, wick to base, with the violet oil. The other partner lights the candle and the charcoal disc. When the disc stops sparking, the first partner places some amber resin incense on the charcoal. Both should breathe deeply and relax. The partner who was offended by the harsh words should speak the following:

> My brother/sister, your cruel words stung me
> As would the bite from a scorpion
> One kind word from your lips
> Shall take this pain from my soul
> Take me in your arms, my brother/sister
> Take me to your bed
> And all shall be forgiven
> For I cannot bear the silence
> That blankets your heart.

The partner who spoke harshly should speak of why he or she was upset or angry and both should work on ways to alleviate the problem. Tend to the offended partner with a tender massage of the shoulders, neck and back. Pamper him or her with the feathers on various parts of the body. Make the offended partner feel special again. But be gracious to the partner who offended you – do not be harsh or disrespectful. This is your lover and you should do your best to accept this gift of love and affection.

This activity may be taken as far as both of you desire and feel appropriate, even to mutual sexual gratification. When you both feel the situation is resolved, you may extinguish the candle.

Your words betray you spell

This spell is designed to avoid a parting, though when a relationship has reached this point it may require more than a spell to heal the heartache. Go into this activity with the best of intentions, but keep in mind that the outcome may not be reconciliation.

Items needed
A yellow pillar candle
Basil oil
Lemon verbena incense
A censor
Matches

The partner trying to effect the reconciliation will be doing most of the work. He or she anoints the candle with the basil oil and lights the lemon verbena incense. Both partners should breathe deeply and relax. The partner desirous of the reconciliation shall look at the other and speak the following:

> *Your words betray you*
> *You speak of love*
> *Yet you can not meet my gaze*
> *My heart leaps at your voice*
> *But my soul is troubled*
> *I see in your eyes*
> *That you do not want my kiss*
> *My touch, my embrace*
> *You are my life and breath*
> *Tell me how to win your heart*
> *And make our love burn yet again.*

Speak to your partner from the heart. Say why you feel the relationship is worth saving. Keep a clear head and do not lose your temper; you need to clear the air and exacerbating the problem will not help. When you have finished, let your partner speak of his or her feelings, including whether the relationship can be salvaged. This activity may become very emotional and both partners need to be able to step back if the words become heated. Open up your hearts to each other to try to resolve the issue at hand. Express your feelings for each other honestly, but do not purposely hurt one another.

When both of you feel you have sufficiently expressed your feelings, extinguish the candle. This activity may not end with a resolution; you both may wish to repeat the spell if you feel it will aid your relationship. If it is the decision of one or both parties not to continue with the activity or the relationship, it may signal that it is time to move on in peace and without malice towards each other.

CHAPTER 13

Egyptian Spells to Ease Heartache

At one time or another, we have all had to face the facts. Things didn't work out as we had hoped, the blush was soon off the rose and it was time to move on. As human beings, we tend to analyse things far too much and obsess over things that we need to let go of. Remember, you are the most important person in your universe – you are not a doormat, nor are you a convenient port in a storm for another to breeze into and out of your life. If your friend, lover or spouse does not have enough respect for you and your needs, then your relationship is bound to flounder.

I do not advocate giving up at the least little hurdle. Relationships are a fragile gift that have to be nurtured and worked at. But you do expect that, when the tough times hit, your partner will be there for you with tenderness, compassion and support – not off drinking with friends or flying off on a solo vacation. There has to be give and take in a relationship, but one person should not always do the compromising. If you have tried all rational means to keep the relationship together, but things are just going from bad to worse, then separating may be the best option. Never stay in a relationship where there is physical, emotional, or mental abuse. I cannot stress strongly enough that abuse is not a form of love.

Many people make the mistake of hanging on to issues long after the relationship is over. When we are hurting, it is not always easy to wish positive things for the person who has hurt us, and some will even speak negatively about the person they were with. However, if you approach the parting with positive energy, you will heal faster and will attract the right person for you. It is not easy to change negative behaviour or feelings and it may not happen immediately, but it will happen in time. These spells are designed to help you move on in a positive direction and to wish your former partner all the best. Relax, take time for yourself and know that you are a person who deserves love and respect.

Traditional Wiccans celebrate 'marriage' with a Handfasting (see pages 204–5 for Handfasting rituals) and they may also perform a Handparting when a relationship ends. For example, you and your lover agreed that your Handfasting would be for a year and a day. That time has come to an end and now the two of you have to make a choice: if the relationship is strong, you may wish to have another Handfasting for a further period of time; if you feel the relationship has run its course, you may wish to perform a Handparting.

If you were legally married, it is best to perform the Handparting when all legal issues have been resolved. Both parties should be present and, if you both approached your relationship with the proper guidance from the deities, you will both approach the Handparting with respect and positive intentions for one another. However, I am not naïve enough to believe all separating couples will graciously agree to a Handparting. My personal beliefs are strong enough that I have been able to wish my former partners well and move on. If you and your partner share similar beliefs, a Handparting, or Parting of Souls ritual, may suit you. A Handparting is not a 'celebration'; it is a helpful ritual to heal any hurts between two former lovers and to release both parties so that they are open to all the possibilities of a new life without their former lover.

Freedom from a lover spell

This is designed to help you and your current partner deal with the end of your relationship. It is also good for when you have met someone new and feel it is time to move on with your life. The best time to perform this is on a Saturday during the Waning Moon.

Items needed
A black 10 cm/4 in taper or votive candle
Cypress oil
Camphor incense
A censor
Paper from a brown paper bag
A nail
A pen
A cauldron or other fire-safe container
Matches

Light the incense and relax. Clear your mind and let the loving energy of the deities help you in your time of need. Using the nail, carve your name and the name of your current lover on the black candle and anoint it, base to wick, with the cypress oil. Light the candle and recite three times:

> I wish only for your happiness
> And all I know now is despair
> I no longer desire you
> I wish to be free of you
> And give my love to another
> For he has captured my heart
> And it is now he that I long for.

Sit for a time and remember all the good and bad times you had together. If it makes you feel better, write your current partner a letter, expressing all your thoughts, fears and desires for the future. Wish him or her well. Place the letter under the candle and let the candle burn out of its own accord. Take any remains of the candle, wrap it in the letter and burn it all in your cauldron. Collect up the ashes and scatter them to the winds, knowing that you and your current lover have released your bonds to each other.

Parting lovers' spell

This spell is designed to heal the heart during a separation or divorce – the green of the candle corresponds with healing. The best time to perform it is a Sunday on the night of the New Moon or during the Waning Moon.

Items needed
A green taper or votive candle
Sandalwood oil
Frankincense incense
A censor
A candle snuffer
Matches

Light the incense and clear your mind of all other thoughts. Anoint the candle, base to wick, with the sandalwood oil and recite:

> I have loved you well
> Your pleasure has been my joy

But the time has come
For us to part
I shall leave your house
Without a bitter word or thought
For I have loved you well.

Think only positive thoughts about your former partner. Let the candle burn for an hour before you extinguish it with the candle snuffer. You can repeat this spell any time you feel the need for a little extra strength when you are going through a stressful or painful separation or break-up.

Release from love spell

This spell is designed to heal and help you move on with your life. The best time to begin it is a Sunday or Friday of the New Moon or during the Waning Moon.

Items needed
A green taper or pillar candle
Yarrow oil
Dill incense
A censor
Dried marjoram
A candle snuffer
Matches

Light the incense and breathe deeply to relax. Close your eyes and think positive thoughts about your former partner and yourself. When you are ready, open your eyes and anoint the candle, base to wick, with the yarrow oil while reciting at least once:
Release me, my beloved
Set me free of your snare
I am like a captive bird
Who longs to soar the heavens
Release me, my beloved
So I may spread my wings
And know the joys of new love.

Place the candle in front of you and sprinkle a circle of dried marjoram around the base in a clockwise direction. Light the candle and envision yourself free of all worry and anxiety about the relationship. Hold that image for as long as you wish. Extinguish the candle with the candle snuffer and leave everything where it is.

Repeat the incantation as you light the candle each day or evening for one week. Sit for a time and focus your thoughts on your new life and your former lover or spouse being able to move on.

At the end of the week, sweep up the marjoram and dispose of it outside to return it to the Earth. If the candle is not completely burned out, store it with your other ritual items. It will be available for your use if you need added strength during this difficult time.

When love ends spell

This spell is designed for former lovers to make a clean break. It would be ideal if you could each say these words to the other, but when love ends it is not always that easy. The rue in the incense will help to ease painful separation: the yellow candle represents your confidence to move on. If you don't have fresh sage, you can use dried. The best time to begin this spell is on a Saturday during the Waning Moon.

Items needed
A black votive candle
A yellow taper or pillar candle
Rue incense
Basil oil
Sage incense
Lemon balm oil
Sage leaves
A censor
A nail
A photograph of the two of you together
A snippet of hair from each of you (optional)
Paper from a brown paper bag
A pen
Scissors
A small brown paper bag
A cauldron or other fire-safe container
A candle snuffer
Matches

Light the rue incense and breathe deeply to relax. Clear your mind of all thoughts except the work at hand. Using the nail, carve your lover's name on the black candle. Anoint it, base to wick, with the basil oil, light it and place it in front of you. Write the following incantation on the piece of paper, kiss it once and anoint it with one drop of basil oil:

> *My heart aches at the thought of leaving*
> *But I know it must be so*
> *Your touch no longer makes me tremble*
> *Your kiss no longer fans my passion*
> *Your body no longer stirs my desire*
> *Your words no longer sound so sweet*
> *My heart aches at the thought of leaving*
> *But I know it must be so.*

Take the photograph and think of all you have meant to each other. When you feel ready, cut the photograph in two with the scissors, so that each of you is alone in the picture. Place the half with your lover's picture on top of the paper, add the snippet of his hair if you have one, fold it up and light it from the candle flame. Drop it in your cauldron and make sure it burns completely to ash. Extinguish the black candle with the candle snuffer. Empty the ashes into the paper bag, add the black candle and close up the bag and put it behind you.

Using the nail, carve the words 'My healing is complete' on the yellow candle and anoint it, wick to base, with the lemon balm oil. Kiss the image of yourself that is alone in the photograph and place it under the yellow candle. Light the sage incense and think of how you envision your life without your former partner. When you are ready, light the yellow candle and repeat the incantation aloud as many times as you feel the need.

Let the candle burn for an hour, then extingish it with the candle snuffer. Leave the candle where it is. Take the bag with the black candle and go to a secluded spot near a body of water. With all good intentions for your former lover/spouse, throw the bag into the water, thus releasing your bonds.

Light the yellow candle each day or evening for one hour and speak the incantation aloud once. When the candle has burned out completely, take any candle remains, your picture and the snippet of your hair and place them all in your cauldron. Sprinkle everything with sage leaves and light it. Make sure everything burns to ash. Collect up the ashes and cast them to the winds to begin your new life.

A banishing and release spell

This spell is primarily for use to banish an unwanted habit or behaviour; due to the destructive action involved, it is best not to use it with a particular individual in mind. The ramifications of using this spell to banish a person could be great, regardless of your positive intentions. Although the Ancient Egyptians used curse tablets for any number of ills of a personal or behavioural nature, my only intention is to illustrate the nature of their magick.

This spell may be performed at any time, but the best time is on a Saturday during the Waning Moon.

Items needed
A gold taper or votive candle, to represent the god Set
A silver taper or votive candle, to represent the goddess Sekhmet
Cypress incense
Banishing oil (see page 203)
Modelling clay (oven or microwave drying)
A nail or black marker
A censor
A candle snuffer
Matches

Light the incense and then fashion the modelling clay into a plate or tablet. While doing this, reflect on all the reasons why you want this behaviour gone. You might like to share your thoughts with the deities, being as specific as possible.

When you have finished, use the nail to inscribe your request on the clay before it dries, or use the black marker after it has dried. Anoint the plate or tablet with one drop of Banishing oil, then anoint the gold candle, base to wick, with Banishing oil and light it. Pass the dried plate or tablet over the flame of the gold candle and the incense smoke as you recite:

> *Set, God of Destruction*
> *Hear the petition of Your humble servant, (magickal name)*
> *I have suffered long enough*
> *With (what you wish to be rid of)*
> *Use Your immense power*
> *To cause chaos to reign*
> *Lord of Storm*
> *Bring tranquillity from this chaos*

> *Set, God of Suffering*
> *Put an end to my torment*
> *And hear my plea.*

Anoint the silver candle, wick to base, with Banishing oil and light it. Now pass the clay item over the flame of the silver candle and the incense smoke as you recite:

> *Sekhmet, Goddess of Destruction*
> *Hear the petition of Your humble servant, (magickal name)*
> *I have suffered long enough*
> *With (what you wish to be rid of)*
> *Use Your immense power*
> *To give me the courage*
> *To do what must be done*
> *Lady of the Flame*
> *Bring peace to my troubled soul*
> *Sekhmet, Lady of the Bright Red Linen*
> *Put an end to my torment*
> *And hear my plea.*

Put the plate or tablet on your altar and place both hands palm down over it. Recite:

> *I call upon the Ancient Ones*
> *To hear my petition*
> *I cry out to You*
> *From the depths of despair*
> *And ask for Your guidance and protection*
> *In the destruction*
> *Of this earthen plate/tablet*
> *I pray that this action*
> *Will not cause any harm to me*
> *But will make (what you wish to be rid of) vanish*
> *Bring this wish to fruition*
> *I am Your humble servant, (magickal name)*
> *And ask only that You hear my plea*
> *So I may once again*
> *Know peace and tranquillity.*

Snuff out the candles, take up your plate or tablet and go outdoors. With all your might, raise it high above your head and throw it crashing to the ground. Breathe deeply and feel the release of emotion. After a few moments, sweep up as much of the clay as you can and dispose of it in your dustbin.

A banishing desire spell

Many Ancient Egyptian spells were written on papyrus, then soaked in water or wine. When the ink dissipated into the liquid, the liquid was drunk, thus releasing the spell. Since it may be dangerous to drink even diluted ink, I would think twice about trying this method. If you really feel you wish to drink the spell, you could create your own ink out of sugar beet (red beet), pomegranate or grape juice instead.

The ritual burning of items is just as effective. Ideally you want something with the person's essence on or contained within it – a lock or strands of hair, a piece of paper with his or her handwriting or a snippet of clothing from something he or she has worn but has not washed. Please do not burn the person's entire wardrobe!

This spell should be performed on a Saturday during the Waning Moon.

Items needed
A black 10 cm/4 in taper or votive candle
Banishing oil (see page 203)
Sage incense
A censor
A cauldron or other fire-safe container
A nail
Matches
Paper from a brown paper bag
Personal item(s)
A pinch of sulphur
A pen

Using the nail, inscribe the person's name on the black candle and anoint it, base to wick, with Banishing oil. Light the incense and take a few moments to relax and concentrate on the task at hand. Light the candle and recite:

> *As I light this candle*
> *Your love for me shall be consumed.*

When the candle is half-burned recite:

> *As this candle burns down*
> *Your desire for me shall lessen.*

When the candle is coming to its end recite:

> *As this candle sputters out*
> *Your need for me shall die.*

While the candle is still burning but almost out, write the following on the brown paper and pass it through the incense smoke:

I release you, (name of person to banish)
From your bonds of love
Go, my brother
Burden me no more.

Place the personal item(s) and the pinch of sulphur in the paper and fold it to make a small packet. Light the packet from the candle flame before it burns out and drop it into your cauldron. It will flare up so be careful and quick. Recite as it burns:

I release you, (name of person to banish)
From your bonds of love
Go, my brother
Burden me no more.

When the candle has burned out, collect up any candle remains along with the ashes in the cauldron and bury them in the ground away from your house. Turn and walk away without looking back.

Preparation for the parting of souls ritual

This is obviously not a joyous occasion, but it should be as painless as possible for both parties. Holding on to past grievances, hurts and ill-feelings doesn't help anyone move on in life. It's worth making the effort to commemorate both the relationship and its ending for, in the long run, you will find that you feel better about yourself and the time you were together.

I have written two versions of the Parting of Souls ritual: one is to help an individual to heal and move on (see pages 195–9); the other is for both partners who have shared their lives and have now grown apart (see pages 199–203). The individual version may also be adapted for use if someone you love has died suddenly and you need closure before you can open up to another.

The offerings the two parties exchange as a token of parting as friends may be as simple as a flower or feather. You may wish to use the ritual to return the jewellery you exchanged at your Ritual of the Joining of Souls (see page 208) instead of or in addition to any other offerings.

The black candle in the ritual represents the end of the relationship and the coloured candles represent each of the parties involved. You should each choose your own colour, depending upon your desires for the future and the energy involved. The most logical would be blue (healing, hope), green (emotional healing, peace), orange (emotional stability, healing relationships), pink (emotional healing, self-love), purple (healing, respect), white (enlightenment, healing) or yellow (confidence, hope). You may find you both choose the same colour. The rue incense helps to ease a painful love and sandalwood incense is appropriate for most magickal and ritual work. Ritual clothing is not required – you may wear whatever you are most comfortable in.

Items needed
4 white pillar candles, to represent the Elements
4 canopic jars (optional)
A gold pillar candle, to represent the god Osiris
A silver pillar candle, to represent the goddess Isis
A black pillar or taper candle
2 coloured pillar or taper candles (see page 193)
Parting of Souls oil (see page 203)
Rue or sandalwood incense
A small plate of sea salt
A small bowl of spring water
An athame
A chalice of wine or fruit juice
Offerings for each partner (see page 193)
A candle snuffer
A censor
Matches

Prior to the ritual, anoint the black candle and the coloured candles with Parting of Souls oil. In addition, place a drop of Parting of Souls oil on each of the four white pillar candles and on the gold and silver candles. You are now ready to prepare the ritual space.

Starting in the West and proceeding counterclockwise, place the white pillar candles and canopic jars, if you are using them, at the four compass points. Place the gold candle in the upper right of your altar with the plate of sea salt in front of it and the athame next to the plate. On the left side, place the silver candle with the bowl of spring water in front of it and finally the chalice of wine next to the bowl. Place the censor filled with incense between the gold and silver candles and place the anointed black candle between the athame and chalice. The anointed coloured candles should be placed one on each side of the black candle. Finally, place the offerings and candle snuffer on the altar in front of the black and coloured candles. It is time to begin the ritual.

Parting of souls ritual (for one)

Go to the candle in the West, light it and recite:

> *Qebhsennuf, Son of Horus, Element of Water*
> *God of the West, look with favour upon this solemn*
> *ritual.*

Go to the candle in the South, light it and recite:

> *Imsety, Son of Horus, Element of Fire*
> *God of the South, look with favour upon this solemn*
> *ritual.*

Go to the candle in the East, light it and recite:

> *Duamutef, Son of Horus, Element of Air*
> *God of the East, look with favour upon this solemn*
> *ritual.*

Go to the candle in the North, light it and recite:

> *Hapi, Son of Horus, Element of Earth*
> *God of the North, look with favour upon this solemn*
> *ritual.*

Proceed to the altar and face it. Light the incense, breathe deeply and take a few moments before continuing with the ritual.

Light the gold candle and recite:

> *O Great Osiris*
> *God, Father, Magician*
> *I invite You to witness this solemn ritual.*

Light the silver candle and recite:

> *O Great Isis*
> *Goddess, Mother, Enchantress*
> *I invite You to witness this solemn ritual.*

Light the black candle and recite:

> *May this candle serve as a symbol*
> *Of the end of my life with (name of person).*

Take the black candle and use it to light the coloured candle representing your former partner. Recite:

> *And may this candle serve as a symbol*
> *Of his new life parted from me*
> *Without bitterness or despair*
> *With hope and healing for that which lies ahead.*

Next take the black candle and use it to light the coloured candle representing you. Recite:

> *And may this candle serve as a symbol*
> *Of my new life parted from him*
> *Without bitterness or despair*
> *With hope and healing for that which lies ahead.*

Face the altar and speak what is in your heart as if the person were there with you or you may speak the following:

> *I have loved you well*
> *I have loved no other*
> *I have honoured you*
> *I have respected you*
> *I have not harmed you intentionally*
> *I have not spoken ill of you*
> *But all cycles of life*
> *Come to an end*
> *Our life together*
> *Has come to its conclusion*
> *I wish you joy and love*
> *I wish you happiness and peace*
> *I wish you long life and health*
> *You may go, my beloved brother*
> *For I have loved you well.*

Place your offering to your former partner in front of the candle representing him and intone the following:

> *I give/return this to you*
> *As a token of my friendship*
> *May you find ahead*
> *That which you seek*
> *Search for your heart's desire*
> *And know that I shall always carry*

> *The memory of our life together*
> *With me forever and all Eternity*
> *Farewell to you, my beloved brother.*

Take up the athame in both hands, raise it high above your head, point facing up, and recite:

> *This is a sacred symbol*
> *Of the Great God, Osiris*
> *May He consecrate*
> *This most solemn rite.*

Lower the athame and place it back on the altar. Take the chalice in both hands, hold it high above your head and speak the following:

> *This is a sacred symbol*
> *Of the Great Goddess, Isis*
> *May She consecrate*
> *This most solemn rite.*

Lower the chalice to waist level, hold it in your non-dominant hand and pick up the athame in your dominant hand. Insert the tip of the athame into the wine in the chalice as you recite:

> *This wine is blessed*
> *By the God and Goddess*
> *I thank You for Your gift*
> *And my new life to come.*

Remove the athame from the chalice and place it on the altar. Drink some of the wine and leave the rest as an offering to the deities. Face the altar and recite:

> *You may go in peace, my brother*
> *I wish you health*
> *I wish you love*
> *I wish you no harm*
> *Our life together is finished*
> *You may go in peace, my brother.*

Blow out the candle flame that represents your former partner, then the candle flame that represents you and finally the black candle flame. Recite:

> *The life cycle is complete*
> *Our time together has ended*
> *Peace, joy and health to you.*

Face the silver candle and recite:

> *Thanks and praise to You, Isis*
> *Goddess, Mother, Enchantress*

With Your help and guidance
I begin my new life
Alone, yet never alone
For You are with me always.

Extinguish the silver candle flame with the candle snuffer. Face the gold candle and recite:

Thanks and praise to You, Osiris
God, Father, Magician
With Your help and guidance
I begin my new life
Alone, yet never alone
For You are with me always.

Extinguish the gold candle flame with the candle snuffer. Go to the white candle in the West and recite:

Qebhsennuf, Son of Horus
Element of Water, God of the West
I thank You for Your attendance
At this most solemn of rituals.

Extinguish the candle and go to the candle in the South. Recite:

Imsety, Son of Horus
Element of Fire, God of the South
I thank You for Your attendance
At this most solemn of rituals.

Extinguish the candle and go to the candle in the East. Recite:

Duamutef, Son of Horus
Element of Air, God of the East
I thank You for Your attendance
At this most solemn of rituals.

Extinguish the candle and go to the candle in the North. Recite:

Hapi, Son of Horus
Element of Earth, God of the North
I thank You for Your attendance
At this most solemn of rituals.

Extinguish the candle. The ritual is complete.

If your lover or spouse is deceased, you may wish to bury your offering with him or her or bring it to the grave site. This simple act may help you in the grieving process, for until you work through your grief, you will be unable to move forward. Your deceased partner may no longer be with you physically, but will always live on in your heart and soul. True love never dies, but it may be interrupted until you are reunited again in eternity. A word of note: in these circumstances, you may wish to omit the lines in the ritual that deal with health or replace the word with 'rest' or 'solace'.

Parting of souls ritual (for two)

Both parties go to the candle in the West. One lights the candle and both recite in unison:

> Qebhsennuf, Son of Horus, Element of Water
> God of the West, look with favour upon this solemn
> ritual.

Go to the candle in the South. Again one person lights it and both recite in unison:

> Imsety, Son of Horus, Element of Fire
> God of the South, look with favour upon this solemn
> ritual.

Go to the candle in the East. One person lights it and both recite in unison:

> Duamutef, Son of Horus, Element of Air
> God of the East, look with favour upon this solemn
> ritual.

Go to the candle in the North. One person lights it and both recite in unison:

> Hapi, Son of Horus, Element of Earth
> God of the North, look with favour upon this solemn
> ritual.

Proceed to the altar and face it, with the man on the right and the woman on the left. One person lights the incense. Both now take a few moments before continuing with the ritual.

The man lights the gold candle and recites:

> O Great Osiris
> God, Father, Magician
> I invite You to witness this solemn ritual.

The woman lights the silver candle and recites:

> O Great Isis
> Goddess, Mother, Enchantress
> I invite You to witness this solemn ritual.

Each partner strikes a match and they light the black candle together. They recite in unison:

> May this candle serve as a symbol
> Of the end of our lives together.

The man takes the black candle and uses it to light his coloured candle.
He recites:

> *And may this candle serve as a symbol*
> *Of my new life parted from you*
> *Without bitterness or despair*
> *With hope and healing for that which lies ahead.*

The woman takes the black candle from the man and uses it to light her
coloured candle. She recites:

> *And may this candle serve as a symbol*
> *Of my new life parted from you*
> *Without bitterness or despair*
> *With hope and healing for that which lies ahead.*

The man and woman then face each other and speak what is in their
hearts or they may recite the following, with the man speaking first:

> *I have loved you well*
> *I have loved no other*
> *I have honoured you*
> *I have respected you*
> *I have not harmed you intentionally*
> *I have not spoken ill of you*
> *But all cycles of life*
> *Come to an end*
> *Our life together*
> *Has come to its conclusion*
> *I wish you joy and love*
> *I wish you happiness and peace*
> *I wish you long life and health*
> *You may go, my beloved sister/brother*
> *For I have loved you well.*

The man hands his offering to the woman and recites:

> *I give/return this to you*
> *As a token of my friendship*
> *May you find ahead*
> *That which you seek*
> *Search for your heart's desire*
> *And know that I shall always carry*
> *The memory of our life together*
> *With me forever and all Eternity*
> *Farewell to you, my beloved sister*

The woman hands her offering to the man and recites:

> *I give/return this to you*
> *As a token of my friendship*
> *May you find ahead*
> *That which you seek*
> *Search for your heart's desire*
> *And know that I shall always carry*
> *The memory of our life together*
> *With me forever and all Eternity*
> *Farewell to you, my beloved brother.*

Both parties turn and face the altar. The man takes up the athame in both hands and holds it high above his head, point facing up. He recites:

> *This is a sacred symbol*
> *Of the Great God, Osiris*
> *May He consecrate*
> *This most solemn rite.*

He lowers the athame and holds it point facing down. The woman takes up the chalice in both hands and lifts it high above her head. She recites:

> *This is a sacred symbol*
> *Of the Great Goddess, Isis*
> *May She consecrate*
> *This most solemn rite.*

The woman lowers the chalice to waist level as the man raises up the athame and inserts the tip into the wine in the chalice. Both recite in unison:

> *This wine is blessed*
> *By the God and Goddess*
> *We thank You for Your gift*
> *And our new lives to come.*

The man removes the athame from the chalice and places it on the altar. He takes the chalice from the woman and drinks some of the wine. The woman takes the chalice back and she, too, drinks some of the wine, leaving some in the chalice as an offering to the deities.

The former lovers face each other and wish each other well once again, with words of their own or they may speak the following, with the man speaking first:

> *You may go in peace, my sister/brother*
> *I wish you health*
> *I wish you love*

> *I wish you no harm*
> *Our life together is finished*
> *You may go in peace, my sister/brother.*

After he has spoken, the man picks up the coloured candle that represents him, blows out the flame and places it back on the altar. After the woman has spoken her own words or recited as above, she picks up the coloured candle that represents her, blows out the candle flame and places it back on the altar. Both then lean over the altar, blow out the flame of the black candle and recite in unison:

> *The life cycle is complete*
> *Our time together has ended*
> *Peace, joy and health to you.*

The woman faces the silver candle and recites:

> *Thanks and praise to You, Isis*
> *Goddess, Mother, Enchantress*
> *With Your help and guidance*
> *I begin my new life*
> *Alone, yet never alone*
> *For You are with me always.*

She extinguishes the silver candle with the candle snuffer, places the snuffer on the altar and turns her back on the man. He faces the gold candle and recites:

> *Thanks and praise to You, Osiris*
> *God, Father, Magician*
> *With Your help and guidance*
> *I begin my new life*
> *Alone, yet never alone*
> *For You are with me always.*

He extinguishes the gold candle with the candle snuffer, places the snuffer on the altar and turn his back on the woman. After a few moments, both walk to the white candle in the West and recite in unison:

> *Qebhsennuf, Son of Horus*
> *Element of Water, God of the West*
> *We thank You for Your attendance*
> *At this most solemn of rituals.*

The woman extinguishes the candle and both proceed to the candle in the South. They recite in unison:

> *Imsety, Son of Horus*
> *Element of Fire, God of the South*

We thank You for Your attendance
At this most solemn of rituals.

The man extinguishes the candle and both proceed to the candle in the East. They recite in unison:

Duamutef, Son of Horus
Element of Air, God of the East
We thank You for Your attendance
At this most solemn of rituals.

The woman extinguishes the candle and both proceed to the candle in the North. They recite in unison:

Hapi, Son of Horus
Element of Earth, God of the North
We thank You for Your attendance
At this most solemn of rituals.

The man extinguishes the candle.

The ritual is now complete. Try not to dwell on any bad feelings or unresolved issues. Now is the time to move on and begin a new life with the help and guidance of the deities.

Oils to ease heartache

Banishing oil
5 ml/1 tsp hemp seed oil
2 drops cypress oil
3 drops rue oil
3 drops sandalwood oil

Parting of Souls oil
2.5 ml/½ tsp olive oil
1 drop frankincense oil
2 drops marigold oil
2 drops myrrh oil

CHAPTER 14

Egyptian Handfasting Ritual

Although marriage was an important part of life in Ancient Egypt, no formal marriage ceremony appears to have existed. Marriages could be arranged by parents, and were often used to solidify treaties and end political disputes, but there is also plenty of evidence that many were based on genuine love and affection between the two parties. Even though love was seen as an illness that could render the 'victim' helpless, monogamy was the norm for the average Ancient Egyptian. Most pharaohs, however, had a primary wife, lesser wives and concubines – rank does appear to have had its privileges. Incestuous marriage among the pharaohs seems to have been commonplace, primarily to keep the Egyptian bloodline pure from outsiders or foreigners.

Many love songs and poems from the New Kingdom speak of young women joining their lovers in their beds prior to marriage, suggesting that sex among consenting adults was an acceptable part of Egyptian life. Women, for the most part, were just as capable as men in matters of owning property, signing contracts and filing for divorce (there are records of divorce proceedings and settlements from that time). Women in Ancient Egypt seem to have enjoyed many of the freedoms we have today. But some things don't change: it was acceptable for married men to consort with prostitutes, but for a married woman to commit adultery the punishment was death, since it called into question the parentage of any children. A rather harsh double standard, don't you think?

Traditional Wiccans and Pagans often celebrate the joining of two persons with a Handfasting ceremony. A Handfasting may be performed by the High Priest/Priestess of a coven: solitary practitioners may celebrate a Handfasting with only their partner or close friends and family present. The Handfasting may be for a specific period of time, such as a year and a day, or for as long as the two partners agree upon. The choice of solidifying your relationship with a Handfasting rests with you and your partner. Please note, though, that Handfasting is not a 'legal' ceremony; check the laws where you reside if legality is important to you. You can always choose to incorporate your Handfasting with a civil ceremony.

Many people choose not to wed for various reasons and same-sex marriages are recognised in only a few countries. Handfasting could give you and your partner a chance to formalise your relationship by planning the celebration that suits you and the life you wish to share together. I am not here to advise you for or against marriage. I was married at a young age and was divorced within two years. I have also been fortunate enough to enjoy a loving relationship, without the benefit of legality, for thirteen years. Marriage is not a piece of paper or a ceremony to please your family, but a commitment to one another.

The following is how an Ancient Egyptian marriage ceremony might have been performed. Although written for a man and woman, it may be adapted for same-sex couples as well. The general ritual is for the couple and their families and friends: the private ritual is intended for the two parties only. Be advised that some of the material in the private ritual is sexually explicit. It is not meant to be lewd, indecent or obscene, but a true expression of love, friendship and commitment between two kindred souls who have pledged their devotion to one another.

You will notice that during the private version of the ceremony and those parts of the general version away from the guests, the handfasting couple address themselves and each other by their magickal names.

You should be aware that during the ritual the couple will drink from the chalice. They can choose to add drops of their blood to the liquid but, because of the risk of blood-borne diseases, they may prefer to omit this from the ritual. Instead, each partner just stirs the wine with a cinnamon stick.

Preparing the potions for a ritual joining of souls

Preparation for the ritual is almost as important as the ritual itself. Both of you need to share responsibility in the mixing of the potions so that they will be infused with the loving energy of you and your spouse. One of you should add ingredients while the other mixes them, and then you switch jobs. The following recipes should be prepared on the evening following the New Moon. For the powder and incense, grind all the ingredients using a pestle and mortar and mix well. Place each mixture in its own labelled airtight container and set them aside. Combine the ingredients for each of the oils and place them in labelled light-blocking glass bottles (see page 90).

Once the ritual oils, powder and incense have been prepared, place them all in their containers on a windowsill where they can absorb the moonlight for several hours. Then store them in a cool, dry, dark place during the day and shake them each evening before placing them on the windowsill again for several hours to absorb the moonlight. On the night before the next Full Moon, place all the containers on the windowsill right after sunset and leave them in the moonlight until just before midnight, then store them away and leave them undisturbed until the ritual.

Making a nemyss

The item of ritual clothing to be worn by the man, a nemyss, is a traditional Ancient Egyptian head covering. The nemyss is quite often seen in tomb paintings as a piece of cloth of blue and gold stripes; present-day colour choice is entirely up to the parties involved, but I have always been partial to gold, or white and gold, as these colours represent the God and male energy.

A nemyss is fairly easy to make and should be created during the two-week period between the New Moon and the Full Moon. The material is cut in the shape of a truncated pyramid. The top is the narrow edge and the bottom the wide. The distance from the top to the bottom should be about 35 cm/14 in – more if you like.

Measure across the man's forehead and slightly down towards the nape of his neck. The 'top' should be 5 cm/2 in larger than the head measurement. From each end of the top, cut at about a 45° angle to the bottom. Make a 2 cm/¾ in hem all the way around. Sew a good length of ribbon or bias tape to each side of the top to make ties.

To wear, place the top of the nemyss against your forehead, bring the ties around to the back under the rest of the nemyss, then tie.

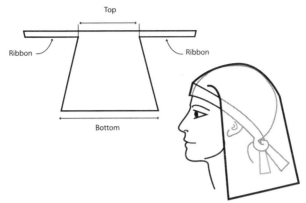

Illustration reprinted, with permission of the publisher, from Reed, Ellen Cannon, *Circle of Isis,* 2002. Published by New Page Books, a division of Career Press, Franklin Lakes, NJ. All rights reserved.

Preparation for the ritual joining of souls (general)

The headscarf for the woman can be in any colour, but white and silver is a good choice. The man, of course, will be wearing his nemyss. Other garments can be those you use for spellwork, or ones chosen especially for this ritual.

Items needed
A gold pillar candle, to represent the gods Osiris, Horus of Edfu and Min
A silver pillar candle, to represent the goddesses Isis, Hathor and Bast
A red pillar candle, to represent the man
A pink pillar candle, to represent the woman
A green pillar candle, to represent both partners
4 white pillar candles, to represent the Directions
4 canopic jars (optional)
A large candle holder or plate
Spring water in a small bowl

Sea salt in a small dish
A chalice of wine or fruit juice
An athame or wand
Joining of Souls incense (see page 228)
A charcoal disc
A censor
A nail
A sewing needle or pin
Matches
A candle snuffer
Joining of Souls oil (see page 228)
Passion powder (see page 228)
Gold, silver, red and green glitter
Roses: one each in white, yellow, pink and red (more if desired)
2 cinnamon sticks
A slice of wholewheat bread
Refreshments for the guests
Rings or appropriate jewellery to exchange
Music
Ritual clothing
A headscarf for the woman
A nemyss for the man
Sexual Magick massage oil (see page 229)

Set up a ritual space in a large room or outside, depending on the weather and time of year and the number of guests you have invited to bear witness to your declaration of love and devotion for one another.

The man takes the nail and uses it to inscribe the red candle with his given (legal) name, then anoints it, wick to base, with Joining of Souls oil. The woman then does the same with the pink candle. After this, both inscribe their given or magickal names on the green candle and both should anoint it, wick to base, with the oil. They may also place a few drops of oil on the top of the gold and silver candles.

They place the gold candle on the altar or table on the right side and the silver candle on the left. They position the dish of sea salt in front of the gold candle and the bowl of spring water in front of the silver. Next, they place the athame next to the sea salt and the chalice next to the water bowl. The two cinnamon sticks and the slice of bread should be situated next to the chalice. The censor containing the charcoal disc is placed between the gold and silver candles. Then place the anointed red and pink candles side by side, red on the right and pink on the left, on the candle holder or plate. The green candle is positioned in front of the red and pink candles. The candle holder or plate is set in the centre of the altar. They place the rings or jewellery and the sewing needle on the altar in front of the group of three candles. Finally the couple lay one rose at each corner of the altar.

Starting in the North and moving clockwise, the couple use the four white candles and canopic jars, if they are using them, to designate the compass points and define their ritual space. They may, if they wish, place a few drops of Joining of Souls oil on the top of each of the white candles. They may also add incense to the censor at any time during the ritual so they should ensure that those items, and the glitter, candle snuffer and Passion powder, are within the ritual space.

The refreshments table for your guests can be set up outside the perimeter of the ritual space. The Sexual Magick massage oil should be placed in the room where the couple will be enjoying their sexual encounter after all the guests have departed.

The next step is the ritual shower or bath, which the couple may do separately or together – though they should refrain from intercourse. They should place a muslin bag of sea salt on the shower head or in the bath water, shampoo and wash thoroughly with unscented soap, then towel dry and use no lotions or perfumes. (They will be using the Sexual Magick massage oil after the ceremony and any other products may have conflicting scents.) Both parties apply make-up in the Ancient Egyptian style and any ritual jewellery of choice may be worn. They then dress in the clothing chosen for the ritual. The headscarf is placed on the woman's head and wrapped in such a way that her head and face are entirely covered, with only her eyes unveiled. If the woman wishes to wear her Egyptian headdress as well, this should be placed on the head first and the headscarf placed on top and wrapped as above. Finally, the nemyss is placed on the man's head.

The couple and guests proceed to the ritual area. Only the two persons sharing the ritual occupy the sacred space; all invited guests stand outside the perimeter designated by the white candles. It's a good idea to have a guest in charge of the music, or to have a CD carousel player loaded with the music.

All preparations are now complete and the ritual can begin.

Ritual for joining of souls (general)

The ritual should begin at sunset on the night of the Full Moon or during the Waxing Moon and as close to the Full Moon as possible.

Start the music. One partner takes the Passion powder and, in a clockwise direction, sprinkles a circle on the altar and around the group of three candles, the rings and the needle. The other partner takes the glitter and sprinkles a small amount of each colour, also in a clockwise direction, on the Passion powder circle.

Both partners go to the white candle in the North, light it and recite in unison:

>*We call upon Hapi, Son of Horus, Element of Earth*
>*God of the North, look with favour upon this ritual.*

They go to the candle in the East, light it and recite in unison:

>*We call upon Duamutef, Son of Horus, Element of Air*
>*God of the East, look with favour upon this ritual.*

They go to the candle in the South, light it and recite in unison:

>*We call upon Imsety, Son of Horus, Element of Fire*
>*God of the South, look with favour upon this ritual.*

Finally, they go to the candle in the West, light it and recite in unison:

>*We call upon Qebhsennuf, Son of Horus, Element of*
>*Water*
>*God of the West, look with favour upon this ritual.*

Both partners go to the altar and stand in front of it, the man on the right, the woman on the left. Either one lights the charcoal in the censor and sprinkles some incense on the disc after it stops sparking. They should take a few moments to relax and breathe deeply before entering the next stage of the ritual.

The man lights the gold candle and recites:

>*I call upon the Mighty Ones*
>*Osiris, Horus of Edfu, Min*
>*Hear Your loyal disciple*
>*Known in the mundane world as (legal name)*

> Look with favour upon my union
> With Your devoted servant
> Known to those present as (legal name).

The woman lights the silver candle and recites:

> I call upon the Great Ladies
> Isis, Hathor, Bast
> Hear Your devoted handmaiden
> Known in the mundane world as (legal name)
> Look with favour upon my union
> With Your faithful servant
> Known to those present as (legal name).

The man lights the red candle and, with the partners facing each other, he recites:

> Today, a day unlike any other
> I represent the Great Osiris
> My love for you is undying
> And shall survive throughout Eternity
> Today, a day unlike any other
> I represent the God Horus of Edfu
> My joining with you shall be
> A time of festivity and celebration
> Today, a day unlike any other
> I represent the Fruitful Min
> My pleasure shall be your pleasure
> And I shall revel in our passion.

The woman faces the altar, lights the pink candle and turns back to face her partner. She recites:

> Today, a day unlike any other
> I represent the Great Isis
> My love for you is undying
> And shall survive throughout Eternity
> Today, a day unlike any other
> I represent the Goddess Hathor
> My joining with you shall be
> A time of festivity and celebration
> Today, a day unlike any other
> I represent the Joyous Bast
> My pleasure shall be your pleasure
> And I shall revel in our passion.

The man and woman turn to face the altar and, using the red and pink candles, both light the green candle and recite in unison:

Joined together, forever and all Eternity
Our light shall shine throughout the ages
May our love never waiver
May our passion never fade.

They place the candles back on the altar in their places. With the needle, the man gently pricks his finger to draw blood. The woman holds the chalice and the man adds one or two drops of his blood to the wine. The woman stirs the wine with one of the cinnamon sticks, then hands the chalice to the man. She then takes the needle and gently pricks her finger to draw blood. She places the needle back on the altar, then adds one or two drops of her blood to the wine. The man stirs the wine with the other cinnamon stick. He hands the chalice back to the woman and picks up the athame. Holding the athame, point up, high above his head with both hands, he recites:

I invoke the Mighty Ones
Osiris, Horus of Edfu, Min
Consecrate this athame
For it represents the Fertile God.

The man lowers the athame and holds it point down. The woman raises the chalice high above her head with both hands and recites:

I invoke the Great Ladies
Isis, Hathor, Bast
Consecrate this wine
For it represents the Fertile Goddess.

The woman lowers the chalice to waist level. The partners face each other and the man raises up the athame and inserts the tip into the wine. Both recite in unison:

Joined together, God and Goddess
Man and woman
May this joining of our bodies and souls
Be fruitful and joyous
And may we always serve You
And praise You for all Eternity.

The man removes the athame from the wine and places it on the altar. He then takes the chalice, drinks some of the wine and recites:

Our lives are forever intertwined
You have nourished me with your body
And I shall cherish you
Throughout the ages.

He hands the chalice to the woman. She also drinks some of the wine and then recites:

> *Our lives are forever intertwined*
> *You have nourished me with your body*
> *And I shall honour you*
> *Throughout the ages.*

The woman places the chalice on the altar and takes up the slice of bread. She breaks it in half and hands one half to her partner. He dips it in the consecrated wine and recites:

> *Food of the God*
> *Nourish my body and soul*
> *Provide me with strength and fortitude*
> *For our blessed union to flourish.*

He bites off the wine-dipped portion of bread and eats it. The woman dips her half in the consecrated wine and recites:

> *Food of the Goddess*
> *Nourish my body and soul*
> *Provide me with compassion and wisdom*
> *For our blessed union to flourish.*

She bites off the wine-dipped portion of the bread and eats it. The remaining bread is placed back on the altar, next to the chalice.

The man takes up the ring or other article of jewellery to be exchanged. He places it in the sea salt and recites:

> *Hapi, bless this (name of item) with the Element of*
> *Earth.*

He passes it through the incense smoke and recites:

> *Duamutef, bless this (name of item) with the Element of*
> *Air.*

He passes it carefully over the flame of the gold candle and recites:

> *Imsety, bless this (name of item) with the Element of Fire.*

Finally, he dips it in the water and recites:

> *Qebhsennuf, bless this (name of item) with the Element*
> *of Water.*

The partners face each other and the man places the ring on the woman's finger (or hands her the article of jewellery). He recites:

> *I give this to you as a symbol of my devotion*
> *To you and to the Ancient Ones*
> *May I always provide you with*
> *Friendship, strength, shelter, passion and love.*

The woman takes up the other ring or other article of jewellery. She places it in the sea salt and recites:

> Hapi, bless this (name of item) with the Element of
> Earth.

She passes it through the incense smoke and recites:

> Duamutef, bless this (name of item) with the Element of
> Air.

She passes it carefully over the flame of the silver candle and recites:

> Imsety, bless this (name of item) with the Element of Fire.

Finally, she dips it in the water and recites:

> Qebhsennuf, bless this (name of item) with the Element
> of Water.

The partners face each other and the woman places the ring on the man's finger (or hands him the article of jewellery). She recites:

> I give this to you as a symbol of my devotion
> To you and to the Ancient Ones
> May I always provide you with
> Friendship, strength, shelter, passion and love.

The partners then express their love for each other, either using their own words or by reciting the following, with the man speaking first followed by the woman:

> You are my life and breath
> Your eyes are the Sun and Moon
> Your body is my sustenance
> You are my greatest joy
> Your embrace is my comfort
> Your passion fuels my desire
> I wish to remain with you forever
> One body, one heart, one soul.

It is now time to complete the formal part of the ritual. The man removes his nemyss, faces the woman and recites:

> Come, my sister
> Gaze upon the face of your beloved
> My eyes shine as the sun
> Gaze upon my body
> It is a temple for your worship
> Come, my sister
> Let me hold you in my embrace
> And feel the passion in my soul
> My strength shall protect you from harm

> *My body shall be your shield and shelter*
> *Come, my sister*
> *Join with me, your cherished brother*
> *One heart, one soul, one body*
> *May our union be fruitful*
> *And may our love endure for all the ages.*

The woman removes her headscarf, faces the man and recites:

> *Come, my brother*
> *Gaze upon the face of your beloved*
> *My eyes shine as the sun*
> *Gaze upon my body*
> *It is a temple for your worship*
> *Come, my brother*
> *Let me hold you in my embrace*
> *And feel the passion in my soul*
> *I shall be your partner in life*
> *Your comfort, your sustenance*
> *Come, my brother*
> *Join with me, your cherished sister*
> *One heart, one soul, one body*
> *May our union be fruitful*
> *And may our love endure for all the ages.*

Both turn to face the altar and, using the candle snuffer, extinguish the green, pink and red candles in that order. The woman faces the silver candle and recites:

> *Isis, Hathor, Bast*
> *Praise to You, Great Ladies*
> *For gracing us with Your presence*
> *At this most blessed rite*
> *May our life together*
> *Be a celebration to You.*

The woman extinguishes the silver candle and hands the candle snuffer to the man. The man faces the gold candle and recites:

> *Osiris, Horus of Edfu, Min*
> *Praise to You, Mighty Ones*
> *For gracing us with Your presence*
> *At this most blessed rite*
> *May our life together*
> *Be a celebration to You.*

The man extinguishes the gold candle and puts the snuffer down. Both partners go to the candle in the West and recite in unison:

> We thank You, Qebhsennuf, Son of Horus, Element of Water
> God of the West, for Your attendance at this blessed rite.

The woman extinguishes the candle and picks it up. They go to the candle in the South and recite in unison:

> We thank You, Imsety, Son of Horus, Element of Fire
> God of the South, for Your attendance at this blessed rite.

The man extinguishes the candle and picks it up. They go to the candle in the East and recite in unison:

> We thank You, Duamutef, Son of Horus, Element of Air
> God of the East, for Your attendance at this blessed rite.

The woman extinguishes the candle and picks it up. Finally, they go to the candle in the North and recite in unison:

> We thank You, Hapi, Son of Horus, Element of Earth
> God of the North, for Your attendance at this blessed rite.

The man extinguishes the candle and picks it up. All four are placed on the altar according to their directional correspondence.

The altar, along with the candle snuffer, Passion powder and Joining of Souls incense, should be carefully moved to the room where sexual intercourse will take place when the couple are alone. (Or it can be moved to another safe location where the items will be undisturbed during the celebration.) The couple then celebrates with family and friends.

When all the guests have departed, the couple may complete the ritual. They prepare the room for their sacred act of intercourse by sprinkling Passion powder on the bed or floor and placing the white candles in the room to designate the compass points. If they feel they might need food items, the food table should be prepared next to the area where intercourse will take place.

The couple relight the incense and all the candles in the order they lit them for the ceremony. The man faces the gold candle and recites:

> I call upon the Mighty Ones
> Osiris, Horus of Edfu, Min
> To witness this sacred act
> As I join with my beloved sister, (magickal name)
> One body, one heart, one soul
> Forever and all Eternity.

The woman faces the silver candle and recites:

> *I call upon the Great Ladies*
> *Isis, Hathor, Bast*
> *To witness this sacred act*
> *As I join with my beloved brother, (magickal name)*
> *One body, one heart, one soul*
> *Forever and all Eternity.*

The man and woman face each other and slowly undress until completely naked. They should really look at their partner, for they have pledged their lives to each other. They can gently stroke each other's cheeks and lightly kiss each other's fingertips. Each should lovingly explore each other's body while the passion mounts. Using the Sexual Magick massage oil will increase their enjoyment and pleasure. If they have food they might wish to use some chocolate sauce or honey on any portion of each other's body for their mutual enjoyment. As they embrace each other tightly and kiss deeply, the passion will build to a fever pitch – but they should slow down a bit. The exploration of each other should last as long as possible.

When they are ready to join for the sacred act of intercourse, they should both silently offer their ultimate expression of love and intimacy as a gift to the deities. Ideally both partners will orgasm, perhaps even at the same moment. They can revel in the release of their passion, lust and desire. When the sexual act is complete, both silently thank the deities for their blessing upon them. The sacred rite has been consummated. If they wish to enjoy the sacred sexual act again, they should leave all candles lit.

When they are ready to retire for the evening, they should extinguish the green, pink and red candles first. Then the woman extinguishes the silver candle with the candle snuffer and recites:

> *Thank You, Great Ladies*
> *Isis, Hathor, Bast*
> *For blessing this sacred act*
> *And bearing witness to our joining*
> *Our love and devotion shall be*
> *A celebration to You and to all the deities.*

The woman hands the candle snuffer to the man. He extinguishes the gold candle and recites:

> *Thank You, Mighty Ones*
> *Osiris, Horus of Edfu, Min*
> *For blessing this sacred act*

And bearing witness to our joining
Our love and devotion shall be
A celebration to You and to all the deities.

Both go to the candle in the West. One partner extinguishes it and both recite in unison:

We thank You, Qebhsennuf, Son of Horus, Element of Water
God of the West, for bearing witness to this sacred act.

Both go to the candle in the South. One partner extinguishes it and both recite in unison:

We thank You, Imsety, Son of Horus, Element of Fire
God of the South, for bearing witness to this sacred act.

Both go to the candle in the East. One partner extinguishes it and both recite in unison:

We thank You, Duamutef, Son of Horus, Element of Air
God of the East, for bearing witness to this sacred act.

Finally, both go to the candle in the North. One partner extinguishes it and both recite in unison:

We thank You, Hapi, Son of Horus, Element of Earth
God of the North, for bearing witness to this sacred act.

They may feel the desire to shower together and then hold each other until they drift off to sleep. It is perfectly acceptable to leave everything where it is and clear up in the morning. However, no candles should be left to burn themselves out while they are both sleeping so they must ensure all are extinguished.

Preparation for the ritual joining of souls (private)

The headscarf for the woman can be in any colour, but white and silver is a good choice. The man, of course, will be wearing his nemyss. Other garments can be those you use for spellwork, or ones chosen especially for this ritual. The refreshments I have listed are just my suggestions – this is a private ritual and you have only to please yourselves.

Items needed

A gold pillar candle, to represent the gods Osiris, Horus of Edfu and Min

A silver pillar candle, to represent the goddesses Isis, Hathor and Bast

A red pillar candle, to represent the man

A pink pillar candle, to represent the woman
A green pillar candle, to represent both partners
4 white pillar candles, to represent the Directions
4 canopic jars (optional)
A large candle holder or plate
Spring water in a small bowl
Sea salt in a small dish
A chalice of wine or fruit juice
An athame or wand
Joining of Souls incense (see page 228)
A charcoal disc
A censor
A nail
A sewing needle or pin
Matches
A candle snuffer
Joining of Souls oil (see page 228)
Passion powder (see page 228)
Sexual Magick massage oil (see page 229)
Gold, silver, red and green glitter
Roses: one each in white, yellow, pink and red (more if desired)
2 cinnamon sticks
A slice of wholewheat bread
Refreshments: Fresh fruit: apples, bananas, cherries, grapes, oranges,
peaches, pears, pomegranates, strawberries. Fresh mint leaves. Honey.
Chocolate sauce in a warming dish. Slices or cubes of cheese. Wine,
apple juice, grape juice, water. Unshelled nuts: almonds, brazils,
cashews, walnuts.
Napkins
Rings or appropriate jewellery to exchange
Music
Ritual clothing
A headscarf for the woman
A nemyss for the man

The ritual space can be set up in the bedroom, living room or any other
room liked. Since the ritual will culminate in sexual intercourse, the
room should be comfortable and warm and allow complete privacy.

Using the nail, the man inscribes the red candle with his given (legal)
name and his magickal name. He then anoints it, wick to base, with

Joining of Souls oil. The woman then does the same with the pink candle. Next, both inscribe their magickal names only on the green candle and both anoint it, wick to base, with the oil. They may also wish to place a few drops of oil on the top of the gold and silver candles.

The man places the gold candle on the altar or table on the right side and the woman places the silver candle on the left of the altar. They position the dish of sea salt in front of the gold candle and the bowl of spring water in front of the silver. The athame is placed in front of the sea salt and the chalice in front of the water bowl. The two cinnamon sticks and the slice of bread should be situated next to the chalice. The censor containing the charcoal disc is placed between the gold and silver candles. They place the anointed red and pink candles side by side, red on the right and pink on the left, on the candle holder or plate. The green candle is positioned in front of the red and pink candles. The candle holder or plate is set in the centre of the altar. The couple lay one rose at each corner of the altar. Finally, they place the rings or jewellery and the sewing needle on the altar in front of the group of three candles.

All the food items are placed on a separate table, along with the matches, napkins, Joining of Souls incense, Passion powder, Sexual Magick massage oil and glitter. If they have chosen music for the entire ritual, they should try to have a carousel CD player already stacked so they don't have to interrupt the ritual to change the music.

Starting in the North and moving clockwise, the couple use the four white candles and canopic jars, if they are using them, to designate the compass points and define their ritual space. They may, if they wish, place a few drops of Joining of Souls oil on the top of each of the white candles. They may also add incense to the censor at any time during the ritual so they should ensure that it is handy.

The next step is the ritual shower or bath, which the couple may do separately or together – though they should refrain from intercourse. They should place a muslin bag of sea salt on the shower head or in the bath water, shampoo and wash thoroughly with unscented soap, then towel dry and use no lotions or perfumes. (They will be using the Sexual Magick massage oil after the ceremony and any other products may have conflicting scents.) Both parties apply make-up in the Ancient Egyptian style and any ritual jewellery of choice may be worn. They then dress in the clothing chosen for the ritual. The headscarf is placed on the woman's head and wrapped in such a way that her head and face are entirely covered, with only her eyes unveiled. If the woman wishes to wear her Egyptian headdress as well, this should be placed on the head first and the headscarf placed on top and wrapped as above. Finally, the nemyss is placed on the man's head.

All preparations are now complete and the ritual can begin.

Ritual for joining of souls (private)

The ritual should begin at sunset on the night of the Full Moon or during the Waxing Moon and as close to the Full Moon as possible.

Start the music. One partner takes the Passion powder and, in a clockwise direction, sprinkles a circle on the altar and around the group of three candles, the rings and the needle. The other partner takes the glitter and sprinkles a small amount of each colour, also in a clockwise direction, on the Passion powder circle.

Both partners go to the white candle in the North, light it and recite in unison:

>*We call upon Hapi, Son of Horus, Element of Earth*
>*God of the North, look with favour upon this ritual.*

They go to the candle in the East, light it and recite in unison:

>*We call upon Duamutef, Son of Horus, Element of Air*
>*God of the East, look with favour upon this ritual.*

They go to the candle in the South, light it and recite in unison:

>*We call upon Imsety, Son of Horus, Element of Fire*
>*God of the South, look with favour upon this ritual.*

Finally, they go to the candle in the West, light it and recite in unison:

>*We call upon Qebhsennuf, Son of Horus, Element of*
>*Water*
>*God of the West, look with favour upon this ritual.*

Both partners go to the altar and stand in front of it, the man on the right, the woman on the left. Either one lights the charcoal in the censor and sprinkles some incense on the disc after it stops sparking. They should take a few moments to relax and breathe deeply before entering the next stage of the ritual.

The man lights the gold candle and recites:

>*I call upon the Mighty Ones*
>*Osiris, Horus of Edfu, Min*
>*Hear Your loyal disciple, (magickal name)*
>*Look with favour upon my union*
>*With Your devoted servant, (magickal name).*

The woman lights the silver candle and recites:

> *I call upon the Great Ladies*
> *Isis, Hathor, Bast*
> *Hear Your devoted handmaiden, (magickal name)*
> *Look with favour upon my union*
> *With Your faithful servant, (magickal name).*

The man lights the red candle and, with the partners facing each other, he recites:

> *Today, a day unlike any other*
> *I represent the Great Osiris*
> *My love for you is undying*
> *And shall survive throughout Eternity*
> *Today, a day unlike any other*
> *I represent the God Horus of Edfu*
> *My joining with you shall be*
> *A time of festivity and celebration*
> *Today, a day unlike any other*
> *I represent the Fruitful Min*
> *My pleasure shall be your pleasure*
> *And I shall revel in our passion.*

The woman faces the altar, lights the pink candle and turns back to face her partner. She recites:

> *Today, a day unlike any other*
> *I represent the Great Isis*
> *My love for you is undying*
> *And shall survive throughout Eternity*
> *Today, a day unlike any other*
> *I represent the Goddess Hathor*
> *My joining with you shall be*
> *A time of festivity and celebration*
> *Today, a day unlike any other*
> *I represent the Joyous Bast*
> *My pleasure shall be your pleasure*
> *And I shall revel in our passion.*

The man and woman turn to face the altar and, using the red and pink candles, both light the green candle and recite in unison:

> *Joined together, forever and all Eternity*
> *Our light shall shine throughout the ages*
> *May our love never waiver*
> *May our passion never fade.*

They place the candles back on the altar in their places. With the needle, the man gently pricks his finger to draw blood. The woman holds the chalice and the man adds one or two drops of his blood to the wine. The woman stirs the wine with one of the cinnamon sticks, then hands the chalice to the man. She then takes the needle and gently pricks her finger to draw blood. She places the needle back on the altar, then adds one or two drops of her blood to the wine. The man stirs the wine with the other cinnamon stick. He hands the chalice back to the woman and picks up the athame. Holding the athame, point up, high above his head with both hands, he recites:

> *I invoke the Mighty Ones*
> *Osiris, Horus of Edfu, Min*
> *Consecrate this athame*
> *For it represents the Fertile God.*

The man lowers the athame and holds it point down. The woman raises the chalice high above her head with both hands and recites:

> *I invoke the Great Ladies*
> *Isis, Hathor, Bast*
> *Consecrate this wine*
> *For it represents the Fertile Goddess.*

The woman lowers the chalice to waist level. The partners face each other and the man raises up the athame and inserts the tip into the wine. Both recite in unison:

> *Joined together, God and Goddess*
> *Man and woman*
> *May this joining of our bodies and souls*
> *Be fruitful and joyous*
> *And may we always serve You*
> *And praise You for all Eternity.*

The man removes the athame from the wine and places it on the altar. He then takes the chalice, drinks some of the wine and recites:

> *Our lives are forever intertwined*
> *You have nourished me with your body*
> *And I shall cherish you*
> *Throughout the ages.*

He hands the chalice to the woman. She also drinks some of the wine and then recites:

> *Our lives are forever intertwined*
> *You have nourished me with your body*
> *And I shall honour you*
> *Throughout the ages.*

The woman places the chalice on the altar and takes up the slice of bread. She breaks it in half and hands one half to her partner. He dips it in the consecrated wine and recites:

> Food of the God
> Nourish my body and soul
> Provide me with vigour and passion
> For the blessed union to come.

He bites off the wine-dipped portion of bread and eats it. The woman dips her half in the consecrated wine and recites:

> Food of the Goddess
> Nourish my body and soul
> Provide me with tenderness and passion
> For the blessed union to come.

She bites off the wine-dipped portion of the bread and eats it. The remaining bread is placed back on the altar, next to the chalice.

The man takes up the ring or other article of jewellery to be exchanged. He places it in the sea salt and recites:

> Hapi, bless this (name of item) with the Element of Earth.

He passes it through the incense smoke and recites:

> Duamutef, bless this (name of item) with the Element of Air.

He passes it carefully over the flame of the gold candle and recites:

> Imsety, bless this (name of item) with the Element of Fire.

Finally, he dips it in the water and recites:

> Qebhsennuf, bless this (name of item) with the Element of Water.

The partners face each other and the man places the ring on the woman's finger (or hands her the article of jewellery). He recites:

> I give this to you as a symbol of my devotion
> To you and to the Ancient Ones
> May I always provide you with
> Friendship, strength, shelter, passion and love.

The woman takes up the other ring or other article of jewellery. She places it in the sea salt and recites:

> Hapi, bless this (name of item) with the Element of Earth.

She passes it through the incense smoke and recites:

> Duamutef, bless this (name of item) with the Element of Air.

She passes it carefully over the flame of the silver candle and recites:

> Imsety, bless this (name of item) with the Element of Fire.

Finally, she dips it in the water and recites:

> Qebhsennuf, bless this (name of item) with the Element
> of Water.

The partners face each other and the woman places the ring on the man's finger (or hands him the article of jewellery). She recites:

> I give this to you as a symbol of my devotion
> To you and to the Ancient Ones
> May I always provide you with
> Friendship, strength, shelter, passion and love.

The partners then express their love for each other, either using their own words or by reciting the following, with the man speaking first followed by the woman:

> You are my life and breath
> Your eyes are the Sun and Moon
> Your body is my sustenance
> You are my greatest joy
> Your embrace is my comfort
> Your passion fuels my desire
> I wish to remain with you forever
> One body, one heart, one soul.

It is now time to complete the formal part of the ritual. The man removes his nemyss and ritual clothing. Completely naked, he faces the woman and recites:

> Come, my sister
> Gaze upon the face of your beloved
> My eyes shine as the sun
> Gaze upon my body
> It is a temple for your worship
> Come, my sister
> Let me hold you in my embrace
> And feel the passion in my soul
> My strength shall protect you from harm
> My body shall be your shield and shelter
> Come, my sister
> Join with me, your cherished brother
> One heart, one soul, one body
> I desire to plant my seed
> In the fertile plain of my sister.

The woman removes her headscarf and ritual clothing, including her headdress if she was wearing one. Completely naked, she faces the man and recites:

> Come, my brother
> Gaze upon the face of your beloved
> My eyes shine as the sun
> Gaze upon my body
> It is a temple for your worship
> Come, my brother
> Let me hold you in my embrace
> And feel the passion in my soul
> Suckle as a child to his mother
> And I shall quench your desire
> Come, my brother
> Join with me, your cherished sister
> One heart, one soul, one body
> Enter the gateway of my desire
> And fill me with your love.

The two must really look at each other – for they have each pledged their life to the other. The woman slowly raises her hands, palms facing the man, to shoulder height. The man slowly mimics what she has done so that their palms are facing each other. They move their hands closer and closer to each other without ever touching to feel the passion and energy passing between them. They should separate a little, pause for a few moments, then slowly walk towards each other, again without touching to enjoy the sensation of the building passion and heat.

The woman gently strokes the man's cheek, and he does the same to her. They lovingly explore each other with gentle stroking, using the Sexual Magick massage oil to let the desire build. They embrace each other tightly and kiss deeply, feeling the sensation and connection with the other person. They are forever one body, one heart, one soul. If either feels the passion is building too fast, they should slow down.

If they wish, they can feed each other some fruit or nuts dipped in chocolate or honey, or have some bread, cheese and wine. One or both partners can put some chocolate or honey on their fingers, or any other body part, for the their partner to enjoy. Food and intimacy is a very sensual combination and will add to sacred sexual pleasure. The exploration of each other should be prolonged for as long as possible.

When they are ready to join for the sacred act of intercourse, they should both silently offer their ultimate expression of love and intimacy as a gift to the deities. Ideally both partners will orgasm, perhaps even at the same moment. They can revel in the release of their passion, lust and desire. When the sexual act is complete, both silently thank the deities for their blessing upon them. The sacred rite has been consummated. If they wish to enjoy the sacred sexual act again, they should leave all candles lit.

When they are ready to retire for the evening, they should extinguish the green, pink and red candles first. Then the woman extinguishes the silver candle with the candle snuffer and recites:

> *Thank You, Great Ladies*
> *Isis, Hathor, Bast*
> *For blessing this sacred act*
> *And bearing witness to our joining*
> *Our love and devotion shall be*
> *A celebration to You and to all the deities.*

The woman hands the candle snuffer to the man. He extinguishes the gold candle and recites:

> *Thank You, Mighty Ones*
> *Osiris, Horus of Edfu, Min*
> *For blessing this sacred act*
> *And bearing witness to our joining*
> *Our love and devotion shall be*
> *A celebration to You and to all the deities.*

Both go to the candle in the West. One partner extinguishes it and both recite in unison:

> *We thank You, Qebhsennuf, Son of Horus, Element of Water*
> *God of the West, for bearing witness to this sacred act.*

Both go to the candle in the South. One partner extinguishes it and both recite in unison:

> *We thank You, Imsety, Son of Horus, Element of Fire*
> *God of the South, for bearing witness to this sacred act.*

Both go to the candle in the East. One partner extinguishes it and both recite in unison:

> *We thank You, Duamutef, Son of Horus, Element of Air*
> *God of the East, for bearing witness to this sacred act.*

Finally, both go to the candle in the North. One partner extinguishes it and both recite in unison:

> *We thank You, Hapi, Son of Horus, Element of Earth*
> *God of the North, for bearing witness to this sacred act.*

They may feel the desire to shower together and then hold each other until they drift off to sleep. It is perfectly acceptable to leave everything where it is and clear up in the morning. However, no candles should be left to burn themselves out while they are both sleeping so they must ensure all are extinguished.

Incense, oils and powders

Joining of Souls incense
1.5 ml/¼ tsp aloes wood powder
Pinch amber resin
2.5 ml/½ tsp benzoin resin powder
5 ml/1 tsp copal resin
2.5 ml/½ tsp dragon's blood resin
2 pinches gum arabic
Pinch sulphur powder
2 pinches wormwood powder
Mix well by shaking in a glass jar. After it has absorbed the Moon's energy for the time between the New Moon and the Full Moon, you may wish to grind it into a fine powder or use it as it is.

Joining of Souls oil
15 ml/1 tbsp hazelnut (filbert) oil
10 drops frangipani oil
8 drops lotus oil
6 drops rose oil
3 drops vanilla oil
11 drops violet oil
Add one gemstone of amber and one gemstone representing each partner's birthstone for extra intensity.

Passion powder
60 ml/4 tbsp talc
2.5 ml/½ tsp carob powder
5 ml/1 tsp ground cinnamon
1.5 ml/¼ tsp ground coriander (cilantro)
1.5 ml/¼ tsp ground damiana
2.5 ml/½ tsp ground ginger
1.5 ml/¼ tsp ginseng powder

1.5 ml/¼ tsp ground liquorice root
1.5 ml/¼ tsp ground lovage root
1.5 ml/¼ tsp ground mandrake
5 ml/1 tsp mistletoe powder
1.5 ml/¼ tsp ground patchouli
1.5 ml/¼ tsp pure vanilla powder
1.5 ml/¼ tsp ground sassafras
Pinch ground violet leaf
Mix well and place in a glass jar.

Sexual Magick massage oil
60 ml/¼ cup unscented massage oil
11 drops carnation oil
11 drops cinnamon oil
8 drops jasmine oil
8 drops orange oil
10 drops vetivert oil
Add one gemstone each of amber, aquamarine, emerald, garnet and topaz for extra intensity.

CHAPTER 15

Eternal Love

Strange as it may sound, death was probably the most important event in Ancient Egyptian life and I feel I would be doing a disservice to the Ancients and to those who today really wish to pursue the Egyptian path not to share with you all aspects of their rich legacy.

Traditional Wiccans tend to believe in reincarnation after a period of rest in 'The Summerland', a place of happiness and joy. Those who have mastered all the Karmic lessons no longer need to be reborn but may find eternal peace. The Ancient Egyptians did not so much believe in reincarnation as rebirth. The afterlife they spent their entire lives preparing for was much as life was on Earth, but with beautiful lakes, lush oases and eternal happiness. The Egyptians mummified their dead in the belief that the body had to be as intact as possible for rebirth, for a body not properly preserved would be doomed to everlasting death. Offerings were made daily to deceased relatives and incantations recited to ensure their rebirth in the afterlife. The deceased could also be called upon, much like a deity or saint, to intercede for the living in matters of the heart, health and prosperity.

The following are not really spells, but incantations or prayers that may be coupled with burning candles and incense to honour the dead and the deities who watch over us and guide us on our path to the afterlife. I have included guidelines for candle colour and incense but use your own judgement. Only you know how devastating your loss is and what may help you cope with it. You may wish to burn candles for several days or several months. You may wish to speak to the deceased as if they were still with you; it can be a very moving and cathartic experience. I still feel my mother's presence in many ways, still ask for her advice and guidance, and still regret the experiences she has missed and all the things she will not share with me. I find true solace in connecting with her, with the help of Ma'at and Anubis, Isis and Osiris, Nephthys and Set and Amun and Amenti.

Death is a fact of life and one I feel should be dealt with as openly and honestly as the wonderful, happy feelings we share in new and ongoing love. Death is not really an ending, but the beginning of another form of existence. Open your mind to the possibilities and the deities will guide you in your search, for through them you can find your way past the grief and mourning of your loss to a gentler regret, and even gratitude to the gods and goddesses for their continuing care for your loved one.

Prayer for the terminally ill

If the person you wish to pray for is in hospital, please ask permission to perform this rite. Explain that this is a religious ritual. If they refuse, you may perform this at home, at any time during the illness. You can use a different incense from the ones I have suggested if another feels more appropriate to the ill person or would express your feelings better.

Items needed
2 gold taper or pillar candles, to represent the gods Imhotep and Set
A silver taper or pillar candle, to represent the goddess Nephthys
A purple taper or pillar candle, to represent the ill person
Lotus, musk, nutmeg or sandalwood incense
A censor
A candle snuffer
Matches

Light the incense of your choice and breathe deeply. Light one of the gold candles and recite:

> Great Imhotep, Skillful Physician and Magician
> Hear the plea of Your humble servant, (magickal name)
> Assist my loved one, (name of ill person)
> You have the power
> To ease his/her pain.

Place the gold candle on the table or altar, light the silver candle and recite:

> Benevolent Nephthys, Goddess of Peace
> Hear the plea of Your humble servant, (magickal name)
> Assist my loved one, (name of ill person)
> You have the power
> To grant him/her peace.

Place the silver candle to the left of the gold and light the second gold candle. Recite:

> *Mighty Set, God of Suffering*
> *Hear the plea of Your humble servant, (magickal name)*
> *Assist my loved one, (name of ill person)*
> *You have the power*
> *To end his/her suffering.*

Place the gold candle to the left of the silver and light the purple candle. Recite:

> *I beg Your divine intercession*
> *Not for myself*
> *But for my loved one*
> *Ease his/her suffering*
> *Grant him/her peace*
> *And put an end to his/her pain*
> *Hear my plea and answer me.*

Place the purple candle in front of the silver candle and sit for a time with the candles and your loved one. When you both feel ready, you may extinguish the candles with the candle snuffer. If you are able to leave the candles where they are, you should leave them undisturbed.

This prayer can be performed as often as you both desire. If any of the candles burns out completely, you can replace it with another of the same colour.

Prayer at the moment of death

Holding someone in your arms as their life ebbs away before your eyes can be the most humbling experience of your life. When I was a young woman, I cared for my terminally ill mother and was grateful to have been present at the moment of her death.

If the person you wish to pray for is in hospital, please ask permission to perform this rite. Explain that this is a religious ritual similar to the Last Rites in the Catholic Church. If they refuse, perform this as soon as you return home, to speed the soul on its way.

Items needed

A black taper or pillar candle, to represent death
A gold taper or pillar candle, to represent the God
A silver taper or pillar candle, to represent the Goddess
Sandalwood incense
A censor
A candle snuffer
Matches

Light the incense and breathe deeply. Light the black, gold and silver candles in that order. Recite the following incantation to your lover before he or she expires:

For a woman

> *Rest your head upon my broad chest*
> *It is time to rest, my sister*
> *I shall be your comfort*
> *Let me enfold you in my loving embrace*
> *And I shall hold you in my arms*
> *Forever and all Eternity*
> *Parted in life yet not parted in my heart*
> *You live on in my soul*
> *And one day we shall join together again*
> *When my time has come*
> *Your lovely face will be the face I see*
> *At the end of my days*
> *And I shall rejoice.*

For a man

> *Rest your head upon my ample breast*
> *It is time to rest, my brother*
> *I shall be your comfort*
> *Let me enfold you in my loving embrace*
> *And I shall hold you in my arms*
> *Forever and all Eternity*
> *Parted in life yet not parted in my heart*
> *You live on in my soul*
> *And one day we shall join together again*
> *When my time has come*
> *Your handsome face will be the face I see*
> *At the end of my days*
> *And I shall rejoice.*

Hold your lover in your arms for as long as you can. Kiss him or her tenderly and silently wish him or her a speedy journey. When you must leave, extinguish the candles with the candle snuffer and place the candles on a table or your altar when you arrive home. Light the incense and the candles in the same order and sit for a time with the lit candles. Feel your lover's presence and know that he or she is with you always in your heart and soul. Grieve for your lover; the emotional release is painful but will help you to heal. When you are ready, snuff out the candles with the candle snuffer.

Leave the candles where they are and light them and the incense each day or evening. If any of the candles burns out completely before you feel ready to stop performing this offering to your lover, just place another candle of the same colour in its place. You may wish to change the black candle to a grey candle, to help to alleviate the loneliness and sorrow. When you feel it is appropriate, you may replace the grey candle with one in a healing colour, such as blue, green, pink, purple or white. This offering may be performed as long as you feel the need; mourning does not cease after the funeral, but may last for months. You may also wish to seek professional grief counselling if you are finding it difficult to cope with your loss.

Prayer for a deceased child

Items needed
A grey taper or pillar candle, to represent sorrow
A silver taper or pillar candle, to represent the goddess Isis
A pink or blue taper or pillar candle, to represent the child
Cedarwood incense
A censor
A candle snuffer
Matches

Light the incense and breathe deeply. Light the grey, silver and pink or blue candles in that order. Recite as many times as you wish:

> *My child*
> *Fruit of my womb*
> *Your life has ended*
> *Before it had begun*
> *My arms ache with emptiness*
> *My breast no longer suckles you*
> *Heartbreak has enveloped me*
> *Great Mother, Isis*
> *I entrust my precious one*
> *To Your loving care*
> *Take this lifeless little body*
> *Into Your divine embrace*

And issue forth life eternal
For my beloved child.

Sit for a time with the lit candles. When you are ready, extinguish the candles with the candle snuffer. You may wish to leave the candles where they are and light them and the incense each day or evening. If any of the candles burns out completely before you feel ready to stop performing this offering to the child, just place another candle of the same colour in its place.

Prayer for a deceased older or adult daughter

Items needed
A pink taper or pillar candle, to represent your daughter and healing
A silver taper or pillar candle, to represent the goddess Nephthys
Cinnamon incense
A censor
A candle snuffer
Matches

Light the incense and breathe deeply. Light the pink and silver candles and recite as many times as you wish:

No longer a child
You had grown graceful and lovely
But you were still my child
Now you are gone
I am left with only your memory
An empty heart and empty arms
My grief envelops me
Like darkness on a moonless night
I shall no longer hear
Your voice, your laughter
I shall no longer see
Your smile, your tears
Rest now, my daughter
May you find eternal life
With Nephthys, Protectress of the Dead
And may She welcome you
With open arms.

Sit for a time with the lit candles. When you are ready, extinguish the candles with the candle snuffer. You may wish to leave the candles where they are and light them and the incense each day or evening. If any of the candles burns out completely before you feel ready to stop performing this offering to your daughter, just place another candle of the same colour in its place.

Prayer for a deceased older or adult son

Items needed
A blue taper or pillar candle, to represent your son and healing
A gold taper or pillar candle, to represent the god Osiris
Peppermint incense
A censor
A candle snuffer
Matches

Light the incense and breathe deeply. Light the blue and gold candles and recite as many times as you wish:

> *No longer a child*
> *You had grown tall and strong*
> *But you were still my child*
> *Now you are gone*
> *I am left with only your memory*
> *An empty heart and empty arms*
> *My grief envelops me*
> *Like darkness on a moonless night*
> *I shall no longer hear*
> *You voice, your laughter*
> *I shall no longer see*
> *Your smile, your tears*
> *Rest now, my son*
> *May you find eternal life*
> *With Osiris, Lord of the Dead*
> *And may He welcome you*
> *With open arms.*

Sit for a time with the lit candles. When you are ready, extinguish the candles with the candle snuffer. You may wish to leave the candles where they are and light them and the incense each day or evening. If any of the candles burns out completely before you feel ready to stop performing this offering to your son, just place another candle of the same colour in its place.

Prayer for a deceased mother

I was a young woman when my mother died and it took me many years to accept her death, some of which were filled with self-destructive behaviour as a way to blot it out or to cope with the loss and pain. In speaking her name, I keep her alive in my heart and feel her spirit with me. Although I cannot ask for her wisdom, I can sense her guidance and love in many of my activities. She was not only my mother; she was also my friend, my anchor, my solace.

Items needed
A grey taper or pillar candle, to represent sorrow
A gold taper or pillar candle, to represent the god Osiris
Combined frankincense and myrrh incense
A censor
A candle snuffer
Matches

Light the incense and breathe deeply. Light the grey and gold candles and recite as many times as you wish:

Dearest mother
I crave the comfort of your embrace
The soothing sound of your voice
You have attained eternal rest
I should rejoice
For you know peace
And have joined with Osiris
Yet I weep at the thought
Of not looking upon your face
Until we are at last reunited
In the Land of Holiness
Fairest one
I shall honour your memory
And praise your name
Until at last I gaze upon you once more.

Sit for a time with the lit candles. When you are ready, extinguish the candles with the candle snuffer. You may wish to leave the candles where they are and light them and the incense each day or evening. If any of the candles burns out completely before you feel ready to stop performing this offering to your mother, just place another candle of the same colour in its place.

Prayer for a deceased father

Items needed
A grey taper or pillar candle, to represent sorrow
A blue or purple taper or pillar candle, to represent healing
Acacia incense (or gum arabic)
A censor
A candle snuffer
Matches

Light the incense and breathe deeply. Light the grey and blue or purple candles and recite as many times as you wish:

> *Beloved father*
> *I have watched you age*
> *Grow weaker and die*
> *Knowing that death is just*
> *Another part of life*
> *Yet powerless to stop time*
> *From taking you away from me*
> *I shall no longer feel your protective hand on my shoulder*
> *But I shall look forward to the day*
> *When we are reunited again*
> *In eternal peace and rest.*

Sit for a time with the lit candles. When you are ready, extinguish the candles with the candle snuffer. You may wish to leave the candles where they are and light them and the incense each day or evening. If any of the candles burns out completely before you feel ready to stop performing this offering to your father, just place another candle of the same colour in its place.

Prayer for a deceased lover or spouse

Items needed
A black taper or pillar candle, to represent death
2 silver taper or pillar candles, to represent the goddesses Ma'at and Nephthys
Copal resin incense
A charcoal disc
A censor
A candle snuffer
Matches

Light the charcoal disc. When it stops sparking, place some of the incense on it and breathe deeply. Light the black and silver candles and recite as many times as you wish:

> May Ma'at find your heart
> To be as light as a feather
> May Nephthys enfold you
> In a loving embrace
> I pray your journey is swift
> And know that some day
> We shall join again as one
> And I shall gaze once more
> Upon the face of my lover
> Together, for all Eternity.

Sit for a time with the lit candles. When you are ready, extinguish the candles with the candle snuffer. You may wish to leave the candles where they are and light them and the incense each day or evening. If any of the candles burns out completely before you feel ready to stop performing this offering to your lover, just place another candle of the same colour in its place.

Prayer to ease grief

Each of us handles bereavement in our own way and it may take one person longer than another to deal with the grieving process. There is no magick that can bring a loved one back to life, but this incantation is designed to help us deal with the death of a loved one, most specifically the loss of a lover.

Items needed
A white taper or pillar candle, to represent healing
A silver taper or pillar candle, to represent the goddess Isis
Rue incense
A censor
A candle snuffer
Matches

Light the incense and breathe deeply. Light the white and silver candles and recite as many times as you wish:

> *The pain of my loss is great*
> *I miss the sound of your voice*
> *Your touch, your taste*
> *Life is so empty without you*
> *Great Isis, hold me in Your care*
> *Show me the way through my grief*
> *So my heart may heal*
> *And I can learn to smile again*
> *At the sound of his/her name.*

Sit for a time with the lit candles. When you are ready, extinguish the candles with the candle snuffer. You may wish to leave the candles where they are and light them and the incense each day or evening. If any of the candles burns out completely before you feel ready to stop performing this offering to the deceased, just place another candle of the same colour in its place.

Glossary

Anoint: To rub essential oils on to a candle with your fingers or hands to infuse it with your energy and desire. Another term often used in place of anoint is 'dress'.

Banishing spell: A spell or ritual to rid oneself of a negative habit, influence or person. It is not meant to be performed with malice but with the intent to learn from the experience and move on. The Ancient Egyptians relied quite heavily on banishing spells; they were used primarily to destroy a rival or enemy and, in my opinion, with such an intent can only be destructive for all involved.

Binding spell: A spell or ritual to stop someone or something from harming themselves or others. This should also be approached with the best of intentions and should not be used without trying all other avenues available. The Ancient Egyptians relied quite heavily on binding spells for love and lust; they were used primarily to tie an individual to the person performing the spell and, in my opinion, with such an intent can only be destructive for all involved.

Canopic jars: Vessels used to hold the internal organs of mummified Ancient Egyptians. The heads on the stoppers corresponded to the Four Sons of Horus – Duamutef, Hapi, Imsety and Qebhsennuf.

Correspondences: Two or more items, tools, or 'forces' which, when used in conjunction with one another, generate additional energy in spellwork.

Coven: A group of like-minded individuals who have dedicated themselves to Wicca and who meet to perform rituals.

Craft: A shortened form of the word witchcraft. The word has a much more 'friendly' connotation and does not frighten the uninformed.

Divination: A method to predict or tell future events by inspiration and the use of various aids or tools.

Elements: The primary powers and components of nature: Earth, Air, Fire, Water and Spirit.

Esbat: The Wiccan practice of Full Moon celebration to the Goddess. You may wish to perform a ritual combined with spellwork on these days.

Handfasting: The Pagan marriage ritual.

Handparting: The Pagan divorce or separation ritual.

Incantation: A magickal charm or spell that may be recited or written to bring about a desired result.

Invoke: To call upon or appeal to a deity for assistance or guidance.

Magick: This spelling of the word generally refers to the practice of witchcraft as opposed to the stage magic that is performed for entertainment.

Magickal name: The name a person takes when he or she becomes a Wiccan. It is not a necessity, although many Wiccans do have a magickal name. A Wiccan may have more than one magickal name during the course of his or her lifetime.

Pagan: A person who practises an Earth-based religion. The term may sometimes be used in the same context as Wiccan.

Poppet: An item crafted to resemble a person you wish to perform a spell upon. It may be fashioned out of cloth (stuffed with herbs), wax, clay, a piece of fruit or the root of a herb such as ginger or mandrake.

Ritual: An act of magick. A ritual is usually more time-consuming and more structured than a spell. Ritual work should incorporate the Elements and is generally designed to honour the deities for Esbats and Sabbats.

Sabbat: One of the eight major days celebrated by Wiccans: Samhain (Halloween) on 31 October, Yule (Winter Solstice) on or about 23 December, Imbolc (Candlemas) on 2 February, Ostara (Spring Equinox) on or about 23 March, Beltane on 30 April, Midsummer (Summer Solstice) on or about 23 June, Lammas on 31 July, and Mabon (Autumn Equinox) on or about 23 September. These days comprise the Wheel of the Year; the Ancient Egyptians observed the Cairo Calendar and their festivals centred on the annual inundation of the Nile.

Scrying: A method of divination using a black mirror or a bowl of water that has been darkened with ink.

Smudge: To cleanse. You may wish to cleanse your ritual tools prior to use and your sacred space prior to ritual or spellwork. Most Wiccans use incense to clear away any negative influences that may be present.

Spell: The raising of energy designed to cause a desired result. Spells can be fairly simple and rely on candles and/or words alone.

Wicca: Another term for witchcraft. It appears to come from the Anglo-Saxon Wicce, which has been defined as 'wise one' or 'one who practises sorcery'.

Witchcraft: The practice of magick.

Bibliography and Suggested Reading

Not all of the books listed here are Egyptian in nature but they will give you a well-rounded view of Wicca in general and some books are specific in their topics. All should be useful in making your spellwork more rewarding. This is just a portion of my library and every 'Good Witch' should have an extensive library for resources and ideas.

Aldred, Cyril. *The Egyptians* (3rd edition). London: Thames and Hudson, 1998.

Almond, Jocelyn & Seddon, Keith. *An Egyptian Book of Shadows.* London: Thorsons, 1999.

Ball, Pamela. *Spells, Charms, Talismans and Amulets.* Edison, NJ: Castle Books, 2001.

Barrett, Clive. *Egyptian Gods and Goddesses.* London: Diamond Books, 1996.

Bennett, James & Crowley, Vivianne. *Magic and Mysteries of Ancient Egypt.* New York, NY: Sterling Publishing, 2001.

Brier, Bob. *Ancient Egyptian Magic.* New York: William Morrow, 1980.

Bruce, Maire. *Candleburning Rituals.* Quantum/Foulsham, 2001.

Bruce, Marie. *Everyday Spells for a Teenage Witch.* Quantum/Foulsham 2002.

Bruce, Marie. *How to Create a Magical Home.* Quantum/Foulsham, 2004.

Bruce, Marie. *Magical Beasts.* Quantum/Foulsham, 2004.

Bruce, Marie. *The Witch's Almanac.* Quantum/Foulsham, 2004.

Budge, E. A. Wallis. *Gods of the Egyptians* (2 volumes). Mineola, NY: Dover Publications, 1969.

Bunson, Margaret. *Dictionary of Ancient Egypt.* New York: Oxford University Press, 1995.

Clayton, Peter. *Chronicle of the Pharaohs.* London: Thames and Hudson, 2001.

Collier, Mark & Manley, Bill. *How to Read Egyptian Hieroglyphs.* Berkeley, CA: University of California Press, 1998.

Conway, D.J. *Magick of the Gods and Goddesses.* St. Paul, MN: Llewellyn Publications, 1997.

Cunningham, Scott. *The Complete Book of Incense, Oils and Brews.* St Paul, MN: Llewellyn Publications, 1997.

Cunningham, Scott. *Cunningham's Encyclopedia of Crystal, Gem and Metal Magic.* St Paul, MN: Llewellyn Publications, 2001.

Cunningham, Scott. *Cunningham's Encyclopedia of Magical Herbs.* St Paul, MN: Llewellyn Publications, 1996.

Cunningham, Scott. *Magical Herbalism.* St. Paul, MN: Llewellyn Publications, 1998.

Cunningham, Scott. *Wicca Guide for the Solitary Practitioner.* St Paul, MN: Llewellyn Publications, 1996.

Dolnick, Barrie. *Simple Spells for Love.* New York, NY: Harmony Books, 1994.

Drew, A.J. *Wicca for Couples.* Franklin Lakes, NJ: Career Press, 2002.

Dunwich, Gerina. *Herbal Magick.* Franklin Lakes, NJ: Career Press, 2002.

Eason, Cassandra, *Complete Book of Spells.* Quantum/Foulsham, 2004.

Eason, Cassandra, *Every Woman a Witch.* Quantum/Foulsham, 1996.

Eason, Cassandra, *Fragrant Magic.* Quantum/Foulsham, 2004.

Eason, Cassandra, *Magic Spells for a Happy Life.* Quantum/Foulsham, 2003.

Eason, Cassandra, *A Practical Guide to Witchcraft and Magick Spells.* Quantum/Foulsham, 2001.

Eason, Cassandra, *Psychic Protection Lifts the Spirit.* Quantum/Foulsham, 2001.

Eilers, Dana D. *Practical Pagan.* Franklin Lakes, NJ: Career Press, 2002.

Farrar, Janet & Stewart. *The Witches' God.* Blaine, WA: Phoenix Publishing, 1998.

Farrar, Janet & Stewart. *The Witches' Goddess.* Blaine, WA: Phoenix Publishing, 1987.

Fletcher, Joann. *The Egyptian Book of Living and Dying.* London: Thorsons, 2002.

Garrison, Cal. *Old Girl's Book of Spells.* York Beach, ME: Red Wheel/Weiser, 2002.

Gray, Deborah. *The Good Witch's Guide to Wicked Ways.* Boston, MA: Journey Editions, 2001.

Gray, Deborah. *How to Turn Your Boyfriend Into a Love Slave and Other Spells.* San Francisco, CA: HarperSanFrancisco, 2001.

Gray, Deborah. *Nice Girl's Book of Naughty Spells.* Boston, MA: Journey Editions, 1999.

Hart, George. *Dictionary of Egyptian Gods and Goddesses.* New York, NY: Routledge, 1986.

Hayes, Michael. *The Egyptians.* New York, NY: Rizzoli International Publishers, 2000.

Heath, Maya. *Ceridwen's Handbook of Incense, Oils and Candles.* San Antonio, TX: Words of Wizdom International, 1996.

Holland, Eileen. *The Wicca Handbook.* York Beach, ME: Samuel Weiser, 2000.

Horne, Fiona. *Witch: A Magickal Journey.* London: Thorsons, 2000.

Jacq, Christian. *Fascinating Hieroglyphics.* New York: Sterling Publishing, 1998.

Jordan, Michael. *Encyclopedia of Gods.* New York: Facts on File, 1993.

Kemp, Gillian. *Good Spell Book.* New York, NY: Little, Brown and Company, 1999.

Lawless, Julia. *Complete Illustrated Guide to Aromatherapy.* London: Element, 2002.

Lawless, Julia. *The Encyclopedia of Essential Oils.* London: Thorsons, 2002.

Love Lyrics of Ancient Egypt, translated by Barbara Hughes Fowler. Chapel Hill, NC: University of North Carolina Press, 1994.

Love Songs of the New Kingdom, translated by John L. Foster. Austin, TX: University of Texas Press, 1974.

Lurker, Manfred. *An Illustrated Dictionary of Gods and Symbols of Ancient Egypt.* New York: Thames and Hudson, 1996.

McColman, Carl. *Well-read Witch.* Franklin Lakes, NJ: Career Press, 2002.

McColman, Carl. *When Someone You Love is Wiccan.* Franklin Lakes, NJ: Career Press, 2003.

McDermott, Bridget. *Decoding Egyptian Hieroglyphs.* San Francisco, CA: Chronicle Books, 2001.

McFarland, Phoenix, *Complete Book of Magical Names.* St Paul, MN: Llewellyn Publications, 1996.

Mercatante, Anthony S. *Who's Who in Egyptian Mythology* (2nd edition). New York, NY: MetroBooks, 2002.

Moon, Sister. *The Wiccaning.* New York: Kensington Publishing, 2001.

Morgan, Michele. *Simple Wicca.* Berkeley, CA: Conari Press, 2000.

Reed, Ellen Cannon. *Circle of Isis.* Franklin Lakes, NJ: Career Press, 2002.

Reed, Ellen Cannon. *Invocation of the Gods.* St Paul, MN: Llewellyn Publications, 1992.

Rhea, Lady Maeve. *Handfasted and Heartjoined.* New York: Kensington Publishing, 2001.

Rodway, Marie. *Wiccan Herbal.* Quantum/Foulsham, 1997.

Rosean, Lexa. *Supermarket Sorceress.* New York, NY: St Martin's Press, 1996.

Rosean, Lexa. *Supermarket Sorceress's Enchanted Evenings.* New York, NY: St Martin's Press, 1998.

Rosean, Lexa. *Supermarket Sorceress's Sexy Hexes.* New York, NY: St Martin's Press, 1997.

Ryan, Donald P. *Complete Idiot's Guide to Ancient Egypt.* Indianapolis, IN: Alpha Books, 2002.

Sabrina, Lady. *Exploring Wicca.* Franklin Lakes, NJ: Career Press, 2000.

Sellar, Wanda. *The Directory of Essential Oils.* Essex, UK: C. W. Daniel, 2001.

Sergiev, Gilly. *5 Easy Steps to Becoming a Witch.* London: Thorsons, 2000.

Singer, Marian. *The Everything Wicca and Witchcraft Book.* Avon, MA: Adams Media Corporation, 2002.

Spence, Lewis. *Ancient Egyptian Myths and Legends.* Mineola, NY: Dover Publications, 1990.

Starwoman, Athena & Gray, Deborah. *How to Turn Your Ex-Boyfriend into a Toad and Other Spells.* New York, NY: HarperCollins, 1996.

Telesco, Patricia. *Exploring Candle Magick.* Franklin Lakes, NJ: Career Press, 2001.

Tempest, Raven. *How to Bewitch.* London: Cassell and Company, 2001.

Wildwood, Chrissie. *The Encyclopedia of Aromatherapy.* Rochester, VT: Healing Arts Press, 1996.

Wilson, Hilary. *Understanding Hieroglyphs.* Lincolnwood (Chicago), IL: Passport Books, 1996.

Worwood, Susan. *Essential Aromatherapy.* Novato, CA: New World Library, 1995.

Zauzich, Karl-Theodor. *Hieroglyphs Without Mystery.* Austin, TX: University of Texas Press, 1992.

Zimmerman, Denise & Gleason, Katherine A. *Complete Idiot's Guide to Wicca and Witchcraft.* Indianapolis, IN: Alpha Books, 2000.

Suppliers

I have included some of my favourite suppliers, as well as other reputable companies. Since I haven't had a chance to use every one of them, you should always check these, or any other sources you find, before ordering.

Candles and candle-making equipment

Canada
Crafty Candles
3919 Seminole Street
Windsor
Ontario N8Y 1Z1
www.craftycandles.ca

UK
Price's Candles Ltd
16 Hudson Road
Elms Farm Industrial Estate
Bedford MK41 0LZ
Tel: +44 (0) 1234 264500
www.prices-candles.co.uk

Collectibles

Australia
M&M Treasures
PO Box 133
Kippas
ACT 2615
Tel: +61 (0) 2 6254 3503
www.treasures.com.au
(Fantasy figures, pewter figurines and more.)

UK
The Faerie Shoppe
www.fairyshop.co.uk
(All things faerie.)
105 High Street
Marlborough
Wiltshire SN8 1LT
Tel: +44 (0) 1672 515995
and
3 Montpelier Walk
Cheltenham
Gloucestershire GL50 1SD
Tel: +44 (0) 1242 230833
and
6 Lower Borough Walk
Bath
Avon BA1 1QR
Tel: +44 (0) 1225 427773

Snapdragon
12 South Park
Sevenoaks
Kent TN13 1AN
Tel: +44 (0) 1732 740252
www.giltedgedgoblins.com
(All kinds of faerie collectibles, dragons etc.)

USA
Design Toscano Inc.
Outlet Store
40 Scitico Road
Somersville CT 06072
Tel: +1 (1) 860 749 1213
www.designtoscano.com
(Telephone or visit the website for
catalogue information. They carry a
wide variety of statuary, including
Egyptian deities, as well as jewellery,
clothing, cloaks, chalices and
artwork.)

The Pyramid Collection
Altid Park
PO Box 3333
Chelmsford
MA 01824-0933
Tel: +1 (1) 800 333 4220
www.pyramidcollection.com
(Telephone for catalogue
information or order online. They
carry a wide assortment of statuary,
including Egyptian deities, as well as
jewellery, clothing, cloaks, candles,
resins, cauldrons and many other
items.)

**Crystals, amulets, magical items
etc.**

Australia
Mysterys
Level 1
314 Darling Street
Balmain
NSW 2041
Tel: +61 (0) 2 9818 2274
www.mysterys.com.au
(Wiccan supplies by mail order.)

The Mystic Trader
125 Flinders Lane
Melbourne 3000
Tel: +61 (0) 3 650 4477
(Mail order and personal service.)

South Africa
The Wellstead
1 Wellington Avenue
Wynberg
Cape 7300
Tel: +27 (0) 797 8982
(Mail order.)

UK
Futhark Esoteric Specialists
18 Halifax Road
Todmorden
Lancashire OL14 5AD
Tel: +44 (0) 1706 814205
(Occult, magical and alchemical
supplies of all kinds by mail order.)

Mandragora
Essex House
Thame
Oxfordshire
OX9 3LS
Tel: +44 (0) 1844 260990
www.mandrakepress.com
(Mail order worldwide.)

Mysteries
9–11 Monmouth Street
Covent Garden
London
WC2H 9DA
Tel: +44 (0) 20 7240 3688
www.mysteries.co.uk
(Shop and mail order for absolutely
everything New Age, plus good
advice.)

USA
AzureGreen/Abyss
PO Box 48-WEB
Middlefield
MA 01243-0048
Tel: +1 (1) 413 623 2155
www.azuregreen.com
(Order catalogue online or by
telephone. They carry a wide variety
of magickal items, including essential
oils and blends, books, incense,
jewellery and ritual items.)

Earth Spirits
3 Arnold Road
Fiskdale
MA 01518
Tel: +1 (1) 508 347 1180
www.earthspirits-herbals.com
(Their website is available for
ordering bulk herbs, essential oils,
books, candles, crystals and many
other items.)

Pacific Spirit
1334 Pacific Avenue
Forest Grove
Oregon
OR 97116
Tel: +1 (1) 800 634 9057
www.pacificspiritcatalogs.com
(Statuary and jewellery, books and
gifts.)

Sacred Source
PO Box 163WWW
Crozet
VA 22932
Tel: +1 (1) 434 823 1515
www.sacredsource.com
(Call for catalogue information.
They carry statuary for many
different paths, including Egyptian
deities, as well as wands, jewellery,
books, sistra, bowls and CDs.)

Herbs and oils – products

UK
G Baldwin & Co
171–173 Walworth Road
London
SE17 1RW
Tel: +44 (0) 20 7703 5550
www.baldwins.co.uk
(Largest range in the UK of herbs
and herbal products, aromatherapy
oils, tinctures, incenses and
ingredients for cosmetics. Extensive
mail order.)

Butterbur & Sage
Aroma House
7 Tessa Road
Reading
Berkshire RG1 8HH
Tel: +44 (0) 1189 505100
www.butterburandsage.com
(A comprehensive range of high-
quality essential oils.)

Gerard House Ltd
475 Capability Green
Luton
Bedfordshire LU1 3LU
(Dried herbs by mail order.)

Neal's Yard Remedies
8–10 Ingate Place
Battersea
London SW8 3NS
Tel: +44 (0) 20 7498 1686
www.nealsyardremedies.com
(Oils by mail order.)

USA
AromaTherapeutix
PO Box 2908
Seal Beach
CA 90740
Tel: +1 (1) 800 308 6284
(Call for catalogue information.
They carry a variety of carrier oils,
essential oils and blends, as well as
light-block bottles, sprayers,
disposable droppers and muslin
bags.)

Ceridwen's Magickal and New
Age Supplies
630 South Huttig
Independence
MO 64053
Tel: +1 (1) 816 461 7773
(Send $2.00 for a catalogue. They
carry many hard-to-locate essential
oils and Egyptian deity blends. Diana
and Bob are always available to
answer any questions.)

Joan Teresa Power Products
PO Box 442
Mars Hill
NC 28754
(Unusual herbs, plants, oils, incenses
etc. by mail order.)

Quintessential Oils
847 35th Street
Richmond
CA 94805-1707
Tel: +1 (1) 510 215 2750
www.quintoils@earthlink.net
(They carry blue and white lotus
essential oils. Kate and Sherry will
assist in any way possible and send
out special sale flyers on a regular
basis.)

The Sage Garden
PO Box 144
Payette ID 83661
(Herbs, oils, amulets and incenses by
mail order.)

**Herbs and oils – professional
organisations**

Australia
National Herbalists Association
of Australia
13 Breillat Street
Annandale
NSW 2038
Tel: +61 (0) 2 9555 8885

UK
The Herb Society
Sulgrave Manor
Sulgrave
Banbuy
Oxfordshire OX17 2SD
Tel: +44 (0) 1295 768899
www.herbsociety.org.uk

The International Federation of
Professional Aromatherapists
82 Ashby Road
Hinckley
Leicestershire LE10 1SN
Tel: +44 (0) 1455 637987
www.ifparoma.org

The National Institute of
Medical Herbalists
56 Longbrook Street
Exeter
Devon EX4 6AH
Tel: +44 (0) 1392 426022
www.nimh.org.uk

USA
The American Herbalists Guild
1931 Gaddis Road
Canton GA 30115
Tel: +1 (1) 770 751 6121
www.americanherbalistsguild.com

Index